Business Leader

"Ron's proven approach to leadership training makes the reality of a fulfilling and successful life available to everyone. He presents these timeless principles professionally, yet practically in a down-to-earth way that is easy to understand and put into practice. His message is greatly needed throughout our world today."

Norm Miller, Chairman of Interstate Batteries

"I felt the content of your book, *Make a Life, Not Just a Living*, is not only timely for me at this point in my career, but for our entire organization and the nation as a whole. The life skills and action steps you are presenting will help everyone build an outstanding foundation for a truly successful life."

Hugh Maclellan Jr., Chairman of the Executive
Committee, Provident Companies

"I am most impressed with the leadership principles found in *Make a Life, Not Just a Living*. Principles such as these are foundational in personal growth and in the success which companies and countries experience. My knowledge of you gives me great confidence that you will be successful in your worldwide ventures to help families and organizations rebuild a desperately needed solid infrastructure."

David Hentschel, Former Chairman and CEO,
Occidental Oil and Gas Corporation

"Dr. Jenson has written an owner's manual to take each and every reader to the next level of life. Highly recommended!"

Sam Hardage, Chairman and CEO,
The Hardage Group of Companies

"For too long America has been focused on the bottom line. Now Dr. Jenson's book focuses on the bigger and more important issues of making a more effective and complete person."

Anthony M. Wilson, Former Chief Executive Officer,
Hobie Cat Company

"It is the best program I have seen internationally for starting at ground zero and building a value system. You have created a new paradigm of success."

Dr. Jerry Curtis Nims, Chairman, NIMSTECH

"Concise, to the point, and relevant to today's marketplace."
Jeffrey W. Comment, President,
Helzberg's Diamond Shops, Inc.

"Dr. Ron Jenson has the unique gift of formulating and communicating in a practical and relevant manner principles that allow and encourage his readers to maximize their personal and business success."
Charles L. Collings, President/CEO,
Raley's Supermarkets and Drug Centers

"Never in modern history have moral standards and nonnegotiables been more important than today. I believe this book, *Make a Life, Not Just a Living*, is 'must reading' for all leaders and would be leaders today."
Dr. D. S. Reimer, Reimer Express World Corp.

"Dr. Jenson has written a blockbuster of wisdom profoundly needed today. I have known Ron personally for twenty-three years. He exemplifies the principles espoused in his book."
Robert O. Safford Sr., Senior National Sales Director,
PRIMERICA Financial Services,
a member of Travelers Group

"Don't just buy copies and give them to your associates. Build an organization that lives these principles and you will have a successful company—an investment for generations to come."
Bunker Hunt, International Businessman

"A profound book that defines true success based on authentic principles. A must-read for anyone desiring to make a difference."
David Cavan, President, Cavan Investments, Ltd.

"You reminded me how important it is to keep our priorities straight and to actively plan for a balanced life. It was easy to see how 'success' often leads us away from that objective—to our detriment. You stimulated me to reevaluate my priorities and be more conscious of my daily decisions."
Mary L. Walker, Partner-San Diego Office, Brobeck,
Phleger, and Harrison, Attorneys at Law;
Former Assistant Secretary,
United States Department of Energy

"If people would just consider the title *Make a Life, Not Just a Living*, they would understand why Ron says in his book, 'man's money can buy him a bed, but not a good night's sleep.' A must-read!"
Dwight L. Johnson, President, Sturgeon Systems, Inc.

"Jenson has produced a book that gets right to the heart of modern pursuits. What a refreshing and informative set of principles to make a life by!"
J. David Rae, Former Vice President, Apple Computer

"Ron Jenson has captured some of the most important lessons anyone can learn. Our society distracts us from the essence of life as we pursue living. Not only has he discovered these truths, but his experience in communicating them to a worldwide audience makes his presentation and insights even more powerful."
James L. Sheard, Ph.D., Former Senior Vice President,
Director of Human Resources,
Federated Insurance Company

Public Service and Military Leaders

"A refreshingly wise and workable prescription for helping us in all facets of life. Ron has truly delivered tools with which we can craft a more meaningful and fulfilling life."
Elizabeth Dole, President, American Red Cross

"The ten principles which you have articulated are both exciting and essential for building a foundation for positive, productive lives."
The Honorable Don Nickles,
United States Senator, State of Oklahoma

"A powerful communicator whose message is so appropriate for today. I have used his material with colleagues in the Senate and all of us have greatly benefited from its relevance."
The Honorable William L. Armstrong,
Former United States Senator, State of Colorado

"Finally—an author who crafts timeless truths into life skills that work. A coming together of the intellectual and the practical that achievers everywhere will embrace."
The Honorable Bob McEwen, Former United States
Representative, State of Ohio

"You are a respected communicator whose message has influenced chief executives in a powerful way. Your approach has been practical, convincing, and relevant to the real world. I, along with hundreds of key business leaders across our nation, have benefited significantly from the powerful thrust of your efforts."

Richard G. Capen Jr., Former U.S. Ambassador to Spain,
1992–93, Former Vice Chairman, Knight-Ridder, Inc.

"The principles presented in this book form the foundation for successful and inspirational leadership. Individuals need them and business and government organizations need to create an environment that encourages their use."

William R. Nelson, Lieutenant General (Ret.),
United States Air Force

"*Make a Life, Not Just a Living* hits at the very heart of our motivations and causes us to reevaluate our moral and ethical foundations of life. Ron Jenson captures and highlights in his book the truth that leadership is needed more than ever in our nation and in the world, but leadership that is directed, not at the leadership themselves, but at those served."

Brigadier General Dick Abel, USAF (Ret.); Director,
Military Ministries, Campus Crusade

"Dr. Jenson has an uncanny ability to lay out an easy-to-follow formula for successful living through personal growth. His practical approach and insights will challenge any reader regardless of age and background."

Rear Admiral William L. Schachte Jr., USN (Ret.)

"Families, businesses, and societies around the world desperately need to be exposed to these universal principles of life. I am confident that everyone practicing these ten principles will see immediate and continuing success as I have in my life."

Thomas D. Conrad, Ph.D., Executive Director,
Government Employees Association, Inc.;
Former Deputy Assistant Secretary, USAF

Education and Professional Leaders

"*Make a Life, Not Just a Living* provides specific inspirational direction for those who seek to win in all areas of life. Informative and practical, the book is loaded with common sense and the realistic side of inspiration. GOOD stuff!"

Zig Ziglar, Chairman, The Zig Ziglar Corporation

"Dr. Ron Jenson's approach to leadership is what companies are really needing—this book needs to be on every manager's desk. I have seen him with top worldwide business leaders and what he has written really works and helps people win big. Very Big."

Dr. Ken Blanchard, Best-selling Author,
The One Minute Manager, *Speaker*

"Working with thousands of men around the world, we have seen the critical need for the kind of life skills articulated by Ron Jenson in this exciting book. Not only are these principles practical, they work. We have seen Ron in action and the changed lives that have resulted speak for the power of his work. We urge men and women alike to study this book and to become "craftsmen at life.""

Dr. E. Glenn Wagner, Vice President,
and Dr. Rod Cooper, National Director of Education,
PROMISEKEEPERS

"This is one of the most important books written in many years. It gives you a series of practical, powerful steps that you can follow to become a far more effective person on the *inside* and a far greater success on the *outside*. Every success-oriented person in America should read and reread this book and apply its practical ideas to every part of life."

Brian Tracy, Brian Tracy Learning Systems,
Author and Speaker

"I have long taught methods and strategies for success in a sales career. However, the foundation of my message has always been that you must have *balance* in your life in order to truly succeed. Knowing Dr. Ron Jenson as I do and of his phenomenal life's work, this book promises to give you the answers to help you achieve a balanced, successful life."

Tom Hopkins, International Sales Trainer,
Million-selling Author, How to Master the Art of Selling

"Few people have Dr. Jenson's capacity to motivate inner success and affect positive change. This book is a must read for anyone grappling with what success should look like in his own life."
Robert Seiple, President, World Vision

"These [principles] seem to be imminently basic, clear, concise and valid. I do not believe that there is much hope for any society, our own or any other, unless these fundamental principles can be internalized, universalized, and practiced. In this period of momentous cultural change, revolutionary beginnings and reformation of societies, both East and West, nothing could seem more important than the high ground staked out by these principles and your energizing leadership."
Glenn Olds, Former Commissioner, State of Alaska,
Department of Natural Resources;
Former President, Kent State University

"Here are carefully crafted and experiential helps for all of us to live out those values we hold as strategic and critical in lives that make a difference."
Ted W. Engstrom, President Emeritus, World Vision

"Ron Jenson is a winner and so is his book. Seldom, if ever, will you read a book which has more credibility in terms of the author's own life. Ron is a man who has built his life upon proven principles . . . and now they're available here in transferable form. If you thirst for an authentically successful and effective life, this is a must-read."
Stu Weber, Pastor, Author

"*Make a Life, Not Just a Living* is a captivating, humorous, and personally helpful look at how to bring order to the chaos of living in the fast lane. Ron Jenson has captured and distilled the best ideas from the most insightful thinkers who have ever written on the subjects of purpose, priorities, and living life successfully. I found myself reading with pen in hand, jotting down quotes and ideas to share with my team. The action steps at the end of each chapter are intensely practical and guaranteed to turn the concepts into habits."
Stan Oaks, National Director, Christian Leadership

"In an age when we are inundated with distractions and diversions, Ron has created a crisp, easy-to-read mind filter that helps keep us focused on priorities built around our individual unique core competencies. It is a must read for people involved in solving problems."

William E. Anderson II, Character Training Consultant,
and Ann Kiemel Anderson, Speaker and Author;
President, William Anderson Company

Sports and Entertainment Leaders

"Dr. Jenson has written a comprehensive and do-able achievement program for following through with one's personal and professional goals with emphasis on inner success versus outward success."

Joe Gibbs, Former Head Coach, Washington Redskins;
Joe Gibbs Racing

"Ron is a 'lifestyle coach' for me in my business and personal life. The message and teaching he shares is now in book form, giving many others the chance to grow from his leadership as well. *Make a Life, Not Just a Living* will undoubtedly serve as a 'handbook' for anyone who wants direction in getting his priorities straight."

Rolf Benirschke, Former NFL Place-kicker,
San Diego Chargers;
Partner, Eastman and Benirschke Financial Group

"Working with top executives in film and television for fifteen years has convinced me that people who get to the top of the ladder seldom ask if it's leaning against the right wall. Dr. Jenson's book makes the right wall, the right ladder, and the right rungs crystal clear. Every exec should know these principles."

Larry W. Poland, Ph.D.,
Chairman and CEO, MasterMedia International, Inc.

"As many of us make the transition from success to significance, we can find useful guidance in Ron Jenson's ten practical and highly actionable skills. Ron communicates with clarity, enthusiasm, and depth of understanding."

Bob Buford, Chairman of the Board,
Buford Television, Inc.; Author, Halftime; Changing
Your Game Plan from Success to Significance

"I have read *Make a Life, Not Just a Living,* and I am very excited about the contents of this book. Ron Jenson has taken ten very practical, individual skills and shown how they are foundational to building authentically successful and effective lives. The book really challenged me in many areas of my life. I am going to be recommending it widely."

Pat Williams, Chief Operating Officer/General Manager,
Orlando Magic, National Basketball Association

"The ten points you have developed are a great concept for building or rebuilding the individual, family, business, and government. I believe that there must be principles such as these for people to be able to develop their highest potential while at the same time supporting and leading other people."

Stan Smith, Professional Tennis Champion

International Leaders

"Ron Jenson is a great communicator and has significantly influenced my perspective on what it means to be truly successful."

Kevin Jenkins, Former President and CEO, Westaim
Canadian Airlines International, Ltd.

"Your work is extremely timely and relevant in our age of cardinal social and political transformations. We need to change with the times, too, but we should also focus on the roots, stick to our principles, and refine them unceasingly. *Make a Life* communicates the truth directly to the human soul.

"It makes me think of life's real meaning; of what I can and should change in myself, and how. You have provided a benchmark from which I can think further to find solutions to dilemmas facing every one of us daily. I would recommend *Make a Life* with the utmost warmth to anyone striving to lead a meaningful life. Every library, college, business person, and leader should have a copy."

Nicolai S. Stolyarov, Major General,
Dean of the Graduate School of Business for Servicemen,
International University, Moscow, Russia

"Ron Jenson's book is arresting, inspiring, and interesting, just as he is in real life."

Peter J. Daniels, President and Founder,
World Centre for Entrepreneurial Studies,
Adelaide, Australia

"It has been conclusively established that holistic, spiritually-founded social patterns and behaviors provide the only known hope for the future of our civilization. This book is poised to bring mankind to new planes of internal personal peace, interpersonal relationships, and social harmony."

The Honorable Matthew Nrukikaire,
Minister of State for Finance and Economic Planning,
Republic of Uganda

"When he [Ron] comes alongside, he really causes one to reflect upon one's quality of life, purpose, and values. I really believe that many people will grow through his insight and wisdom."

Ralph Zielsdorf, President,
Zielsdorf Financial Group, Ltd.,
Calgary, Alberta, Canada

"I subscribe to the Maximizers model in my life and I am sure that everyone who reads this book will want to find practical ways to design this model into his own future. As busy as I am traveling around the world, there are only a few select books that make it into my 'must read' list—this is definitely one of them!"

R. Scott Zimmer, President, EchoStar International,
The Republic of Singapore

"Ron's aim at redefining the traditional measures of success is forcefully communicated because he is specific in blending values with standard achievement goals. Understanding and applying these principles will make readers want to rethink their path to success."

Joseph G. Kass, Vice Chairman,
REPAP Enterprises, Inc., Montreal, Canada

"We have found that there is an extremely great need for the materials you communicate in our country. In fact, I am confident to say that what you are sharing is foundational for the rebuilding of this country. People need what you call 'straight lines.' You are providing those. On behalf of the people of Russia, I thank you for your immeasurable assistance."

Iouri Minaev, First Deputy Chairman, Radio Moscow

"Thanks Ron, for helping me to understand what authentic success is really all about. It is easy to succeed on a balance sheet but lose in life. Your book adds a meaningful perspective to what the 'bottom line' should be . . . a significant life."

Gordon D. Wusyk, President, The Wusyk Financial
Group; Chairman of CAFE (Canadian Association of
Family Enterprise), Edmonton, Alberta, Canada

"We as leaders in emerging democracies need to redefine our personal definition of success, rethink our priorities, and reestablish the moral and ethical foundations of our lives, because that is the only way we can alleviate the causes of human need and transform the structures of our nations. *Make a Life, Not Just a Living* provides the foundations for such effective leadership. It is a must reading for leaders in the two-thirds world and those aspiring into leadership everywhere."

Dr. Appianda Arthur, Former Chairman,
Parliamentary Committee on Presidential Affairs,
Ghana, West Africa;
Director, Distinguished Leaders Commission (AD 2000)

"Readers will gain a sense of purpose in life. They will learn how to discipline themselves to manage priorities within the time they have. We learned to think beyond ourselves and the present. We believe this book will be a positive motivational tool with which readers will change their lives for the better."

Dina H. and R. Brooks Loomis, Owners,
Southeast Asia Speakers and Trainers Bureau,
Manila, Philippines

"Ron walks his talk. His life is ordered by that which he teaches and has left an indelible imprint on my life. His Maximizers principles are easy to grasp, practical, yet challenging to put to work."

Dr. Henry Tan, President,
ACTS International, Philippines

MAKE A LIFE

NOT JUST A LIVING

MAKE A LIFE

NOT JUST A LIVING

10 Timeless Life Skills
That Will Maximize Your Real Net Worth

Dr. Ron Jenson

BROADMAN
& HOLMAN
PUBLISHERS

Nashville, Tennessee

0-8054-1196-8

Published by Broadman & Holman Publishers, Nashville, Tennessee
Acquisitions and Development Editor: William D. Watkins
Typesetter: TFDesigns, Mt. Juliet, Tennessee

Dewey Decimal Classification: 248.84
Subject Heading: CHRISTIAN LIFE \ LIFE SKILLS

Unless otherwise noted, Scripture quotations are taken from the Holy Bible, New International Version ®. Copyright © 1973, 1978, 1984 by International Bible Society. Used by permission. Scripture quotations noted TLB are from the Living Bible (Wheaton, Illinois: Tyndale House Publishers, 1971) and are used by permission.

Library of Congress Cataloging-in-Publication Data

Jenson, Ron.
    Make a life, not just a living / Ron Jenson.
        p. cm.
    Originally published: Nashville, TN : T. Nelson, 1995.
    Includes bibliographical references and index.
    ISBN 0-8054-1196-8
    1. Christian life. 2. Conduct of life. I. Title.
[BV4501.2.J438   1998]
158—dc21

95-40913
CIP
Rev.

1 2 3 4 5 02 01 00 99 98

To some of those special people who have helped me make a life:

My mom, Maxine,
who taught me to work hard

My dad, Bob,
who models gentleness

My wife, Mary,
who makes daily living a delight

My son, Matt,
who helps me build "straight lines" in my life

My daughter, Molly,
who makes life fun

My longtime friend, Bob Safford,
who keeps "making things happen"

My inner-life mentor, Bill Bright,
who best models to me the power of "energizing the inner life"

My friend, Kevin Jenkins,
who illustrates daily the ability to adjust to constantly changing situations

And my associates over the years
who have grappled with and sought to model "authentic success"

Contents

Section 1: Root Attitudes

Section 2: Root Beliefs

Section 3: Root Commitments

Preface

If you could have anything in the world, what would it be? All sorts of myths and other stories throughout history have tried to resolve that question. Some people have gone after power, some people have gone after great fame, others have pursued wealth, and then many have chosen just to have more choices.

But if I could have anything in the world, I believe I would choose wisdom. For you see, wisdom is really the art of living. If we learn how to live, if we develop the craftsmanship of making a life, then we'll have everything we've ever wanted and ever needed. Beyond that we'll have a life of great success and true significance. And that's what I want for myself personally and what I desperately want for my family, my friends, and those I have the opportunity to touch in some fashion.

In a day when the world culture is rapidly falling apart, we desperately need to learn again how to live.

That's what this book's all about. I spent the last number of years doing research among leaders from around the world to discover those absolute nonnegotiables that were true in their lives that enabled them to make not only a great living, but to have a successful life and lifestyle. Through that research, as well as the reading of thousands of books and communication with literally millions of people around the world, I've come to the conclusion that there are ten universal organizing principles to making a life. I've been able to distill my thoughts at least in a summary form in this book. My goal is to create a book that brings truth, principles, and life change to all people from every frame of reference, faith, and background.

My passion in life is to help people make a life—to develop the artistry or the craftsmanship of living.

I've sought to build these principles into my life (with various levels of success) and seek to communicate these through every vehicle I possibly can. In fact, I have taken the material in this book and built it into multiple seminars, audio tapes and manuals, video tapes, and educational programs that are presently being used in places as far away as Russia.

I hope that you'll grapple with these truths.

I want to urge you to not only read the book, but study it and consider ordering other materials and reading some of the other resource books I recommend. My real desire is that you begin to develop a framework based on these ten principles that will give you a philosophy of life and upon which you can build an even more solid foundation, leading to success and significance in every area of your life.

I truly believe that you and I are both here to make a difference, and that happens as we're able to get our lives together.

Acknowledgments

I want to particularly thank my wife, Mary, who has given time and energy to putting together these principles. She is my friend, my confidante, my wife of twenty-seven years, my editorial director, my associate, and my partner. This book, as is true about any area or production of my life, wouldn't happen without her. She is intertwined in every page and paragraph and was my primary editor.

I also want to thank my son, Matt, and my daughter, Molly, for allowing Mary and me the opportunity to build these qualities into their lives and for their feedback. In fact, Matt and I coauthored a book called *Fathers and Sons*. This book is all about what we've done to grow together as father and son in the development of these principles.

I also want to thank all of those whom I have interviewed (too many to mention here) over the years and my associates and friends who have helped by reading the manuscript and giving me their feedback: Kin Clinton, Bob Safford, John Maiorino, Bill Kimball, Ty Miller III, Michael "Hutch" Hutchison, and my son, Matt Jenson. In addition to this, I want to thank Bill Kimball for his help in providing the graphics for the book.

Introduction

> *The battle for control and leadership of the world has always been waged most effectively at the idea level. An idea, whether right or wrong, that captures the minds of a nation's youth will soon work its way into every area of society, especially in our multimedia age. Ideas determine consequences.*
>
> *—The American Covenant*

Two elderly ladies were sitting on their porch one summer evening, enjoying the warm breeze. The crickets were awake in the field, and their music competed only with that of the church choir down the road, which was practicing for Sunday morning. One of the women, who was enraptured by the choir's singing, commented dreamily, "Isn't that a beautiful sound?" The other woman, who rocked gently in time to the sounds of the crickets, replied, "Oh, yes. I understand they do it by rubbing their hind legs together."

Communication can be a funny thing. Often it's hard for us to know whether we're truly getting our thoughts across. So, as I begin this book, I do so with caution—because I want to communicate to you as effectively as I can the essential factors for becoming a successful, fulfilled, maximized individual.

But before going any further, I want to develop a clear understanding of what success is and isn't. If I'm going to help you achieve your goal of making a life and not just a living, I need to ensure that you start with a firm foundation. And that involves your idea of what success is.

One of my overarching assumptions about life is that we all move toward our definition of success.

"Hold on!" you may be saying. "I don't even have a definition of success."

> **You are moving toward your concept of success—but is it the right concept?**

Yes, you do! Everyone does. You may not be able to articulate it or write it down. But you and I are *always* trying to succeed at something. That "something," whatever it is, drives our thoughts, feelings, and actions. We are constantly focused on what we want to accomplish, whether we realize it or not.

Your concept of success has been developed and conditioned over the years by the media, your family upbringing, your peers and associates, and your various experiences. The net effect can be either positive or negative. Therefore, the questions to ask yourself are: What are you trying to accomplish? How will you know if you have succeeded once you "get there"? And, moreover, can you *ever* "get there" or is it all just a process?

How Are You Defining Success?

Whenever I present seminars on this topic, I ask for definitions of success. Most of the time I get the usual answers: "money," "position," "influence," "climbing the ladder," "the one who has the most toys wins." Usually I can group the definitions into five basic areas: power, prosperity, position, prestige, and pleasure.

Let's consider these five "elements of success":

What about power? Is power the secret to success? Hitler had a lot of power, but calling him a success would be to condone his actions!

Think about the stories Wall Street provides. There are hundreds of "successful" businesspeople with enormous power—along with broken marriages and failing families. The common philosophy is that if you're going to succeed in business, you have to forfeit success in other areas of life. I don't buy that. A truly successful person doesn't have to sacrifice his or her family.

What about prosperity? Materialism is a major problem today. Yet possessing things and having money aren't wrong. It is only when we become preoccupied with those things—with seeking truth and fulfillment in our accumulation—that we begin to miss the purpose and meaning of life.

In the comic strip "Cathy," an interesting dialogue takes place between Cathy and a young man regarding a collection of "have-to-have" items. The two characters point to each item and comment by turns:

> "Safari clothes that will never be near a jungle."
>
> "Aerobic footwear that will never set foot in an aerobics class."
>
> "Deep-sea dive watch that will never get damp."
>
> "Keys to a four-wheel-drive vehicle that will never experience a hill."
>
> "Architectural magazines we don't read filled with pictures of furniture we don't like."
>
> "Financial strategy software keyed to a checkbook that is lost somewhere under a computer no one knows how to work."
>
> "Art poster for an exhibit we never went to of an artist we never heard of."
>
> Finally, with a blank stare, one character says, "Abstract materialism has arrived."
>
> The other rejoins, "We've moved past the things we want and need and are buying those things that have nothing to do with our lives."

That is a grave but accurate description of our culture. Materialism is eating us alive.

The January 28, 1960, issue of *The Washington Post* records a letter from the author John Steinbeck to the politician Adlai Stevenson. Steinbeck wrote, "A strange species we are. We can stand anything God and nature throw at us save only plenty. If I wanted to destroy a nation, I would give it too much and I would have it on its knees: miserable, greedy, and sick."

What about position? Some people say that position defines success. Ferdinand and Imelda Marcos had prominent positions in the world. But did they succeed? It all depends on your definition of success.

I have a friend who was a U.S. congressman. This senior senator was always my choice for president, but he never ran. During a visit to his office, I saw displayed on his bulletin board many of the "hate letters" written against him. Underneath those letters was a quotation from the Bible: "Woe to you when all men speak well of you" (Luke 6:26).

This great man had enough humility and wisdom to know that a responsible position inevitably carries with it substantial criticism, both fair and unfair. Therefore, position alone isn't a worthy measuring stick for success.

What about prestige—being known and recognized? Many people who have it can tell you that prestige can be very fleeting. Baseball star Pete Rose was a man of prestige at one moment and a man of notoriety the next. Prestige certainly is no guarantee of success.

In fact, those who have prestige normally receive an equal or even greater amount of denigration. Think about what the tabloids do to "beautiful people." They portray them in the worst possible light! Is that success?

Finally, *what about pleasure?* "The rule of life is to make business a pleasure, and pleasure our *only* business," said Aaron Burr. This aptly conveys the rampant attitude of pleasure seeking in our day and age.

Jon Johnston speaks of the insidious infiltration of this striving for pleasure into our every thought and action. He says, "I've had waitresses ask me, 'What is your pleasure?' And we've all heard the ads 'You deserve a break today' (McDonald's) and 'Oh, What a Feeling' (Toyota). We're familiar with terms like *hyped up, turned on,* and *tripped out*—so overused during the seventies. All of these words and expressions are directly related to the national quest for pleasurable experience."[1]

Widespread as this desire for pleasure is, and as well documented in our day and age in particular books such as *Through the Culture of Narcissism,* there is nothing new about it. It's simply a form of hedonism. Hedonism, a philosophical worldview in which the experience and appreciation of pleasure are the highest goals, has been around since the beginning of time. Aristippus (435–356 B.C.), whose motto "Eat, drink, and be merry, for tomorrow you die" could also fit the pleasure seekers of the nineties, was one of the early advocates of hedonism. To be a hedonist is to make a god out of pleasure.

Rabbi Harold Kushner shares this illustration of a woman in his congregation who escaped a bad marriage and seemed to all concerned to be happily in control of her life, content with her singleness and freedom. But in a personal counseling meeting with Mr. Kushner she confided, "I know people envy me—the parties, the vacations, the freedom from responsibility. I wish I could make them understand how much I envy them. I wish I could tell them how soon it all gets to be dull and repetitious, until you find yourself doing things you really don't want to do, just not to be doing the same thing all over again, and how quickly I would trade all of this for the sound of a car door closing and familiar steps coming up the stairs at night."[2]

Building a life around self-focused pleasure is simply not satisfying in the long run.

You can easily see the problem. People put all their eggs in one basket to chase power, prosperity, position, prestige, or pleasure to find success. But once they have it, they realize they haven't succeeded at all in the most significant areas of their lives.

Glenn Bland, in his book *Success,* provides the best example I know of the importance of priorities. He tells of a meeting in 1923 of the world's most successful financiers, at Chicago's Edgewater Beach Hotel. These financial giants literally ruled the world of money: Charles Schwab, president of the largest steel company in America; Samuel Insull, president of the largest utility company; Howard Hopson, president of the largest gas company; Arthur Cutten, the great wheat speculator; Richard Whitney, president of the New York Stock Exchange; Albert Fall, Secretary of the Interior in President Harding's cabinet; Jesse Livermore, the great "bear" on Wall Street; Ivan Krueger, head of the world's greatest monopoly; and Leon Fraser, president of the Bank of International Settlements.

These men were "movers and shakers," the kind many people envy and wish to be like. Yet something went terribly wrong with these men's lives. Twenty-five years later:

- Charles Schwab went bankrupt.
- Samuel Insull died in a foreign land, penniless and a fugitive from justice.
- Howard Hopson was insane.
- Arthur Cutten was insolvent and died abroad.
- Richard Whitney had just been released from Sing Sing prison.
- Albert Fall had just been pardoned from prison and died at home, broke.
- Jesse Livermore committed suicide.
- Ivan Krueger committed suicide.
- Leon Fraser committed suicide.[3]

To be fair, the five Ps—power, prestige, position, prosperity, and pleasure—don't always result in personal devastation. In fact, they are rather amoral—neither good nor bad in themselves. Their use or abuse determines the outcome of a person's life. I don't want to discourage you from enjoying the rewards of your hard work. I want to encourage you to leverage those rewards for the good of others and yourself.

In my research of hundreds of top leaders around the world, I have asked the question: "At the end of your life, how will you know you've succeeded?" Without exception, I have never heard one person answer, "By my power, prosperity, position, prestige, pleasure, or any related areas." Instead, I have heard statements such as, "No one ever said on his deathbed that he wished he had worked more." Or, "I've never seen a hearse towing a U-Haul."

Indeed, these men and women answered:

- "It's important how my kids turned out."

- "Did I live a personally rich and fulfilling life?"

- "Did I positively change lives?"

- "Did I build meaningful and deep relationships?"

- "Did I really love my spouse?"

- "Did I make a difference?"

On the other hand, many people today are like the man Harold Kushner writes about in his book, *When Everything You've Ever Wanted Isn't Enough.* One day Kushner, a Jewish rabbi, received a visit from an executive who was in a depressed stupor. At Kushner's gentle urging, the man unburdened himself. He spoke of a funeral he'd attended in the past week. It wasn't the funeral that bothered him so much; rather, it was that in the brief period since the man's death, his name had been taken off his office door and his desk quickly cleaned out, "as though he were never there."

The executive then described a vision that had come to him during the funeral, "of a small serene forest. Inside that forest was a placid pond, and it was as though a small pebble had been dropped in that placid pond. It quickly fell to the bottom. There were a few ripples, but they were quickly gone. And it was as though that pebble were never there."

What had frightened this executive was the feeling that his own life seemed like that—that, although he had traveled extensively, made a lot of money, met a lot of people, and experienced a lot of things, his life seemed insignificant and meaningless—"as though I'd never lived."[4]

What about you? What is your concept of success? Have you deliberately developed one, or has yours simply evolved through the influence of the culture around you? And is it the *right* concept of success?

If you are not sure, I want to suggest to you a new way of looking at success. It's important to move away from thinking of success as power, prosperity, position, prestige, or pleasure, and to begin building a definition of success that centers on legitimate values: What are the things that ultimately count in life? How do you want people to remember you when you die?

You Determine What It Means to Succeed

Recently, I was one of thirty-five hundred people who attended the annual National Presidential Prayer Breakfast in Washington, D.C. At my table was a close friend of mine, the president of a major international airline. Sitting next to us were top business leaders from Latin America and a European ambassador. The chairman of a major oil company, senators, and heads of state were at the next table. At the front table sat President and Mrs. Bill Clinton, Vice President and Mrs. Al Gore, and other dignitaries.

This was clearly a Who's Who of movers and shakers. These successful people all had power, prosperity, position, and prestige in spades.

Then, in walked the speaker. Within moments, I observed one of the most extreme shifts in perspective I have ever witnessed. Immediately, the true meaning of success became crystal clear. It was blatantly obvious to everyone in the room that the most successful person there was this speaker.

She was not a dynamic speaker. As she read her talk she seldom looked up. She couldn't even be seen because of her diminutive size. And her speech was as politically incorrect as I could imagine. She spoke out strongly against abortion. The President and First Lady squirmed in their seats. The conservatives in the room cheered in a show of approval. But then she blasted birth control. That shut the mouths of many of the conservatives and almost everyone else.

When the speaker finished, she received a thunderous standing ovation. Why? Because she personified a life of authentic success. She didn't have power, prosperity, position, prestige, or pleasure, as we typically know it. But she did have *real* power, *real* prosperity, *real* position, *real* prestige, and *real* pleasure.

Who was this powerhouse? Mother Teresa.

I don't mean to suggest that we all need to become poor and live in squalor and anonymity to experience authentic success. I do suggest that our success has much to do with the values of caring, sacrifice, character, and contribution—values that Mother Teresa embodied.

So, let's look at success by asking the following:

How Will You Be Remembered?

What epitaph do you want written on your tombstone? How should your obituary read?

When you read the name Alfred Nobel, the Nobel Peace Prize probably comes to mind. Yet that famous prize is only half of Alfred Nobel's story!

Nobel was a Swedish chemist who made his fortune by inventing dynamite and other powerful explosives used for weapons. Years later, when Nobel's brother died, a newspaper accidentally printed an obituary for Alfred instead. He was described as a man who became rich by enabling people to kill each other in unprecedented quantities. Shaken by this assessment, Nobel resolved to use his fortune to honor accomplishments that benefited humanity. Thus, he created the Nobel Peace Prize, among others.

Alfred Nobel had had a rare opportunity—that is, to evaluate his life at its end and yet still be alive to change it. *And now you, too, can have this same opportunity!*

Harold Kushner wrote: "Our souls are not hungry for fame, comfort, wealth, or power. Those rewards create almost as many problems as they solve. Our souls are hungry for meaning, for the sense that we have figured out how to live so that our lives matter, so that the world will at least be a little bit different for our having passed through it."[5] Isn't that really the issue when it's all said and done?

You were meant to succeed authentically in all vital areas of your life and to make a positive difference with your life. In short, you were meant to maximize your life.

> **Success is the progressive realization of all that you were meant to be and do.**

Build Success in All Areas of Your Life

Any success you attain must be a holistic success—that is, balanced, integrated success, one that is in harmony with who you are. I believe that if you succeed in work and yet fail in personal relationships, you haven't succeeded. And if you accomplish great things but live miserably in the process, you haven't succeeded. Only a life rooted in *real and lasting values* is successful.

Think about it for a moment. You are a whole person. You have emotional, physical, volitional, spiritual, and relational sides to your being. Beyond that, you have responsibilities in various realms—business, family, community. And each of these areas has its own subresponsibilities. They are all interrelated. You cannot afford to succeed in your finances and yet fail in your marriage. You cannot achieve levels of excellence in your business and yet burn out physically and emotionally. You must be winning in all vital areas to be successful.

You may be thinking, "But you can't have it all!" Oh, yes you can! You were *meant* to have it all. The key is having it all *correctly*.

Now if you're a manager, this idea of holistic success might make you a little nervous. After all, if people give attention to their personal lives, families, places of worship, and communities, won't that hurt your bottom line? No, no, a thousand times no!

First, you have to define your bottom line not only in fiscal terms, but also in human terms. You have to realize that a well-managed life produces a well-managed business. Happy and growing people are more productive; healthy families feed profitable ventures.

My goal is to help you refine, clarify, and articulate a definition of success that is in harmony with the real you and will allow you to lead a balanced, fulfilled, and significant life.

Become a Champion for Positive Impact

Maximizing your impact on yourself and those around you is, in short, *to be a champion for good.*

A number of years ago the great Alexis de Tocqueville, a French philosopher and statesman, made this insightful comment about the United States: "America is great because America is good, and if she ceases to be good she'll cease to be great."

Right now, America *is* ceasing to be good. We have a breakdown in the greatness of our country because of an erosion of moral values, an ignorance of the underlying principles that built our culture.

Society reflects the health of major institutions which reflect the health of our families which reflect the health of individuals. All groups of society, from government to the family, are influenced ultimately by their leadership. Thus, the quality of leadership, or the lack of it, is the root of our problems. We need ethical, value-driven men and women of deep convictions and courage, people who have carefully determined and developed their worldviews and have decided upon a way of looking at life that is based on proven values.

Great cultures fall apart when great prosperity fools the people into apathy. As the people sit back and enjoy their good fortune, their blessing of prosperity turns into a curse of laziness and ingratitude. Eventually that permeates their values and ethics, and, in the end, the entire culture collapses.

Why does this happen? A passage in the Bible teaches that the people fall when there is no leadership (Prov. 29:18). Laurence Cohen, the former mayor of Saint Paul, Minnesota, said, "If cynicism and apathy are to be reversed, the national leadership must take stands from a position of honesty and integrity." Derek Bok, the former president of Harvard University said, "There is a very serious dearth of people who seem able to supply convincing answers, or even point to directions toward solutions."

In every major area of our culture today, people are crying out for leaders of vision, moral courage, values, and ethics—leaders who will say, "I want to make a difference, and I *can* make a difference." Such leaders have lives that are deeply rooted in solid principles and driven by universal values. They have a strong sense of direction because they hold firmly to certain absolutes.

You're probably reading this book right now because you want to become that kind of person—a champion. You want your life to be significant by helping to change your world. You want not only to take something out of the world, but to put something back into it—to make a difference.

This book is the tool you need. I'm writing it because I want you to be complete—whole as a person, balanced in every area. I want you to be significant and to succeed. I want you to be a champion for truth. I want you to be able to help the people around you live more productive, meaningful lives. I want your business to be more successful because of the values that undergird your life. And I want your city and country to be renewed, internally and externally, as you live out an authentic success—one that is based on abiding principles.

Success Depends on What *You* Do with *You*

The three axioms to the right have a common theme: *success is in your hands*. Indeed, all success is based on the way you manage yourself. And the way you manage yourself is only as good as the principles upon which you build your life.

> **Good government is based on self-government. Good business management is based on self-management. Good institutional administration is based on self-administration.**

Therefore, pursue *truth*. By that I mean universal truths. The tendency today is to elevate a relativistic mindset in which no absolutes exist. This viewpoint is nonsense. *Absolute universal principles exist!*

Just as physical laws govern the physical universe, so universal principles govern human existence. If these laws are violated, inevitable repercussions result. These principles are abiding truths—universal, absolute, nonnegotiable. They are as factual as the law of gravity. We may not understand them or buy into them, but that doesn't invalidate them. They simply won't move; they are firm. Our choice is either to discover and fully embrace them and thereby succeed as we are meant to, or to ignore them and fail without ever knowing why.

Let me offer an illustration:

One night a massive battleship was cruising coastal waters in the middle of a raging storm. The OOD (officer of the deck) was keeping a careful watch when he suddenly saw the light of an oncoming ship. He summoned the captain and told him of the situation. At the captain's orders, the OOD directed the radio man to signal the oncoming ship: "We are on a collision course. Move 10 degrees to port." Expecting immediate acknowledgment, the OOD was surprised to hear the reply: "You move 10 degrees to starboard."

"I suggest you move 10 degrees to port."

"I suggest you move 10 degrees to starboard."

"Sir," said the OOD on the battleship, "I am an officer in the United States Navy. You move 10 degrees to port."

"Sir, I am a seaman. You move 10 degrees to starboard."

It was obvious to the OOD that somebody had better do something soon. The light of the other ship appeared closer and closer.

"Sir," he signaled firmly, "I am a battleship!"

"Sir," came the reply just as firmly, "I am a lighthouse!"

What we should seek more than anything else in the search for success is *truth*. truth is more important than power, prosperity, position, prestige, and pleasure combined. truth alone is the source of authentic success.

> **Become a craftsman at making a life by applying right principles.**

If you want to succeed in life, you must passionately pursue the discovery of truth and know how to apply that truth appropriately in your life. This is called *wisdom*. The word *wisdom* in the original Hebrew language referred to craftsmanship. To be wise was to be a craftsman at living, an artisan of life. In short, that is what this book is all about.

I'd like to share a great personal secret with you. In my research of hundreds of leaders, spanning over twenty-five years, I have been most profoundly influenced by one particular leader. She is world-renowned and serves as a consultant to heads of state, Fortune 500 CEOs, and well-known professional leaders. She has given me concise evaluations on every major success, peak performance, leadership development, and personal excellence system I have found. Furthermore, she has consistently guided me toward truth and principles. Indeed, she is my ultimate source of knowledge and experience.[6] Throughout this book I will refer to her as "Ruth." Of course, Ruth is not a real person, but rather my way of personifying wisdom and light principles—fundamental, bedrock truth that has been sought out and applied for centuries.

I once quizzed her about the various authors, authorities, and leaders in fields ranging from success literature to philosophy of life. Ruth stopped me in midsentence with the following admonition: "The value of wisdom is far above the greatest treasures on earth. And wisdom and good judgment dwell together, for wisdom knows where to discover knowledge and understanding. Wisdom gives good advice. It is the strength that allows leaders to lead well and make good rules. If you seek this wisdom with all your might, you will find it. It is the source of unending riches, honor, justice, and life. So, Ron, get wisdom. Whatever it costs, seek it out."[7]

That is exactly what I have been doing for dozens of years. Now I want to communicate some of the insights I have gained to you. I communicate these out of no sense of "having arrived." In fact, one of the major truths I have learned along the way is that seeking wisdom demands an *authentic humility*. I don't believe I am more special than anyone else. I am not a dispenser of all truth, a guru, or a prophet. Quite the contrary. I am a ship on the same sea you are on. However, I have seen the lighthouse, and I know enough to understand that if I let its light guide me, I will be safe. And to the extent that I discover and embrace this principle, I succeed. To the extent that I don't, I fail.

Having said that, I present to you three major assumptions, which comprise my game plan for this book:

- Assumption 1: You are moving toward your definition of success.

- Assumption 2: Authentic success is maximizing all of your life and impact.

- Assumption 3: Wisely applying universal principles is the key to authentic success.

I plan to communicate these truths to you first by providing *motivation* through stories, illustrations, principles, and worksheets that get you involved. It's not enough for you to just read this book. You need to put it to work.

Second, I will provide *methods* for you to work these ideas into your life. I will help you take these principles and add to them motivation to pull them all together. This process includes a twenty-one-day habit-changing system, which I will discuss in an upcoming chapter.

Third, I'm going to provide a *map* for you—a mind-set, a grid, a way of looking at life. I'm going to help you understand how to live in a way that will get the job done. I call this concept, "How to Make a Life, Not Just a Living." It's a new way of looking at life using principles of truth you can count on in all circumstances.

In my interviews with leaders over the past twenty-five years,[8] one of the questions I have asked is: "When you're seventy-five and look back on your life, how will you know you've succeeded?"

Based on the responses I have received and my own personal evaluation and study, I have identified ten nonnegotiable principles that serve as the organizing system around which you can develop all the subsequent truths that should flow in your life. These principles form the framework of the **MAXIMIZERS** acrostic that I will develop for you.

What does it mean to be a "maximizer"? The best way to explain this is with an acrostic. Every letter stands for a phrase, and every phrase states a basic principle about life that I will develop more deeply in this book.

Here is the easy-to-remember **MAXIMIZERS** acrostic:

M ake things happen.
A chieve personal significance.
X out the negatives.
I nternalize right principles.
M arch to a mission.
I ntegrate all of life.
Z ero in on caring for people.
E nergize internally.
R ealign rigorously.
S tay the course.

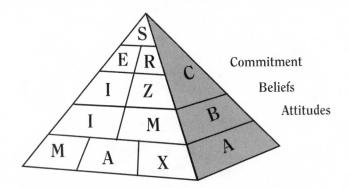

To give clarity to these principles, I have broken them down into three categories of authentic success: attitude, belief, and commitment.

Section 1 of this book deals with the foundational principles of *attitude:* "Make Things Happen," "Achieve Personal Significance," and "X out the Negatives." Attitude, or the way we view life, is essential and foundational to all of the other principles.

Section 2 is built on two principles of *belief:* "Internalize Right Principles" and "March to a Mission." These two chapters include the development of a character-based lifestyle and a clear purpose statement to help you become successful.

Finally, section 3 deals with the five principles that serve as major *commitments* to life: creating balance in life, helping to change people through right relationships, how to experience ultimate personal power, the art of making mid-course corrections, and what I call the ultimate leadership principle—*persistence,* or the ability to stand against all that the world may raise up against you.

Attitude. Belief. Commitment. The power of these three categories comes through aligning them together. Some people have good attitudes but lack commitment and follow-through. Others have solid beliefs, but negative attitudes sabotage their authentic success. Still others are volitionally strong and can will themselves to accomplish things but consistently fall short because either their belief systems or attitudes are inhibited. Finally, others may be solid in all three areas but lack the integration of the ten Maximizers principles I propose.

As our attitudes, beliefs, and commitments become aligned within ourselves, our authentic success grows. These are all in direct proportion to one another.

Focus on Roots of Right Living, Not the Fruit

If you are going to authentically succeed, you must focus on *roots* and not the *fruit* of your life. The fruit in your life includes happiness, fulfilling relationships, prosperity, influence, position, etc. The roots are the nonnegotiable principles around which you build your life. These are the basic attitudes, beliefs, and commitments I will communicate and illustrate throughout this book via the MAXIMIZERS concept. The soil for those roots is wisdom or universal truths.

Perhaps you have spent your life focusing on obtaining fruit. I urge you to stop. Make a commitment now to spend the rest of your life focusing on *roots*—those principles that when fully embraced produce authentic success.

Go back through this chapter now, and remember the challenge I gave to you about how you want to be remembered. Imagine you're writing out the words that will be found on your tombstone. With that vision in mind, commit yourself to the search. I am confident we can get you there.

Action Steps

1. How do you define success now, after having read this chapter? (Consider your use of time, talents, attention, and lifestyle.)

2. Take a few minutes to write your own obituary.

3. How will you know you have succeeded at the end of your life?

4. Rate yourself according to the MAXIMIZER principles listed here in the form of a creed (1 is the lowest rating, 10 the highest):

Make things happen.

> I take charge of my life and am a difference-maker.

> 1 . . . 5 . . . 10

Achieve personal significance.

> I live my life with a sense of destiny.

> 1 . . . 5 . . . 10

X out the negatives.

> I embrace problems as positive opportunities.

> 1 . . . 5 . . . 10

Internalize right principles.

> I center my life on bedrock principles.

> 1 . . . 5 . . . 10

March to a mission.

> I passionately pursue my mission.

> 1 . . . 5 . . . 10

Integrate all of life.

> I keep all vital areas of my life in balance.

> 1 . . . 5 . . . 10

Zero in on caring for people.

> I put others first and honestly serve them.

> 1 . . . 5 . . . 10

Energize internally.

> I cultivate my character and spirit.

> 1 . . . 5 . . . 10

Realign rigorously.

> I keep adjusting to needs.

> 1 . . . 5 . . . 10

Stay the course.

> I never, ever, ever quit.

> 1 . . . 5 . . . 10

ROOT ATTITUDES

Section

1

What you see is what you'll be!

This statement articulates the power of attitude. The following section of this book develops three "root attitudes" you must develop if you are going to succeed in your life and profession.

First, the foundational issue of taking responsibility for your life and making things happen will be addressed. As long as you live as a victim (one who is not responsible for his or her actions and life in general), you are doomed to fail. But, if you take responsibility for your attitudes, beliefs, and commitments, you will achieve success. You cannot control what has happened in the past or what others might think, feel, say, or do. You cannot control the end results or fruits in your life. But you can take responsibility for planting and cultivating the right roots. This "rightness living" will ultimately produce the fruit of authentic success. But you must take charge of your own life and accept responsibility for it.

The second root attitude is the principle of achieving personal significance. Your self-perception determines your behavior. If you see yourself as having a destiny and being of great value, you will act accordingly. Quite frankly, the deep crises in America's inner cities and other locations around the world can be linked directly to self-concept. The answer is not to get the people out of the ghetto; it is to get the ghetto out of the people. The ghetto is merely a faulty, deranged self-concept. This chapter addresses how to change that self-concept through healthy, balanced affirmation and through facing and addressing the reality of your soft spots or weak areas.

The third root attitude in this section is learning to X out the negatives. Here I talk about how to handle problems (don't run from them—embrace them!). Moreover, I articulate how to develop right beliefs toward critical areas in your life. Finally, I clarify how you can confront the difficulties in your life by bashing your fears, doubts, and other inhibitors.

Chapter 1

Make Things Happen

How to Be a Difference Maker

*The best years of your life are the ones in which you
decide your problems are your own. You don't blame
them on your mother, the ecology, or the president.
You realize that you control your own destiny.*
—*Psychologist Albert Ellis*

A college freshman at his first football practice breaks away for an eighty-yard touchdown run. His teammates look at him in amazement and disbelief. His coach says, "You're going to have quite a future around here." Later, his blonde girlfriend kisses him excitedly. Life is completely satisfying, and the future looks bright!

But nothing in this young man's life ever lives up to that day. He doesn't become a big-time football player. His business career is equally disappointing. His marriage sours. And the pain of all these failures is even greater because he remembers thinking, on a perfect day many years before, that life would always be pleasant.[1]

That scenario, written more than fifty years ago by Irwin Shaw in a famous short story, beautifully illustrates a nineties dilemma. Many of us spend our entire lives trying either to recapture something we experienced long ago or to finally stumble upon that elusive perfect future.

Waiting for something just around the corner is merely reacting to life. If you are going to be a difference-maker, a *maximizer*, you need to be assertive and proactive in your thoughts and actions. You need to make things happen—and not just wait for them to engulf you! You need to take responsibility for your life and your future.

This is the beginning place of all success: You must want to control the things that determine success and failure. If this foundational attitude is not firmly set in your mind, you may erupt in moments of brilliance and enlightenment throughout your life, but you will never develop patterns of excellence and achievement. Under pressure, people who merely react to life always fall back into the "blame game."

A Civilization of Victims

Today, like never before in history, much of the world is becoming a civilization of blamers and "victims." We blame our past, our parents, our society, our heritage, our "dysfunctionalities," or anything else we can think of for our existing personal problems.

I recently read a cartoon that shows a defense lawyer seeking to persuade a jury. He says: "My client admits murdering eight people. *But* we'll prove that he was cruelly and mercilessly denied a defense by having a caring and loving father."

In one of the most insightful (and inciteful!) books I have read in recent years, *The Nation of Victims*, author Charles Sykes delineates and documents this problem of a victim mentality.[2] Here is a summary of some of the stories he uses to make his case:

- An FBI agent embezzles two thousand dollars and subsequently loses it while gambling in Atlantic City. Though he is fired, he gets reinstated once he convinces the court that his tendency toward gambling with other people's money is a "handicap" and therefore protected under federal law.

- A young man steals a car from a parking lot and is killed while escaping. His family sues the proprietor of the parking lot for failing to take steps to prevent such thefts.

- A man admits to exposing himself more than ten thousand times (being convicted on more than thirty occasions) and is thus turned down for a job as a parking attendant due to his arrest record. But he sues based on the argument that he has never exposed himself in a parking lot (only in libraries and laundromats). Wisconsin employment officials agree. And, the flasher is called a victim of illegal job discrimination.[3]

Sykes also tells the story of a Chicago man who complained to the Minority Rights Division of the U.S. Attorney's Office that McDonald's violates federal equal-protection laws because their restaurants' seats are not large enough for his unusually capacious backside. Seething with indignation, the aggrieved party announced:

> I represent a minority group that is just as visible as blacks, Mexicans, Latins, Asians, or women. Your company has taken it upon itself to grossly and improperly discriminate against large people—both tall and heavyset—and we are prepared, if necessary, to bring federal litigation against your company to comply with the Equal Rights in Public Accommodations Provision. . . .

> I have a 60-inch waist and am 6 feet 5 inches tall. It is absolutely impossible for me to get service in that restaurant because of the type of seating that you have installed. Furthermore, many of the single seats have such small platforms on the seats that it is impossible for the posterior of an overweight individual to sit on that seat.

> We are very serious in our demands that McDonald's recognize the existence of the large and heavy minority that makes up nearly 20 percent of the American population, and take severe steps to provide at least 20 percent of the seating in your restaurants to be suitable . . . for large and heavy people.

> We will await bringing litigation for 30 days pending the possibility of a suitable plan being developed by McDonald's.[4]

Chicago Tribune columnist Mike Royko rightly points out that the author's attempt to equate his status with that of Mexicans, Latins, Asians, blacks, and women is unacceptable. After all, the writer "was not born with a 60-inch waist and an enormous butt. He created himself and his butt. That was the image he sought for himself. His problems are his responsibility. And even the most liberal of liberals would have to agree that [the writer's] 60-inch waist and awesome butt should not be the responsibility of the United States of America or McDonald's."[5]

As ludicrous and absurd as such stories seem, the fact is, they are happening in increasing measure. And the fire is being fanned by tabloid newspapers and TV shows that pander to the "victimized," the explosive growth of litigation in our society, the overly intrusive hand of government that increasingly penalizes citizens by maintaining an archaic welfare culture, and extremist psychologists who create and support every conceivable dysfunction.

The problem becomes especially destructive when the latter industry categorizes misbehavior as a disease. Suddenly the problem is not mine but someone else's. So I join a group to support my illness and enshrine the problem that is destroying me: Gamblers Anonymous, Pill Addicts Anonymous, S-Anon (relatives and friends of sex addicts), Nicotine Anonymous, Youth Emotions Anonymous, Unwed Parents Anonymous, Emotional Health Anonymous, Debtors Anonymous, Workaholics Anonymous, Dual Disorders Anonymous, Batterers Anonymous, Victims Anonymous, Families of Sex Offenders Anonymous.[6]

Please don't misunderstand me. I know that support groups can be and are very helpful. But the danger in such groups is the tendency to encourage participants to blame others and not take responsibility for their own lives.

If you want to succeed, you must take responsibility. You must be proactive and take charge. And that means, you must be prepared to change. If your problems are not your own, how can you change? But, if they are yours—even if you were abused or affected by an unspeakable outer source—you have *hope*. And your hope is tied directly to this fact: You can change if you apply the right principles—the principles you learn in this book. You are in control. You can change because *you* are in charge of your attitudes, beliefs, and commitments.

You cannot afford to be a *victim*. No matter how much you may feel like a victim or enjoy the sympathy of others, you must take the initiative and make a difference with your life. That is your destiny!

Be Proactive, Not Reactive

Your decision to take charge of your life is the seed of your success. Another way of saying "taking charge" is "being proactive." This word—*proactive*—is a simple combination of two familiar words: *pro*, meaning "for," and *active*, meaning "doing something." In other words: Don't just sit there—do something!

You and I get into trouble routinely by focusing on items over which we have no control—will this meeting be positive, will my child be safe, will people like me, will I close the sale, or will I be happy? This is the *fruit* of our life.

What good is it to focus here? None—absolutely none. In fact, it is harmful, often resulting in worry, fear, manipulation, and worse.

Instead, you need to *focus* on those items you can control: (the roots) right attitudes, right beliefs, and right commitments. By so doing, you will use your emotional energy in a positive way and actually move forward more quickly. This proactivity does make a difference. Reactive people focus on the *fruit* (result). Proactive people focus on the *roots* (principles).

Think of the battery in your car. If you merely turn on your car's radio or lights without turning on the engine, over time your battery will run down. Likewise, if you react to life around you as a victim, without turning on the engine of action, your internal battery—your ability to cope, your flame of hope—also will run down.

But if you turn on the engine in your car before turning on your radio or lights, and you drive around—that is, move and take some action—your battery will recharge itself. So it is with proactive people. If you take charge, the challenges of life won't deplete your battery but will add energy to it—and you will be a beacon for all the world to see!

The choice is yours. Will you see yourself as a victim, who only reacts? Or as a victorious fighter who is in control and driving toward success?

You choose: Victim or victor.

Psychologists tell us that stress is a natural reality. Stress is tension that comes into our lives as part of the process of living. We can respond to stress in two ways: as a victim, who acts in a distressful (inappropriate) way, or as a victor, who acts in a eustressful (appropriate) way. If we respond appropriately, we can control stress and increase our capability for greater energy and a positive outcome.

Ruth's Wisdom

I remember talking to Ruth one day about this concept of victimization, of people not taking responsibility for their lives.

(Remember: Ruth's my personification of the wisdom principles of life.) It happened once when I was in Pittsburgh, speaking to a group of about seven hundred people on relationships, particularly in the context of marriage. Much of what I spoke about had to do with people taking responsibility for their roles in relationships.

When I asked Ruth what root problems stop people from taking responsibility for their lives, she gave me a very cryptic and fascinating response. "It's their view of life," she said. "It's their image of themselves and their lives."

I asked what she meant by "view of life." She answered, "Ron, people today have lost sight of the importance of their lives. You need to realize that you are fundamentally managers, not owners of your lives. I don't mean that we don't own properties and have equity. I mean that you can't take it with you. When you die, you die. You leave this life behind. You have a period of time on this earth in which you manage your assets, your time, your capabilities, your finances—all the blessings and talents you have. That's what you should be doing. This is simply called 'stewardship.'

"People have lost sight of that. As a result, they tend to hold back from taking responsibility for their lives. They tend to blame others or expect others to take the initiative. This is why they fail."

She then told me this story:

"I had a friend once who was a very shrewd businessman. He wanted to find a future successor to manage the company he owned. So he targeted three very capable individuals who oversaw different profit centers of his company.

"All three seemed to have the talents needed to fulfill the role. But my friend wanted someone who would take initiative, someone who had courage like himself, who would not be so immobilized by fear of failure that he or she wouldn't risk at a reasonable level.

"Unbeknownst to these three people, my friend put together a test. He gave each of the three profit centers in his business an infusion of capital proportionate to its size.

"He gave Bill, the manager of the smallest profit center, ten thousand dollars to invest in any way he saw fit. Then he gave Sandy fifty thousand dollars for her larger profit center. Finally, he gave Mark one hundred thousand dollars to invest in any way he wanted in his profit center.

"Each of these managers would be evaluated on how he or she spent the money during a twelve-month period of time. So the owner of the business went out of the country to let them manage on their own.

"Six months later he came back and found out that Mark had taken the money and spent it on very intensive training in the area of human relations and other 'soft' training areas, for the purpose of helping his people grow in their self-mastery and self-concept. The result was twofold: the productivity of that particular profit center doubled during the twelve months, and every indicator pointed to even greater growth in the future.

"Then he looked at how Sandy managed her fifty thousand. She had also spent much of her money in a similar type of training, but with a focus on team relationships, because of the need in her particular group. In addition, she developed a particular marketing strategy and a product line for future growth. She, too, doubled what she had been given.

"Then my friend went to Bill. Bill had taken the smallest amount, ten thousand dollars, and had merely kept things going. At one point that may have not been a bad strategy. But Bill's was the least profitable of all the centers, and Bill had only maintained its low profitability.

"When Bill was asked why he hadn't put the money into something that would create growth and greater profitability, he said he was afraid the CEO would be angry with him for taking such a risk and might even consider firing him if his decision turned out to be a bad one.

"The upshot of the whole thing was that Mark, who had invested the one hundred thousand dollars and created the greatest productivity, was given a greater investment the subsequent year. And so was Sandy, who had had fifty thousand dollars to invest. Today, Mark and Sandy are the CEO and COO of the entire company.

"You see, Mark and Sandy took responsibility for their lives. They were willing to trust their instincts. They knew they could be proactive. They were not afraid like Bill."[7]

Making things happen involves a fundamental choice between two ways of life—the right way and the wrong way. You must do the best with what you have. You must focus on what you can affect rather than on what you cannot affect.

Be Disciplined, Not Lazy

**Focus on the roots—
not the fruit.**

We begin to make things happen when we become *disciplined*. We don't accomplish anything in this life without self-discipline. Richard Shelley Taylor, in his book *The Disciplined Life*, defines self-discipline this way: "The ability to regulate conduct by principle and judgment rather than impulse, desire, high pressure, or social custom." You see, discipline is the ability to *consciously control* your circumstances. It is the ability to control your life—to put first things first.

Now here's a question for you. Are there habits in your life that were acceptable when you were a child but aren't acceptable now? Are you still struggling with giving in to impulse?

Everyone struggles with one or more of three areas: pride, sensualism, and greed. Pride, which has its place, is unhealthy when it is stimulated by self-absorption. Sensualism is being preoccupied with sensual fulfillment—food, sex, sound, thrill-seeking. (Many commercials and advertisements today are geared toward sensualism.) Greed involves people just wanting more for more's sake, or being covetous, that is, wanting what belongs to someone else. This creates a generation of people who live on plastic. They are preoccupied with their credit cards and can't stop spending.

I can relate to pride, sensualism, and greed. Yet my major point of struggle is in the area of the senses. Whether the struggle involves not wanting to exercise or wanting to eat too much or watching too much TV, it all centers on sensual gratification.

Consider your own life: What do you really desire? What makes you salivate the quickest? For me it's donuts. I like donuts. There was a place near my home in Philadelphia called the Donuttery. Whenever I got within a mile of the Donuttery, I visualized a hot cinnamon roll with butter cascading down the sides. I could smell it. I could see it. I could taste it. And like Pavlov's dog, I started to salivate and even froth just thinking about that cinnamon roll. In a very real sense, I was looking for sensual gratification—and the words of Richard Shelley Taylor burned in my gut: "Self-discipline is basically the ability to subordinate."

The word *discipline* comes from the Greek word *gymnatsu*. Now, what does that word sound like? That's right: *gymnastic*.

If you're going to become a person who makes things happen—if you really want to be a difference-maker—then you need to become disciplined. You need to put a coach, a governor over your thoughts and actions. You need to become patterned in your life.

I want to tell you a true story. Many years ago I was walking through Sears with a very close friend. We were talking a bit, and as we walked he looked at me and spat in my face. That's right—he spat in my face in the middle of Sears. I took out my handkerchief and wiped my face clean. I didn't say anything, hoping I would hear something from him. He didn't utter a word. We just walked along.

We began talking again. He looked at me a second time, came to within six inches of my face, and spat in it again. (I promise, this is a true story.) I didn't say anything, trying to be a gentleman. I took off my glasses, wiped them and my face clean, and hoped he would say something, but he didn't.

So we walked along a little farther—and do you know what happened? A third time, my friend looked at me and spat in my face. *A third time.*

Do you know what I did? Nothing. Do you know why? Because he was my six-month-old baby boy.

You may be thinking, "What a stupid story! That's what babies do all the time." But here's my point: When you thought I was talking about an adult, you were horrified because you don't expect adults to act that way. Most adults have patterned and disciplined themselves, and they know that it isn't socially acceptable to spit in someone's face. But when I said he was a baby boy, you didn't think anything of it.

Now let me ask you: How often do you still act like a child in the various areas of your life?

To maximize your personal and professional effectiveness, you need to develop and cultivate right patterns through constant, arduous repetition. How do you do this? You must learn two major skills: First, *work hard*. Second, *develop right habits*. This is how you "gymnasticize" yourself.

1. Work Hard

If you're going to succeed in life, you must work. Indeed, this work ethic must be reflected in every critical area of your life. There simply is no shortcut. John Gardner says, "When people are serving, life is no longer meaningless." "Without work," said Albert Camus, "all life becomes rotten." But with work and hard effort, life becomes meaningful and exciting.

Gary Player won more international golf tournaments in his day than anyone else. Today he's still winning on the Seniors tour, and winning big. Throughout his career, people have said to him, "I'd give anything if I could hit the golf ball like you."

On one particularly tough day, Player was tired and frustrated when once again he heard that comment: "I'd give anything if I could hit the ball just like you." Player's usual politeness failed him as he replied tersely to the spectator, "No you wouldn't. You'd give anything to hit a golf ball like me *if it was easy*. Do you know what you've got to do to hit a golf ball like me? You've got to get up at five o'clock in the morning every day, go out on the course, and hit one thousand golf balls. Your hand starts bleeding, you walk up to the clubhouse, wash the blood off your hand, slap a bandage on it, and go out and hit another thousand golf balls. That's what it takes to hit a golf ball like me."

Gary Player is determined. He is persistent. He doesn't quit. People who have accomplished things in life are people who stick with it no matter how tough the going becomes. Making a difference means making the decision to persevere.

Burn out or fizzle?

A comment by Thomas Paine is so telling: "That which we obtain too easily we esteem too lightly." If you really value something, you've got to work hard at it. You must work hard in your business, work hard in your family, work hard at personal fitness, faith, and friendship. Every area of your life needs this discipline!

An important question to ask is, why do we work? Elbert Hubbard said, "We work to become, not to acquire." Work should be neither your sole source of fulfillment nor something you just do. Your real vocation is your life, and work is a part of it. It is a significant part of it—but still just a part. If you don't take charge of this mind-set, you will not succeed *authentically*. You'll either burn out or fizzle.

Burnout is the outcome for those who have too great a preoccupation with work. Fizzle is what happens when people pay too little attention to work. The latter category is where too many people in our culture fit into. Research says that more than 70 percent of all workers say they could be more productive and 45 percent say they could be twice as productive. Imagine the implications of that to our gross national product, not to mention to the lives of those personally involved in underproducing. One writer said it this way: "Millions are idle—even if they have jobs. Some have great careers while others simply chisel."

According to one Lou Harris poll, 63 percent of American workers believe that people aren't working as hard as they did ten years ago; 78 percent believe people take less pride in their work; 69 percent believe that overall workmanship is inferior; 73 percent believe workers are less motivated. In their fascinating book, *Why America Doesn't Work*, Jack Eckerd, founder and president of Eckerd Drugs, and Chuck Colson, of Watergate infamy and Prison Fellowship Ministries, explore how America has moved away from thrift, industry, diligence, and perseverance—concepts summed up by the words "work ethic."

According to writer Arthur Burns, America was founded on the shoulders of enterprising Jewish, Scottish Protestant, and Italian Catholic immigrants, all of whom believed "their work mattered to God." They saw their lives and work as much more than simply being busy and bringing home a paycheck. In fact, work was a fundamental dimension of their very existence. Work to these individuals was a moral imperative that was the key to the "ethic" in work ethic.

These people saw their work as a gift of God and their task as ultimately working for God, according to Eckerd and Colson. Moreover, they saw significant social implications to their work. As Reformation leader Martin Luther said, "Man does not live for himself alone . . . but he lives also for all men on earth." In this vein, Luther's contemporary in the Reformation, John Calvin, encouraged workers to produce more than they needed so they could meet the needs of others.

This work ethic, which was deeply rooted in the Protestant Reformation, was the very core of what made America great in its early years. But in the mid-nineteenth century this ethic began to erode. As Sherwood Wirt says, "The calling lost its vertical bearings in the incessant whir of machinery and the grime of the mill town. . . . As the modern world awoke to its material strength and shook off the disciplines of the Puritan way of life, it found that the doctrine of secular calling had become unnecessary. . . . Vocation became simply 'occupation.'"

Time Honored View of Work	The Growing View of Work
Work is part of "calling/vocation"	Work is just my occupation
A place to reflect right values	A place to get what you want
Focus on giving	Focus on getting (money, time off, perks)
Vital and exciting place to be	Just a place to get the salary needed for life
An ennobling occupation	A means to an end

As the eighteenth century arrived and the Enlightenment came into full force (with the dawn of human reason), humankind increasingly became the center of all things, and work turned from an ennobling occupation to one that was simply utilitarian—a means to an end. Loving God and caring for others were no longer at the center of work. Labor itself became the shrine.

If you're a manager, how does that make you feel about the people who work with you? How long can you stay competitive with this fact? Not long! The key is a revived view of work. And this view needs to be built on the old concept that life is a calling—that we all are here to fulfill our vocation, and that vocation is to be the very best we can be *in all arenas*. We are destined to maximize our lives, to do all excellently. Our destiny is tied to this!

Let me suggest some specific ways to reprogram your view of work as an act of significance and substance:

First, admit where you are in regard to your view toward work. Do you see work as an activity to endure? Or are you on the other extreme, a workaholic?

Second, commit yourself to be your best in every area, both personally and professionally.

Third, focus on using things and caring for people, versus using people and caring for things. This focus will dramatically affect how you function during a day's work. For instance, managers can easily accomplish overall business objectives and, in the process, use people to achieve those ends. What if, instead, you focused on caring for those who work with you and for you by developing them in their professional and personal lives? The more people you have around you who are developed through your authentic concern, the more effective and productive they will be to accomplish an end. You'll get much more done and be much more productive and profitable when your focus moves from using people to caring for them.

Fourth, keep learning and don't stand still. If you see your job as one that's fulfilling a part of your overall life's vocation, you will be highly motivated to become better and better by constantly growing. Thus, you should be reading books, listening to tapes, watching videos, developing new skills and abilities, and always developing quality. If you keep growing and developing—honing and sharpening your saw—you will not only be much more productive, but much more satisfied in your work.

Fifth, look for opportunities to serve others. If you let your focus become serving people—not only in the business realm, but also in your personal realm—you will find significant satisfaction in all your activities. The principle is universal: You'll get satisfaction and significance out of life in direct proportion to what you put into it. And you'll get productivity and prosperity in your business in direct proportion to what you give to your employees, associates, customers, and stockholders.

At the other extreme of the pendulum, of course, are people who live in what is known today as "careerism." This is when a person tries to find total fulfillment in work and thereby lets the other areas of

You get by giving.

life go by the wayside. This mind-set is equally dangerous. Work was never intended to provide one's entire measure of self-worth, fulfillment, success, or significance. Work without happiness is a sure road to sickness and death.

Work does, however, take a major portion of our time. Probably 40 to 75 percent of our waking hours is work-related. About 30 to 35 percent of our time is spent in the area of family and personal interest, and 5 to 10 percent in the area of church or religious activities. Therefore, we need to put everything into perspective before we can succeed.

Douglas LaBier wrote in *Modern Madness*, "Careerism has become the main work ethic of our time. At root, careerism is an attitude, a life orientation in which a person views career as the primary and most important aim of life. An extreme but not uncommon expression of this is found in the comment of a man who told me that he feared dying mainly because it would mean the end of his career."[8]

I recall a friend of mine, a senior executive whom I knew and admired deeply. He spent much of his life pursuing greatness. He had graduated from a top graduate school and was involved in a business of significant proportion. He had all of the things people want out of life. But in the process of all his achieving, he began to identify his worth as being based on his success in business.

While he was achieving all of these lofty goals, he also had a wonderful marriage and three children, and he was known and loved by many people. But increasingly his preoccupation with work and his desire to achieve engulfed his life. That, coupled with his misunderstanding of what those he loved valued, laid the path to destruction for him.

He hit a period when he lost massive amounts of money, due to a number of circumstances outside of his control and some within it. Instead of refocusing his life and building some balance together with the greatest asset he had—his family—he focused his attention on the level of prestige and success that had once been his and which he thought was necessary to be a good provider.

Though he kept working on projects, his personal life became self-destructive. Ultimately, he committed suicide. The purported reason he took his life was that his life insurance premium was due the next day. How tragic: The only thing of worth that he felt he had left was an insurance policy for his wife and his children.

LaBier says, "One senior executive jumped off the roof of his building when he walked into work one morning and discovered that his desk had been moved. A chemist who failed to receive a grant for a research project returned to his lab one night, concocted a poison and drank it, dying where he felt most at home and most betrayed."[9] As Aldous Huxley stated, "They intoxicate themselves with work so they won't see who they really are."

When work starts to become a god in our lives, we're in trouble. Please don't misunderstand: I want you to succeed in your work. I want you to be excellent. I want you to be much more productive than you are right now. But you can't let work become your god! You can't let *anything* material become your god. If you do, you'll lose balance in all other areas of your life. You'll never have the quality or quantity of impact in any area if there is not some degree of balance in your view toward work and the rest of your life.

Art Williams, the founder of Primerica Financial Services, said: "You beat 50 percent of the people in America by working hard; you beat 40 percent by being a person of honesty and integrity and standing for something; and the last 10 percent is a dogfight in the free enterprise system."[10]

I find it easy to work hard at my business. But at the end of the day, I'm tired emotionally and physically. All I want to do is sit in my favorite chair, put my feet up, and watch the news. It feels so good. After all, I *deserve* it.

A few years ago this was my frame of mind. Yet, one such day I was talking with my fourteen-year-old son. I was leaving for Asia the next day for about two weeks, and I knew my time with him was precious. I hoped he might want to talk. But he said to me, "Dad, do you want to play basketball?" Of course, my first response was, "No." Then he persisted: "Come on, you're going to leave. Can't you play basketball?" I said, "I'm too tired, Matt."

Then I watched his countenance fall. I had done more with that one statement to hurt my son than I probably had done during the past month to help him. I'd crushed his spirit.

As I sat there and thought about it, I admitted to myself how much I valued my son. I was going to be leaving town. I would *have* to neglect him for a period of time. In order to compensate I needed to concentrate on him then, at that moment. "Matt, let's go play," I said, not even minding much having to leave my favorite chair. So we played basketball for about forty-five minutes. I kept that commitment in my life, even though it took hard work. And I even felt better!

2. Develop Right Habits

Aristotle was right: Excellence is not just an act but a habit.

Robert Ringer, in his excellent book *Million Dollar Habits*, builds his thesis around this concept of habit. One of his first premises is that success does not depend upon superior intelligence, special skills, formal education, luck, etc. He states, "The world is saturated with intelligent, highly educated, extraordinarily skilled people who experience ongoing frustration because of their lack of success. Millions of others spend their lives working hard, long hours only to die broke." Rather, as he states, "Success is a matter of understanding and religiously practicing specific, simple habits that *always* lead to success."

> **We are what
> we repeatedly do.
> —Aristotle**

Ringer then makes this telling statement: "Remember, life is nothing more than the sum total of many successful years; a successful year is nothing more than the sum total of many successful months; a successful month is nothing more than the sum total of many successful weeks; a successful week is nothing more than the sum total of many successful days. That's why practicing successful habits day in and day out is the most certain way to win over the long term."[11]

If you want to be excellent, you have to develop the habit of being excellent. Keep doing whatever you do over and over and over. Let's say you have a problem with your tongue—you talk behind people's backs. You have to develop the habit of saying positive things about them. Or, if you have problems not getting the job done because of laziness or procrastination, practice completing things over and over until you develop the habit of finishing them. Horace Mann compared habits with a cable: "We weave a strand of it every day and soon it cannot be broken."

Basically, habits are a combination of three things: desire, knowledge, and skill. Desire is why we do what we do. Knowledge is knowing what to do. Skill is how we do it. Together they establish our habits.

You must begin with the desire to succeed. What is the specific habit you want to build? If you have no idea where to start, ask your spouse. He or she probably knows you best.

The first thing you need to ask is why you want to build a particular habit. Here you need to clearly write out what you gain or what you lose by practicing or not practicing a particular habit. If you don't attach enough pain to quitting a bad habit, you'll continue to do it. Moreover, if you don't attach enough pleasure to practicing a good habit, you'll not begin to do it. So how do we develop habits? Let me suggest several of these core competencies. First, practice *mental repetition*. Habit is when we do something without even thinking about it. For instance, when you button your shirt, do you button it up or down? I still have to think about that, because I do it out of habit.

Now, using this same principle, you want to develop positive habits that make your life easier. Imagine your mind as a great mountain. Attitudes you hold, ways you have of doing and responding to things, and habits you've developed are like water that flowed down that mountain over time and developed little ruts that eventually became deep gouges. Habits are like deep rivers in your mind. They are actions that, under given circumstances, you fall into quite naturally. So if you have bad habits, you need to develop good habits—or new riverbeds—through constant mental repetition. After some time, you will begin to see the water flow down these new rivers versus the old ones.

One of the best ways to develop mental repetition is simply to picture the way you ought to behave. See yourself as a winner (not a loser) in everything you do. For instance, let's say you're trying to develop the habit of responding to people in a kind way. You want your words to build people up, not to tear them down.

However, let's also remember that certain people can push buttons within you that induce a habit of destructive verbal communication on your part. How do you handle this? You make careful notes to determine just when it is that you respond in the wrong way and then decide how you should respond in the right way. Then imagine yourself in a situation where you are provoked—and practice the right response over and over until it becomes natural for you to respond that way. This repetition will establish the new positive riverbed in your mind that you want.

One button my wife, Mary, pushes in me is interrupting me when I'm at work in our home office. Mary occasionally wants to get my feedback on an issue—a perfectly acceptable thing to do, and she does it in a gracious way—but when I'm working I'm focused and don't like being sidetracked. So my tendency has been to get angry when she interrupts me. Instead of treating her in a kind and thoughtful way, I react in a way that says to her, "My time is more important than yours, and it bothers me that you're interrupting me right now." I don't *want* to react that way; I simply have found it the easiest and most natural thing to do.

Recently I've thought about how I should respond to Mary. I know I should be kind. I know I should concentrate and focus on her when she needs me. I also know that if I'm in the midst of something urgent, she'll understand and leave, particularly if I communicate this to her in a way that builds her up and doesn't tear her down.

I have seen substantial improvement in my life in this area by simply rehearsing the appropriate attitude and words until they have begun to become a habit. The net effect is that when this button in me is pushed now, my response more often than not is one of kindness and understanding, instead of insensitivity and impatience.

The second technique for developing good habits is *practice.* You have to understand upfront that you're going to fail many times as you develop new habits. However, if you continue to practice a habit over and over—falling, picking yourself up, and trying again—after a period of time it will become a winning habit.

Many psychologists tell us to practice the twenty-one-day habit, that is, if we can do something for twenty-one consecutive days, it becomes a habit. Add to that the encouragement of William James: "Never suffer an exception to occur until the new habit is securely rooted in your life. Each lapse is like the letting fall of a ball of string which one is carefully winding up; a single slip undoes more than a great many turns will wind again."

The key is to practice. And practice. And practice.

A third technique to develop is a feedback mechanism. Monitor your growth through a chart. Take the new habit you want to develop and write out a very simple chart. Gauge yourself for twenty-one days, and mark when you are successful and when you aren't; when you fall into a bad habit, and when you are able to achieve your good habit.

One reason why many diet clinics are effective is that they create the needed monitoring mechanism. They tell you which foods to eat. They ask you what foods you ate that correspond to their guidance. This mechanism develops positive habits.

I know someone who overcame incredible odds to take control of his business and professional life and build a life of disciplined patterns. He is my good friend Bob Safford. Bob is one of the top leaders and producers for Primerica Financial Service (a subsidiary of the giant Travelers Corporation). Travelers is a 100+-year-old company with $115 billion in assets, far larger than companies like IBM, Exxon, or Sears.

A significant portion of Primerica Financial Service's growth is due to its huge sales force. Bob Safford has been a key player in building that sales force since its early days. Bob's particular piece of the company produces about 15 percent and more than $300 million of the total revenue of all Primerica Financial Services. He has twenty thousand full-time and part-time representatives. Obviously, Bob has succeeded financially—becoming a multimillionaire many times over, living in a magnificently furnished historic estate (George Washington once slept there), and owning two planes he flies himself. Before he stepped into the role with Primerica Financial Services, he was the chief operations officer of a large, direct-sales-force insurance company and a member of its N.Y. stock exchange holding company board of directors. Before that, at age twenty-seven, he cofounded Alexander Hamilton Insurance Company, a well-known and respected insurance company.

Bob also has developed a very successful personal and family life. I had the joy of knowing his first wife, Pat (who died of cancer), a marvelous woman who, along with Bob, raised four very talented and solid children (three of whom are now involved with Bob in his business). I also had the privilege of participating in Bob's wedding to his second wife, Barbara. Theirs is a quality relationship, and they continue to have a wonderful impact on their children and grandchildren, as well as the tens of thousands of other people Bob influences through business.

How did Bob Safford get where he is today?

Bob grew up in a small apartment above a bar. His single mother raised him. He didn't have money to lean upon or a great father figure to respond to. His parents were divorced when he was young, so he became the "father" of the house, taking care of his younger sister.

Bob was short in stature. He used to be called Pee Wee, and later on, even as a lieutenant colonel in the Marines, he was called Feather Merchant (a derogatory statement about his height). As a child, the emotional baggage began to collect. By third grade he had been in eight schools.

Bob sold newspapers door to door to put himself through college. During his college years, one of his most vivid memories is missing the major football games because he was washing windows for sororities. He had to work all hours just to make it through college. He had very little money, and new clothes were rare. But Bob Safford had a dream.

As a teenager, Bob says he came across several quotations that began to change the direction of his life. The first was one by the great motivator Andrew Carnegie: "All riches and all material things that anyone acquires through self-effort begin in the form of a clear, concise mental picture of the thing one seeks." A second axiom was said by industrialist Henry Ford: "I pity the man who just wants to get rich for he will make nary a penny. For he must first concern himself with the service that he'll render to be worth the riches he seeks."

In response to Andrew Carnegie's wisdom, Bob eagerly said, "My goal is to be a millionaire by age thirty-five." But the second one, Henry Ford's advice, was tougher. "I had to figure out what 'service I'd render,'" he said. "I didn't know how to do that until I came across another Andrew Carnegie statement: 'The position a person occupies in the world depends on the quantity and the quality of the service he renders plus the mental attitude which he relates to others.'"

"That's where I learned that success was under *my* control," Bob said, "because quantity of service was the number of appointments I had and the number of sales calls I could make. Quality of service was how well *I* did it. And mental attitude is also under *my* control."

From that point, Bob gave his life to achieving success. He knew how to do it, and he knew it was in his hands.

Graduating from Cornell University, Bob went into direct sales since the quickest money could be made in sales, and he could learn the greatest skills in selling. He began selling kitchenware. His employer sent him to the toughest places, and Bob developed the habit of doing the uncomfortable thing of presenting himself and his wares over and over and over. He didn't like it. He didn't want to do it. But he found another quotation that touched him: "Do the thing you fear the most and the death of fear is certain." Experience comes from habit. And this experience gave Bob the tenacity and fortitude to overcome the most excruciating difficulties he would face throughout the rest of his life.

Bob Safford's goal, to become a millionaire, continued to drive him. But as the years went by he learned to focus more and more on the balance in his life. Today, Bob can look back at every good time and every bad time and know he made the most of what he had. And he is still maximizing all of his resources for positive, significant impact and experiencing authentic success.

Regardless of your circumstances, the authentic success of the rest of your life will be in direct proportion to whether or not you embrace Bob's attitude of making things happen.

I close with the story of two men whose last weeks of life were lived under identical circumstances. One took responsibility and was victorious even in death. The other took no responsibility for his last days and saw himself as a victim.

> There were once two men, both seriously ill, in the same small room of a great hospital. Quite a small room, just large enough for the pair of them—two beds, two bedside lockers, a door opening on the hall, and one window looking out on the world.
>
> One of the men, as part of his treatment, was allowed to sit up in bed for an hour in the afternoon (something to do with draining the fluid from his lungs), and his bed was next to the window.
>
> But the other man had to spend all of his time flat on his back, and both of them had to be kept quiet and still. Which was the reason they were in the small room by themselves, and they were grateful for peace and privacy—none of the bustle and clatter and prying eyes of the general ward for them.
>
> Of course, one of the disadvantages of their condition was that they weren't allowed to do much: no reading, no radio, certainly no television—they just had to keep quiet and still, just the two of them.
>
> Well, they used to talk for hours and hours—about their wives, their children, their homes, their jobs, their hobbies, their childhood, what they did during the war, where they had been on vacations—all of that sort of thing. Every afternoon, when the man in the bed next to the window was propped up for his hour,

he would pass the time by describing what he could see outside. And the other man began to live for those hours.

The window apparently overlooked a park, with a lake, where there were ducks and swans, children throwing them bread and sailing model boats, and young lovers walking hand in hand beneath the trees, and there were flowers and stretches of grass, games of softball, people taking their ease in the sunshine, and right at the back, behind the fringe of the trees, a fine view of the city skyline.

The man on his back would listen to all of this, enjoying every minute—how a child nearly fell into the lake, how beautiful the girls were in their summer dresses, then an exciting ball game, or a boy playing with his puppy. It got to the place that he could almost see what was happening outside.

Then one fine afternoon, when there was some sort of a parade, the thought struck him: Why should the man next to the window have all the pleasure of seeing what was going on? Why shouldn't he get the chance?

He felt ashamed, and tried not to think like that, but the more he tried, the worse he wanted a change. He'd do anything!

In a few days, he had turned sour. He should be by the window. And he brooded, and couldn't sleep, and grew even more seriously ill—which none of the doctors understood.

One night as he stared at the ceiling, the other man suddenly woke up, coughing and choking, the fluid congesting in his lungs, his hands groping for the button that would bring the night nurse running. But the man watched without moving.

The coughing racked the darkness—on and on—choked off—then stopped—the sound of breathing stopped—and the man continued to stare at the ceiling.

In the morning the day nurse came in with water for their baths and found the other man dead. They took away his body, quietly, no fuss.

As soon as it seemed decent, the man asked if he could be moved to the bed next to the window. And they moved him, tucked him in, and made him quite comfortable, and left him alone to be quiet and still.

The minute they'd gone, he propped himself up on one elbow, painfully and laboriously, and looked out the window. It faced a blank wall.[12]

Life and success are what you want them to be. They are not what another person sees, but what you see. They are not in what another person has achieved, but in what you achieve. Stop now and reexamine your image of yourself, before it's too late.

Action Steps

1. How do you view yourself—as victim or victor? Do you believe you are stuck and helpless, or capable of making right decisions and gaining control of your thoughts and attitudes? How? Identify some examples.

2. What areas of your life are most disciplined? In what areas do you lack discipline? Write out one example of each.

3. Identify one area in which you can improve by working hard. How would you like to change in that area?

4. As I pointed out in this chapter, we often do what we do because of poorly developed habits. What bad habits are holding you back from authentic success? Make a list. Now, circle the most persistent one. How can you change this habit using the "take charge" principle?

Chapter 2

Achieve Personal Significance

What You See Is What You'll Be

The average person goes to his grave with his music still in him.

— *Oliver Wendell Holmes*

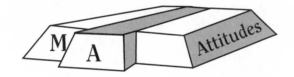

He was a good kid. His parents were honest, hardworking, middle-class Americans from a small town in the Northwest. But as a child he got mixed up with the wrong people. His friends were the tough guys. He didn't like himself much, and as a result he did poorly in almost every area of his life. He got into trouble with his family. He made D's and some C's all the way through grade school. He didn't like the way he looked; he was a little, fat boy, stuck at an early age with the nickname "Jelly Belly."

As he got older he began to get into more and more trouble. At age eleven he began stealing, and he was caught tampering with checks. He clearly was going the wrong direction in his life. His parents and teachers didn't know what to do with him. He had a good home, and his parents had done everything they knew to do. But he still didn't like his life. He was angry at everything and everyone, and he made sure everybody knew it.

At thirteen, however, he had what he describes as a spiritual experience. A young professional took time to build purpose into his life and to give him hope. The boy began to change. His grades went from

D's to A's in one quarter. Instead of fighting, as he'd done in seventh grade, he was elected student body president in his eighth-grade year. People actually liked him! His attitude had about-faced from anger and frustration toward focused productivity. He began to achieve in every major area of his life. He lost weight. It was as though every cell in his mind and body had changed dramatically overnight, like the metamorphosis of a caterpillar to a butterfly. It was a real miracle!

That young man finished high school, college, graduate school, and even postgraduate work, winning honors at each level. He got his doctorate and by age twenty-nine had become the president of a graduate school. In his late thirties he was serving as president and then chairman of two organizations with worldwide impact.

What happened to that little fella? He was confronted with a dramatic realization—that he had a personal destiny.

I know the story well because that boy was me, Ron Jenson. I did grow up in a great home with great parents. And I did have problems when I was young. But because of a deep personal experience and the subsequent realization that I was a person of significance, every area of my life changed. I began to understand that I had a destiny to fulfill, and I began to go for it.

It had nothing to do with intelligence. What I found was my hidden potential.

I was motivated by the realization that I had a destiny, that I could achieve significance in my life. I could make a difference, and I could help change my world. And that's the second principle I want to talk about now—how you can achieve personal significance in your life.

When I saw myself as an angry loser, I reacted as if that was all I ever could be. But when I saw my true potential, I started to see myself as significant—as someone who could make a difference, somebody who had unique gifts and abilities as well as some soft spots that could be changed—and I began to live that way. And so can you.

What influences have forged your self-image? A friend, a job, a positive experience, a failure, a parent? Consider this young man's story:

> When I was around ten years old, my father purchased a 1929 Model A Ford with the idea of restoring it to its original condition. He rented the garage across the street from our house, where he spent evenings and weekends working on his project. I remember sitting for hours watching Dad work, handing him tools when he

needed them, and feeling a happy sense of being with my father as a part of something important. As the months went by, the whole family could feel the excitement build as each new step was completed and the finished product began to take shape.

Finally, one evening, the end was in sight. Dad drove his trophy into the garage, having just picked it up from the paint shop. The new, black paint glistened in contrast with the yellow spoke wheels and the hand-painted, thin, yellow stripe that outlined the car's silhouette. All that remained to do was screw on the white cloth roof.

To allow his only son to play a more central role in the grand finale, Dad asked me to hold the screwdriver in the slot of the screw while he got inside and turned the nut with a wrench. Once the roof was attached to both sides, the project would be finished at last and we'd be free to walk around and "ooh and ah" over the new family masterpiece. "Be careful," Dad added. "I don't want you to scratch the paint."

I carefully held the screwdriver in the slot of the screw with both hands, while Dad began to turn the wrench from inside the car. All of a sudden, the screwdriver slipped and gouged out a two-inch "ravine" in the black paint on the door of the car. (I can still see the exact shape of that scratch as I write this sentence!) I instantly felt sick to my stomach. Dad jumped out of the car and, upon seeing the scratch, began yelling, screaming, and throwing tools. I remember being very glad my mother was there to come to my rescue.

This was one of those traumatic moments in life when personal survival becomes a priority. I was shaken to the core. I had moved into my world and made who I was available, wanting to have a positive impact. The message had come back: "You bumbling idiot, look at the damage you've done! You can't do anything right!"[1]

Perhaps your experience is not as vivid as this young man's. But I'm sure you can remember similar moments in your life when your fragile self-perception was dramatically touched and perhaps indelibly formed. If your experiences have been poor, then most likely the results have been too. But if your encounters have been positive and life-enriching, the likelihood of a positive self-image has been given a powerful boost.

Years ago, a teacher was assigned to the roughest class of boys in the worst area of Harlem. One day she accidentally saw a listing of the boys' IQs and couldn't believe it. These guys were brilliant! So that's how she began treating them—as brilliant, capable human beings with incredible potential. You can finish the story, can't you? They proved her right by graduating from high school and succeeding in great measure throughout their lives.

Yet here's the clincher: This teacher hadn't actually seen the boys' IQ scores. She had misread the paper; it was their locker numbers she had seen! Yet because she thought the numbers reflected their IQ scores and treated the boys as such, she dramatically changed the way those boys lived. And they responded because they had been sold an image of themselves as intelligent people who had potential.

If we see ourselves as people of significance—or if we think someone else believes we are smart—we'll act as if we are just that. But if we don't, we won't. What you see is what you'll be. It's all a matter of your vision of yourself.

What you see about yourself is what you'll be.

Consider a recent survey taken in Russia. A group of teenage girls was asked by a national association of psychologists to state their occupation of preference. More than 70 percent said prostitution. Now, beyond the moral implications of that statistic lies a clear illustration of the point I'm addressing. Prostitution becomes an occupational preference for teenage girls in Russia because they've grown up in a system that regards the body as a clump of flesh to be used for any pragmatic reason necessary. A person has no soul, since there is no God or external power beyond the state. Add to this the Western preoccupation with materialism, instant gratification, and sex, and it's no wonder the girls choose prostitution. It's the easiest and fastest money to be made.

To achieve personal significance, you need to grasp two statements: (1) You are significant, and (2) you must deal with your soft spots or weaknesses.

You Are Significant

Oliver Wendell Holmes said: "The biggest tragedy in America is not the great waste of natural resources, though this is tragic. The greatest tragedy is the waste of human resources. The average person goes to his grave with his music still in him."

What about you? If you were to die today, would you go to the grave with your tune still unplayed? Are the instruments of your life—your talents, skills and abilities, relationships, the resources you've been given—starting to blend into beautiful music, or are they silent? Is the real you being stifled or held back?

1. You Are Special

To recognize your significance, *you need to see that you are special,* unique. Maybe you've been called special by your parents all your life and now consider this to be a superficial compliment. But you had better believe it, because it's absolutely true. You are the only you there will ever be, and regardless of how visible or invisible you are, how popular or unpopular you are, how rich or poor you are, what your background is, you are special. You've heard the phrase, "God don't make no junk." It's true. You aren't junk. You exist to have a special impact on your world, in your area of influence.

You're also the only one with your background, your contacts, and your personality. Therefore, there are many things in this life that only you are qualified to do. This is a reality you must fully embrace!

Consider for a few moments how important it is that you embrace your own specialness. Beyond all the psychological and social benefits, you must consider your impact on the work world. Many of the major economic forces of the past several dozen years are quickly becoming obsolete. As Peter Drucker says, it is increasing "*knowledge* [that] will create wealth. Our primary goal will be to make the knowledge productive."[2] This statement has implications for a new form of leadership and management in the business world, as well as a new form of worker.

In the area of leadership, Drucker states: "We will see management arranged like a jazz combo, in which leadership within the team shifts within the specific assignment and is independent of the rank of each member." Continuing his analogy of music, he says, "The symphony orchestra—with only one 'executive' and no intermediate layers between him and the group members—will be the model for the information-based organization."[3]

Not only will style of leadership dramatically change, but also the style of the worker. Drucker points out, "Each worker or 'musician' will be a high-grade specialist. As a team, they will work toward a common goal. Individual workers, like the individual tuba player or flutist, can make music, but only the entire orchestra can perform a composition. The organization will be harmonious because each player coordinates his or her role with the rest of the group."[4]

You can easily see from Drucker's insights (which are echoed by numerous management consultants and educators today) that your ability to identify and put to work your specialness, uniqueness, gift-edness, and abilities is critical for your own personal well-being as well as your sphere of influence in the days to come.

2. You Can Make a Difference

To appreciate your significance, you need to understand that *you can make a difference.*

I know of a woman from Boring, Oregon, who was concerned about a law that would permit nude dancing in local bars in her community. This mother, who by nature was shy and quiet, felt compelled to attend a county meeting the night the issue came before the County Board of Supervisors.

When the discussion ended, the vote stood evenly split at four to four, with one swing vote remaining. The mother stood up and said, "I'm not eloquent. I'm not used to speaking in public, but I must tell you my experience. My daughter was out with some friends one evening, and they happened to go into one of these bars that allowed nude dancing. She was accosted there, and the physical and emotional scars have been very significant." Then she sat down as quietly as she had stood.

Finally, the one swing vote, a woman, rose and addressed the balance of the committee: "Gentlemen, you've presented a very telling and convincing case. But you have not answered the moral dilemma that this lady has brought to my attention. Therefore I will vote against nude dancing in this community."

One ordinary person had made a difference. Whatever the cause might have been, this mother stood for what she believed, and she made a difference.

What kinds of ambitions do you have? What charges up your inner fire with the awareness that you can do something and make a difference?

3. You Must Fulfill Your Destiny

Once you realize and accept that one person all alone can make a difference, *you must believe that you can fulfill your destiny.* You have been placed on this earth for a reason. And if you are going to be what you are supposed to be—if you are going to maximize yourself and fulfill the purpose you have on this earth—you must fulfill your destiny. This is not optional. If you do not do this, unhappiness and a sense of failure will be your only companions.

One of my major intents in writing this book is to stimulate men and women throughout the world to begin believing again in a personal destiny. I've grappled a great deal with destiny in my own life. I've been involved in five separate careers and have enjoyed all of them. But the older I get, the more intensely I am motivated to fulfill my destiny.

So I have begun to grapple with what I should and should not be doing. This struggle has led me to realize that I need to work in my four areas of strength: conceptualizing, creating, communicating, and connecting resources and people. In addition, I've looked at my life holistically and have seen that I need not only to define, but also to model success in my personal life, my personal and professional relationships, and the various ventures in which I become involved.

You can begin to capture and define your destiny as you grow in your understanding of two major areas—your *unique bent* (gifts, abilities, opportunities, concerns, passions, etc.) and the *pressing needs* in YOUR world. The more you understand these two areas the more precisely you can define your destiny.

Those pressing needs in your world will clearly involve who you are (your own need to grow) and what you do (involving all critical areas in your life).

Fundamentally it is being the BEST YOU you can be.

All of this is part of fulfilling my destiny. And this is what I want you to do!

You Must Deal with Your Soft Spots (Weaknesses)

To establish significance, we must also deal with our weaknesses, which we often choose to ignore. We all have soft spots (weaknesses), such as a bad temper, impatience, or a gossipy tongue. Contrary to popular practice, denying your weaknesses or hiding them under the rug is not an effective way to deal with them. Also contrary to popular belief, these weaknesses are not that difficult to change. You can even benefit from your weaknesses if you follow these three steps:

1. Admit Your Weaknesses

Admit shortcomings to yourself, to others (in the appropriate context), and to God as you know him. Just learn to admit them. Denial exacerbates the problem.

Everyone develops what I call a "box" sense of maturity. We believe that if we live according to a certain socially acceptable "box," then we are accepted and can rise in position or respectability. All of us have certain peer groups that establish the limits of acceptable and unacceptable dress and behavior. Those limits put us in a box. When we measure ourselves against this "box," our focus becomes our external lifestyle, not our internal growth. Consequently, we stop addressing or even being aware of our weaknesses.

I remember once sitting down with a friend who was struggling with worry. I said to him, "What's your greatest problem?" He said, "Money."

I looked at him and laughed. I said, "You're kidding."

"No. Why do you say I'm kidding?"

"In my view, money's not your biggest problem."

"Then what is my biggest problem?"

"It's worry."

He paled. This man worked with a group of people who didn't think worry was acceptable behavior. He said, rather frantically, "Worry? I don't worry. You're wrong. You've got to be wrong!"

"Everybody knows you worry," I said. "Your wife knows you worry. I know you worry. Anyone who meets you for five minutes knows you worry. Your stomach knows you worry. You have an ulcer. Of course you worry! What you need to hear is that it's okay—yes, *okay* to worry. You're not a bad person because you worry. You just don't realize that you don't need to worry."

It's okay to be impatient sometimes. It's okay if we say things we shouldn't say sometimes. I'm not glad to be full of flaws. But I recognize—and so should you—that *everyone is struggling with something,* and it's okay to admit it. In fact, the first principle in growth is to say, "I am helpless. I really am weak and I need help."

Most of us are great con artists. We pretend to be someone we're really not, and we end up playing a game all our lives. Paul Tournier said, "We can conceal our persons behind a protective barrier. We let it be seen only through the bars. We display certain of its aspects. Others we carefully hide."

A number of years ago, a book entitled *Why Am I Afraid to Tell You Who I Am?* became popular.[5] The underlying theme was that people fear exposing themselves because they've concluded their friends and associates will not like what they see. In essence, people are afraid that their inner person—including their thoughts, attitudes, private behaviors, and vulnerabilities—would be rejected if truly understood by others. Therefore, as the author states, individuals develop masks to conceal who they are.

But I find that people respond to vulnerability quite differently. Often when I speak publicly I talk about some weakness in my life. I have plenty of illustrations, and I'm glad to share them. The response is never, "Oh, Jenson, you're worse than I thought!" Instead, people say, "Oh, thank you. I'm so glad to know someone else is struggling in an area where I've struggled." People don't respect me less. They respect me all the more because I admit my weaknesses. We all know we've got problems. We're just too embarrassed to admit them.

Let me caution you here. I am not saying you should tell your deepest, darkest secrets to everyone. To do so would be unwise and inappropriate. However, appropriately sharing real needs to a small band of committed friends can be extremely helpful. Seeking insight and support is positive.

Moreover, having an open spirit to admit when you fail is attractive. It not only frees you to grow, but it provides an openness that can help others grow as well. That is why I speak with a degree of transparency. I want to unlock people's rigid, outer "performance" approach to life and success. And I want to activate their appreciation of authentic success as being growth—stimulated by making mistakes and making positive adjustments to their weaknesses.

So, open up. Admit when you blow it!

An important word here: As you work through articulating your soft spots regularly, you may find that you need to make some kind of reconciliation or restitution. In other words, you may have done something that needs to be made right, or perhaps you may have broken a relationship that needs to be rebuilt.

I urge you to right the wrongs. If you have stolen something in the past, pay for it. If there has been a broken relationship that in some measure was your responsibility, right it.

"But, but, but, but—," I can hear you saying, "If I do this, it will be embarrassing, humiliating. I've done something illegal, like cheating on my taxes. I'll have to pay penalties and fees. Do you mean I have to admit having done some wrong to someone who has wronged me even more? That seems terribly unfair."

My response to you is—yeah, you're right! All those consequences may be true and they may happen. But even if you can't control the outcome, you can control your behavior and your decisions. And those should be based on your being a person of significance who is learning to deal with soft spots and striving for excellence.

I say over and over throughout this book that our job is to concentrate on the *roots* of our lives. In other words, our job is to live in light of *right principles*. Fruit will eventually and permanently abound by our appropriate concentration on roots.

Admitting and overcoming soft spots strengthens the roots of your life the same way fertilizer strengthens plant life. It smells, but as it permeates the growing roots it strengthens the plant. I cannot guarantee where the chips will fall for you, but I can guarantee that your decision to do right will stimulate a tremendous sense of personal integrity in your life and will help to unlock your incredible potential.

I am not speaking theoretically here. I remember when I went through this process many years ago. It involved some money I had finagled out of an older man. Once I acknowledged my unique significance, I was riveted with guilt over my mistakes. I knew I had done wrong. And I knew that every time I saw the person I had wronged, I would want to hide because of the guilt that would overwhelm me. I knew—by the activity of my conscience, as a person who was special and significant—that I couldn't let it slide. I knew I needed to resolve it. So, in trying to make restitution I went to the person, told him how I had wronged him, asked for his forgiveness, and told him I would make restitution for the amount I knew he was out of pocket because of me.

Well, the man laughed! He told me how much he admired my honesty; he said he'd sensed something was wrong, but that he liked me and wanted to help me even though he knew I hadn't been totally honest in the first place.

I never would have known this man's intentions—and I would have carried that guilt no matter how much I tried to sublimate it or deny it for the rest of my life—had I not chosen to do right. Furthermore, once I admitted my wrong to this man and made restitution, I was free to move on.

2. Look for Opportunities to Grow

It's just not enough to be open and admit your soft spots. You need to actively look for areas to change and to ask for help. If you're not a part of an accountability group, you ought to be. Find a group of friends in your business, neighborhood, church, or synagogue who will help you to be more effective. Find people who will build you up, yet will be honest, loving, and caring enough to confront you as a friend. That's one way to grow, mature, and develop.

I've learned that if I'm serious about looking at the weak areas of my life for opportunities to grow, I help my friends become aware of my soft spots. For instance, I have said to several special male friends whom I trust and honor, "Here are five questions I hope to God no one would ever ask me." These five questions represent the five weakest areas in my life. Your weak areas could be things such as how you handle your finances, relational fidelity, struggles with integrity, family difficulties, etc. The fifth question is, "Did you lie about any of the above four?"

I tell my trusted friends, "Whenever you see me ask me these questions."

I know this practice might seem absolutely chilling to think about doing. But accountability to a few trusted friends helps a great deal. It's something I also practice with my son. We have found that it not only binds us together but creates a healthy accountability between us.

My contention is that if I'm serious enough about growing, I will try not only to look for opportunities, but create levers that will help me grow. And practicing accountability is one outstanding lever in my life.

3. Keep Adjusting

You're going to make mistakes. In fact, you're going to fail repeatedly. Just remember that failing doesn't make you a failure. A true failure is a *person who doesn't learn from his failings.*

> **Don't pretend to be perfect, but progress in authentic success.**

The key is to keep admitting you've made a mistake, keep learning, and keep moving on.

Lewis Timberlake tells a great story about achieving personal significance: Nestled back in the hills sat a small cabin inhabited by a carpenter and his barely literate wife. They could scarcely eke out a living from his carpentry work and woodchopping, which were their only means of support.

So when a son was born, it was natural that the father would eventually train him in carpentry and woodchopping as well. The tall, lanky boy chopped wood for his father until he was twenty-one. But chopping wood didn't satisfy his hunger for knowledge. So he borrowed books and read by candlelight during the evening hours. The things he learned in those books planted dreams in his mind of better things, of other occupations, of other worlds beyond his little country town.

At age twenty-three he ran as a candidate for his state's legislature and lost. Yet he continued to study during his spare time, his thirst for knowledge unquenchable. His dream was to become a lawyer, and after many years of studying alone he finally passed his bar exam at age twenty-seven. By then he had worked on a Mississippi ferryboat, in a mill, a general store, and a post office, as a farmhand, and as a surveyor. He also had served in his state's militia.

He found a law partner, went into practice, and went bankrupt, all in a relatively short period of time. He spent the next sixteen years paying off the debts his firm had incurred. He fell in love with a beautiful young lady who broke their engagement and his heart as well. She later died.

At age thirty-three he finally married a young woman with a strong will and a temper to match. Their marriage proved to be stormy and volatile. Of the four sons born to them, three died before reaching adulthood.

At age thirty-five this man reopened his law practice. His desire to serve in public office proved as insatiable as his quest for knowledge. Even though he had lost one election twelve years earlier, he optimistically sought office again and lost again. At age forty-seven his party selected him as its vice presidential candidate. Again he lost. At forty-nine he was nominated for the United States Senate and again lost.

Here was a man whose formal schooling at age twenty-two totaled less than one year. He lost the love of his life, his law practice, and three of his sons. He had a rocky and stormy marriage. He sought public office numerous times, only to be defeated time after time. By most people's definition of a failure, this man certainly must have been one.

However, in spite of all these failures, he did experience a few successes. At age twenty-five, after losing a bid for the state legislature, he came back and won, serving four terms. At age thirty-eight, after losing a bid for a congressional seat three years earlier, he was elected to Congress for one term. And after losing in his bid as vice president and for a United States Senate seat, he was nominated as the Republican Party's presidential candidate at age fifty-one and won. At age fifty-five he was renominated and reelected to a second presidential term.

His name was Abraham Lincoln.

History has testified that Abraham Lincoln not only emancipated the slaves but also became a strong party leader who maintained a faith in democracy that rubbed off on his fellow citizens and people all over the world. He became an international symbol of humankind's quest for freedom. After many failures he remained undaunted, coming back time after time and changing the course of history.

How did he do this? And why do so many like him fail while so few others succeed? I believe one of the pivotal reasons is because successful people learn to achieve personal significance. We all must do it. So join me in the quest. Remember, what you see is what you'll be. You are unique and therefore significant. Now live like it!

Action Steps

1. Take time to complete the following statements. Try to add three specifics for each one.

A. I am special because:

　　1.

　　2.

　　3.

B. I can make a difference in these ways:

　　1.

　　2.

　　3.

C. I must fulfill my destiny (reason for being) by:

　　1.

　　2.

　　3.

Therefore, I see myself as a significant person.

2. Here are three major soft spots I need to admit to myself, to others, and to God:

　　1.

　　2.

　　3.

3. Here's how I will look for opportunities to grow in the coming year:

　　1.

　　2.

　　3.

Place the answers to the above questions somewhere so you can review them throughout the week.

Finally, take time this week to memorize the following creed. Repeat it four or five times each day.

Maximizers' Creed

I will take charge of my life and make a difference.
I will live my life with a sense of dignity.
I will embrace problems as positive opportunities.
I will center my life on universal principles.
I will passionately pursue my mission.
I will keep all vital areas of my life in balance.
I will put others first and honestly serve them.
I will cultivate my character and spirit.
I will keep adjusting to needs.
I will never, ever, ever quit.

Chapter 3

X Out the Negatives

Don't Say Why, Say What

Our doubts are traitors and make us lose the good we oft might win by fearing to attempt.

—Shakespeare

Justifying our actions seems a universally human defense mechanism. I get a kick out of the various crazy responses people have submitted in the name of explanation. For instance, the following are actual statements made on insurance forms by people who were in car accidents. Listen to their explanations:

- The guy was all over the road. I had to swerve a number of times before I finally hit him.

- I pulled away from the side of the road, glanced at my mother-in-law, and went over the embankment.

- I'd been driving my car for forty years when I fell asleep at the wheel and had an accident.

- The pedestrian had no idea which direction to run so I ran over him.

- The telephone pole was approaching fast. I was attempting to swerve out of its path when it struck my front end.

What we call rationalization is often our choice to view things from an untrue perspective—particularly a perspective that might make us look good rather than reveal the ugly truth. In this chapter I want to deal with perspective and attitude. It's the "X" in our MAXIMIZERS model, and I call this approach "X-ing out the negatives." The name of the game in dealing with life problems is not to ask why bad things happen to us. Instead, we should ask, what can I learn from this? How can I use this challenge to grow? It's all a matter of attitude and perspective, of focusing not on the difficulty but on what lessons we can gain from it. The Chinese have a saying: "Crisis creates opportunity." We need to focus on our opportunities.

I think of the two old farmers who lived next to each other. One was an optimist, the other a pessimist. When the sun shone the optimist would say, "Isn't this glorious weather? It's beautiful. The sun's shining. It's healthy for our crops."

But the pessimist would say, "The sun's too hot. It's killing our crops. It's scorching our land."

When it rained the optimist would say, "Isn't this wonderful? Just what we needed." The pessimist would answer, "No, it's too much! Our crops are going to be ruined."

They went back and forth this way for years. Then one day the optimist bought what he considered to be the greatest bird dog ever born. This dog was so great, it literally walked on water to retrieve a bird and bring it back to the boat. Surely the pessimist could find no fault in this fine animal!

The next time the two men went hunting, the dog leaped out of the boat to retrieve a duck. True to form, he ran across the water, grabbed the duck, came back, and put it in the boat. The optimist looked at the pessimist and said, "Well, what do you think about that?"

The pessimist said, "Can't swim, can he?"

Isn't that the way many of us live? We can't see the good side of anything. And that's a key to the principle of "X-ing out the negatives" in life. Don't say why, say what. It's not *why* you are struggling or facing difficult times, but rather *what* you can learn through the process that will advance your authentic success.

The key to putting this principle into practice is your *perspective*, that is, how you look at things. Stephen Covey, one of the wisest business counselors and educators today, tells an interesting story of how his own view changed. As he sat on a commuter train one night, he noticed a father sitting in the corner while his children played in front of him. Apparently the children got louder and louder, and more obnoxious, but the father didn't do anything about it.

It was obvious to Covey and others nearby that the situation was getting out of control. Finally, in desperation, Covey went to the father and said, "Those are pretty active children, aren't they?"

The father turned to him and said, "I guess so. Frankly, I hadn't noticed. We just came from the hospital where their mother died." At that moment Covey's perspective changed. He had seen something one way in one moment and another way the next.

We all have the opportunity to see things from a positive or a negative standpoint. The evidence is overwhelming, however, that if you choose to see things from a negative standpoint, you will almost certainly be the loser. Nobel Prize winning author Isaac Bashevis Singer said: "If you keep saying things are going to be bad, you have a good chance to be a prophet."

Holding on to a pessimistic view will not only make you a prophet of doom, it will also guarantee your doing everything to circumvent the making of an exciting, meaningful, productive life. Martin Seligman, professor of psychology at the University of Pennsylvania, argues this in his book *Learned Optimism*.[1] The book is a compilation of decades of research on depression and the negative impact and sense of hopelessness that prevents its victims from taking action to improve their situation in life. Seligman points out that optimists view unpleasant situations as being caused by external events. For instance, they say things such as, "The dog ate my homework," or "The sun blinded my view of the stop sign," or "The piano was badly tuned."

Pessimists, who tend to be more prone to despair and depression, evaluate circumstances differently. They believe they're at fault in total or at least in the main, and they take less credit for successes and more credit for failures. They blame their own shortcomings for undesirable occurrences. They make statements such as, "I'm not very smart," or "I can't do anything right," or "I'll never get well." Optimists have a significant sense of personal control, while pessimists have a sense of helplessness and despair, which usually leads to depression.

Seligman developed a test called the Attributional Style Questionnaire (ASQ) to compare pessimism and optimism. In this test, subjects are asked to concoct a story explaining the cause of good and bad events in a series of situations. The higher the ASQ score, the greater the likelihood that the test taker is pessimistic.

This test was used with American swimmers who were training for the 1980 Seoul Olympics. After the swimmers took the test, their coaches decided to play a trick on them. They added seconds to the swimmers' real lap times during a practice session. When the swimmers were given these wrong times, they were told to rest and then swim again.

The performance of those who were pessimists deteriorated on the second attempt by two seconds. They believed the bad news. The optimists kept a steady pace, and a few, including Matt Biondi (who ultimately won five gold medals at the Seoul Olympics), swam even faster.[2]

A growing body of evidence also indicates that pessimism has a significant impact on diseases. For instance, a study at the University of Pennsylvania investigated the condition of 120 men who had each suffered one heart attack. After a period of eight years, 80 percent of the pessimists had died with a second heart attack, while only 33 percent of the optimists had died during a second heart attack.

Pessimism can be detrimental at the least and deadly at the most.

Be a critical thinker with a positive attitude.

Think of the productivity that is lost by employees who have pessimistic attitudes. Not only are their tasks done less confidently, but many innovations never take place because of their negative mind-set. Moreover, the toll on relationships that comes out of pessimism and negative attitudes is enormous.

I want to focus on three areas I call the ABCs of right attitudes: *A* is *accept* problems; don't deny them. *B* is *believe* the best. *C* is *cast off* the negatives. These are life's craftsman tools needed to X out the negatives in your life.

Accept Problems

Don't deny problems. It's a simple reality that life is difficult. Richard Leider, in his excellent book *The Power of Purpose*, wrote: "The fact is that life is either hard and satisfying or easy and unsatisfying."[3]

What you make of your life depends on the challenges you choose to accept or seek. Small house, small problems; big house, big problems.

And you ultimately do choose. Do you want a satisfying, challenging life, or do you want to sit back and accept an unsatisfying life? Do you want to build a big house or a little one? Do you want to be significant or insignificant? Your significance will be measured in proportion to your response to the difficulties you face.

"Life is difficult," reads the first sentence of Scott Peck's *The Road Less Traveled.* He reminds us that the minute we accept life as being full of pain as well as joy, the fact that life is difficult no longer becomes a problem. We begin to learn from our struggles when we discover that "it is in this whole process of meeting and solving problems that life has its meaning." Peck writes that "problems are the cutting edge that distinguishes between success and failure. . . . It is only because of problems that we grow mentally and spiritually."[4]

Clyde Reid writes in his book *Celebrate the Temporary:* "One of the most common obstacles to celebrating life fully is our avoidance of pain. We do everything to escape pain. Our culture reinforces our avoidance of pain by assuring us that we can live a painless life. Advertisements constantly encourage us to believe that life can be pain free. [But] to live without pain is a myth. . . . To live without pain . . . is to live half a life, without fullness of life. This is an unmistakable, clear, unalterable fact . . . many of us do not realize that pain and joy run together. When we cut ourselves off from pain, we have unwittingly cut ourselves off from joy as well."[5] This is the sort of understanding you need to be able to start X-ing out the negatives in your life.

Now, let me give you some tools for the task at hand:

1. Learn from Your Mistakes

Don't do what is illustrated in the following poem, entitled "Feeling Blue":

Feeling blue, buy some clothes.
Feeling lonely, turn on the radio.
Feeling despondent, read a funny book.
Feeling bored, watch TV.
Feeling empty, eat a sundae.
Feeling worthless, clean the house.
Feeling sad, tell a joke.
Ain't this modern age wonderful? You don't gotta feel nothing.
There's a substitute for everything.[6]

Poet Lois Cheney says it well here: We tend to dodge our emotions, avoiding the difficulties and substituting anything else that will keep us from our true feelings. Yet when we do this, we miss the joy of growing and life. And we never move on.

Think of the three worst failures in your life. What are they? Maybe one was a marriage that fell apart. Maybe another was becoming trapped in alcoholism. Maybe you failed miserably at a job. Ask the following questions about the failures in your life: What did you learn from these mistakes? And where did they lead you?

I spent eight years as the president of a graduate school. We built a campus in the United States as well as one in Asia and in Africa. The experience was challenging, exciting, difficult, rewarding, and mostly one enormous learning experience for me. I had been through graduate and postgraduate education, taught at the graduate level, and been involved in professional education. But I had never run a graduate school, so, frankly, I was out of my league.

Through the graciousness of my boss, the patient understanding of many faculty members, administrators, and students, the support of a loving wife and family, and certainly the grace of God, I was able to make it through those years without totally demolishing the organization. But I made many mistakes along the way.

When I finally resigned from that job, I stopped at a favorite coffee shop one morning and spent about three hours writing down all the things I had learned. I still have that list and review it routinely. It includes fifty-two things I did wrong. *That's what I learned.* It was *what*

I'd done wrong that taught me what I should not repeat in the future and how I needed to change if I wanted to be more effective.

My hunch is that you also are growing from your mistakes. Whether you've suffered from a mistake or a failure, you can benefit from Mary Craig's words: "The only cure for suffering is to face it head on, grasp it around the neck, and use it."

As I now look back, I can clearly see how I needed those failed experiences for the things I am doing today. In a sense I didn't fail because I *learned*.

2. Choose Joy

Tim Hansel, an articulate, creative writer, and a disciplined, motivated leader, fell down a mountainside during one of his climbing expeditions. Although in constant, difficult pain ever since, he has written a delightful and uplifting book, *You Gotta Keep Dancin'*. Hansel begins one of his chapters with the following quotation by Lewis Smede: "You and I were created for joy, and if we miss it, we miss the reason for our existence. If our joy is honest joy, it must somehow be congruous with human tragedy. This is the test of joy's integrity. It is compatible with pain. Only the heart that hurts has a right to joy."[7]

"Honest joy" is the type of joy we need to embrace. I'm not talking about happiness; happiness comes and goes. Joy is the continually sustaining emotion that's rooted in the sense that I will be able to handle the things I have to handle, and that I'm progressing the way I ought to be progressing. It is knowing that things are going to come together. Happiness is circumstantial; joy comes even in the midst of sorrow, grief, and confusion.

So how do you handle mistakes and problems? Do you react to them or do you respond to them? Do you get better or do you get bitter?

In one of my times of reflection with Ruth, I gained an important insight. As we discussed how a person should handle difficulties and struggles, she smiled and said, "Treat them as friends."

"What?" I responded.

"Treat your problems as friends, Ron. Embrace them. Accept them. See them as opportunities, not obstacles." Then she gave me an equation that has forever changed my life:

$$\underline{Problems + Joy = Patience}$$
$$Patience + Time +$$
$$Repetition =$$
$$Completeness$$

"Ron," she continued, "everyone wants to be complete and whole at the end of his or her life. The trouble is that we try to find this satisfaction, this wholeness, in the wrong ways. The way we really gain completeness is to learn contentment regardless of circumstances. You need to have the same joy whether you're healthy or sick, whether your emotions are up or down, whether events are good or bad. This is the most meaningful, dynamic life that any person can experience. In fact, *if you have to go more than three feet from wherever you are to find fulfillment, something's wrong.*"

She then explained her equation: "The way we become complete is by responding appropriately to problems over time. As I choose to embrace those problems as friends—to choose joy, to believe that things are going to work out, that there's a significant purpose for every difficulty, if only to make me be a better person—I develop patience. And as that patience is tested and perseveres through time and repetition, I gain completeness."

What Ruth said reminded me of an illustration in my own life. I once worked with some Merchant Marines who unloaded docks in the Northwest. I asked these diehard seamen what it was like going back and forth to Southeast Asia. They said that on the way over it was easy, because even though they hit storms and rough seas, their hull was full, so they rode deep in the water. But on the way back the ship was empty, and when stormy weather came the ship was tossed back and forth because it was riding on the top of the water.

It occurred to me—and Ruth concurred—that we need to allow our ship of life to go deeper into the water. That will happen as we respond with contentment when more and more difficulties arise. The deeper we go, the more stability, the more fulfillment, the more completeness, and the more joy we have in our lives.

3. Take Risks

If you are going to learn from your mistakes and failures, you first have to be willing to fail. You must be willing to *take risks*. Don't play it safe; learn to live on the edge. If you are willing to accept difficulties with maturity, you will take risks—not foolish risks, but calculated ones. You should not fear failure when you take a risk. Rather, you should see risk taking as an opportunity to be stretched and to grow.

One problem facing the former Communist world today is that people under the old collectivist mind-set were never rewarded. The net result of this today is a people who have stopped believing, stopped growing, and stopped reaching because of fear of retribution.

There are glimmers of hope, however. I think of my friend who runs Radio Moscow. He is a young forty-year-old, who—along with his associate and general manager—started a new radio station called Open Radio. They converted the same station that was used to block Radio Free Europe before the fall of Communism in Russia.

I've been in the station on a number of occasions. The building is broken down and the equipment is antiquated. Yet these two men who were once a part of the establishment now have broken out to try to create a cutting-edge news radio station.

They don't have adequate funding, they work night and day, and they're trying to do something that many people in Russia said was impossible. But they're growing, they're developing, and their work is beginning to bear fruit. They have not run away from their problems. They've learned to accept them and even to embrace them. They can see only opportunities among all the debris that is now left from seventy years of Communist rule.

Believe the Best

As we think, so we act. Therefore, you must take control of your thought patterns by believing the best about the following areas: yourself, life, problems, people, time, and God.

The key to having the right view toward each of these areas is to use the right methodology to support and cultivate this view.

1. Right View toward Self: Affirming

When you want to think the best about yourself, practice the art of affirming. Affirm yourself. The way to do this is to apply what I said in chapter 2 about achieving personal significance. On the one hand you're to say, "I'm significant"; on the other you're to say, "I have soft spots." You have to constantly admit both of these truths. One does not exist without the other. You're significant, and you have soft spots that need midcourse correction. And you affirm yourself by believing both of these aspects of your humanness. When you keep them before you daily and live in light of them, you can know you're doing all you can.

There's a great story about a young man who fell asleep during a math class. He woke up as the bell rang, looked at the blackboard, and copied the two problems he saw on the board, assuming they were the homework for the week. Then he went home and labored all day and night. He couldn't figure out either problem, but he kept trying for the rest of the week. Finally, he got the answer to one and brought it into class. The teacher was stunned. The problem the student had solved was supposedly unsolvable. If the student had known that beforehand, he wouldn't have solved it. But since he didn't tell himself it couldn't be done, he was able to find a way to do it.

Life is the same way. We've been told our whole lives we can't do it, we can't do it—and as a result we've stopped believing in ourselves.

Fleas are trained by being put in a jar with a lid. The fleas jump up and down for a while before finally saying to themselves, "This is stupid. We keep hitting our heads on this lid. We're going to get smart—we're not going to jump as high, and then we won't hit our heads on the top." When the lid is taken off the jar, the fleas, who could easily escape, jump only as high as the lid had allowed.

Isn't that the way most of us live? As we're growing up we're told, "You can't do it!" And we stop believing because we've been conditioned to set our sights low.

But the truth is, you can fly like an eagle. You can take off and shoot out of that jar! You can reach levels you don't even know are possible, if you'll just start to believe the best about yourself.

Therefore, *affirm* yourself. X out all the misconceptions clouding your mind, and start afresh!

2. Right View toward Life: Thanking

Establish the right view toward life. A key word here is *thankfulness.* Someone said that instead of living in the present tense, we need to live in the pleasant tense. We need to go about life living it to the fullest with a sense of gratitude.

Frederick Buechner suggests that the way to live life to the full is by asking how fully we experience it day in and day out. Buechner asks: "Have you wept at anything during the past year? Have you thought seriously about the fact that someday you're going to die? More often than not, do you really listen when people are speaking to you instead of just waiting for your turn to speak? Is there anybody you know, to whom if one of you had to suffer great pain, you would volunteer yourself?"[8]

The point is that living life to the full involves thanksgiving. It's called the attitude of gratitude.

We must live with an expressed thanksgiving to whatever form God takes in our mind. We must say, "Thank you, God, for my life and my health. Thank you for my opportunities. And thank you for my problems." The way to develop a right perspective and believe the best about life is by constantly being thankful.

Someone has said, "He who laughs, lasts." Humor is a powerful tool for life. Certainly one of the best-known stories concerning the effects of humor on our lives—and particularly on illness—is the story of American author Norman Cousins. In his book, *Anatomy of an Illness*, Cousins tells of his recovery from a long, languishing illness by literally laughing his way back to health.[9] He made a substantial portion of his daily routine immersing himself in films, television programs, and books that made him laugh. Over time, this routine changed his internal perspective, that in turn changed his physical condition. His pain was decreased, he slept better, and he improved in overall well-being.

When I discussed this issue with Ruth, she told me that laughter and a happy heart are strong medicines. I've had this message repeated to me time after time by top business executives and achievers. These individuals, who are excelling in both their professional and their personal lives, have learned to work hard and play hard. And almost always, they have a great sense of humor.

Take a moment now to read some of the following comments, which I have picked up over the years in my reading. Watch what happens to you! See if your state of mind changes as you read. (My friend Tim Hansel, in his book *You Gotta Keep Dancin'*, identifies these outstanding stories of laughter.) Here are some interesting notices culled from church bulletins:

- This afternoon there will be a meeting in the north and south ends of the church, and children will be christened at both ends.

- Tuesday at 7:00 P.M. there will be an invitation to an ice-cream social. All ladies giving milk, please come early.

- Wednesday, the Ladies Literary Society will meet and Mrs. Lacy will sing, "Put Me in My Little Bed," accompanied by the Reverend.

- This Sunday being Easter, we will ask Mrs. Daily to come forward and lay an egg on the altar.

Or, you know you're having a bad day when . . .

- You call your answering service, and they tell you it's none of your business.

- You put your pants on backwards—and they fit better.

- Your horn goes off accidentally and remains stuck as you follow a group of Hell's Angels on the freeway.

- You sink your teeth into a beautiful steak, and they stay there.[10]

We not only need to learn to laugh in our personal lives, but also in our professional context. You've probably heard someone around the office say, "The competition is killing us." "We're dead serious about getting this project done on time." "She'd die to win that promotion." These commonplace phrases actually have some hidden meaning. Since 1988 nearly two thousand deaths from overwork have been reported in Japan. The Japanese call this *klaroshi*.[11]

The fact is, times are tough. Companies are experiencing significant layoffs. People are working longer hours just to keep up. *The Wall Street Journal* reported that employment disability cases related to stress have doubled in the past ten years. And "a Northwestern National Life Insurance survey found in 1991 that 46 percent of U.S. workers described their jobs as highly stressful, twice as many as in 1985. Thirty-four percent of U.S. workers said they considered quitting their jobs in 1990 because of excessive stress; and 14 percent did quit their jobs because of excessive stress."[12]

In his helpful book, *Lighten Up: Survival Skills for People under Pressure,* C.W. Metcalf urges CEOs and business leaders to infuse humor into the workplace. Metcalf identifies humor as "a set of survival skills that relieves tension, keeping us fluid and flexible instead of allowing us to become rigid and breakable, in the face of relentless change." In the midst of serious situations, he says, we have to learn to step back and gain perspective through humor. Psychiatric nurse Donna Strickland, who heads a Denver consulting firm and conducts seminars on the importance of humor in the workplace, has developed the quintessential compilation entitled: *A How-To Primer to Stimulate More Humor in the Workplace.*[13]

Our attitude is strongly affected by our perspective of the world, and our perspective needs to be positive, upbeat, and buoyant. A good perspective begins with developing a thankful, grateful heart about life. Humor helps us down that road.

3. Right View toward People: Building Up

The key to believing the best about people is to have the building up of others as your modus operandi. When you think of people, think of building up. When you're talking to or about people, use words that build up, not ones that tear down.

I have a friend who confronted me one day as we were having lunch. We had spent a lot of time together and were good friends, but he obviously was agitated with me on this particular day. He said, "I've got a problem with you—a problem with your integrity. I think you're a thief!"

"A thief? What do you mean?"

"All those books in your living room have the Dewey Decimal System on their spines. It's obvious to me that when you left your position at that graduate school, you siphoned off a lot of their books. You stole them and brought them to your house."

After gasping with disbelief, I was filled with an almost pungent dose of anger. I said, "Is it possible there's another explanation for why they're catalogued like that?" I explained that my books had been systematized by a volunteer at the same time as the school's library books were. But my friend hadn't thought of that. He only saw the negative.

I cannot tell you how many times I have misread things because I didn't "X" out this particular negative in my own life. I'm sure you've done the same. Let's learn to assume the best when it comes to people. If you have a question, go ask it!

Cast Off the Negative

Now you must learn to (1) reject fears, (2) root out doubts, and (3) realize your possibilities.

1. Reject Fears

I've found through my research in education programs over the years that even though I can help people accept problems and truly embrace them, those same people can be completely immobilized by the negatives they allow to rule their lives.

Zig Ziglar says, "Fear is the darkroom where negatives are developed." Sometimes our fears are quite profound, complicated, and deep. At other times, they're very simple.

I have a close friend who has been virtually immobilized by the recent discoveries that he was a victim of incredible abuse when he was young. He has coped over the years by developing perfectionistic tendencies, knowing that if he can do things just right, maybe he won't experience additional hurt.

The ramifications in his life are astounding. I have listened in awe and sometimes horror as I've heard him recount a day's activities and the immense guilt and shame he feels over the smallest things he's done improperly. Moreover, the dark cloud that has hung over his head and fractured his relationships, as well as robbed him of joy in his life, is obvious and painful to see.

Yet, this man is learning how to reject his fears. He is allowing himself to remember and identify his awful childhood experiences and is thus dealing with them. He's going through some healthy grief therapy, and the light is shining from his life again. He's becoming unshackled.

Perhaps you're in a situation in which you need to address similar difficulties. Certainly the support of a group and wise counsel can help. But ultimately, you must take responsibility to focus your thoughts on the positive. Remember that your emotions flow out of the way you perceive life. And you can learn to reject your fears by attaching new meaning to your experiences.

Let me tell you of my own much more mundane, but nevertheless immense fear.

When I was in high school, I sang my first solo in front of a group of several hundred people. I was scared to death, and my voice was trembling, but I thought I did okay. Then I sat down and noticed over my left shoulder one of my friends rushing to my side. I thought he was there to affirm me, but his first statement to me was, "Jenson, you were so flat!"

Now, that was just a teenage friend being honest. Nevertheless, his words devastated me. And they created a tremendous fear in me; I attached great pain to singing from that moment on. But through some wise counsel, I realized that if I was ever going to sing publicly again, I needed to replace the pain I attached to that activity with pleasure. Therefore, I continued singing. I sang the lead in our high school musical, in front of thousands of people. Though I was nervous, I sang. And the more I worked at singing, the more pleasure I attached to the experience of singing, and my fear began to fade.

Another experience that hit even closer to home for me involved my daughter, Molly. At one point, Molly was fearful of her mother and me being away from her. This fear manifested itself both emotionally and physiologically and had built up in her mind in greater and greater proportions, until finally it began to overwhelm her. So my wife and I began to work on technology Molly could use to change her thinking and reject this fear.

The first thing we did was to help Molly begin identifying this fear. I asked her to visualize what went on in her mind when she thought about our leaving. When she began to feel the emotion, I told her to jump up and say, "Hallelujah! My feet don't stink!"

Now, before you're ready to assign me a room in a mental hospital, let me tell you what I was doing. *I was trying to get Molly to change her state*, or the way she saw things when her mother and I were away from her. And one way to change such a state of mind is to use the ludicrous. Have you noticed that something as simple as the way you stand or speak—your tone of voice—can change your state of mind? Or the way you perceive things—the emotional, mental mind-set that you find yourself in?

To change Molly's state of mind we simply helped her to develop a state-breaker. As soon as she said, "Hallelujah! My feet don't stink!" she started to laugh. Now she had a breakthrough with her problem.

The next step was to get her to begin to attach pleasure instead of pain to her thoughts about our leaving. So I asked Molly to think of positive things in her life—music she enjoyed, colors that made her happy, pictures that excited her, sitting in a certain chair. Then I asked her to focus on these while she thought about our leaving, until she started to develop a positive, pleasurable attitude toward the circumstances of our leaving.

The key with Molly—and for you—is to learn to handle fears in a tangible way. Until you learn to reject your fears, you can be inhibited from being all that you can be.

2. Root Out Doubts

You now need to deal with your doubts. We all have doubts; no one is free of them. Much of energetic and positive living is making the decision *not* to doubt, and instead to think optimistically about even the difficult things in our lives.

We can learn a lot in this regard from the cognitive therapy field. The basis of cognitive therapy is that we have emotional problems because we think wrongly. The key to positive emotions, once again, is positive, accurate thinking—having the right image of oneself and thinking right. Dr. David Burns, in his classic book, *Feeling Good,* explains the impact of this thinking. He writes that what happens in our minds are cognitive (thinking) distortions. One of these is called "all or nothing" thinking. In this mind-set, an individual sees everything in black-and-white categories. If his performance falls short of perfect, he sees himself as a total failure. Another distortion is overgeneralization. This is when a single, negative event is seen as a never-ending pattern of defeat. Another is disqualifying the positive. Here you reject positive experiences by insisting they don't count for some other reason or doubt. A person with such distortions can maintain a negative belief that is contradicted by his everyday experiences. There are multiple cognitive distortions. The point here is that the way to deal with your doubts is to start thinking accurately about a situation. If you doubt you can do something, articulate in your mind the reasons why you can't do it, and then write down plausible reasons why you think you can do it.[14]

3. Realize Your Possibilities

In the 1952 Olympics, a young Hungarian boy peered down the barrel of his gun and hit the bull's-eye repeatedly. He was flawless. His perfect hand and eye coordination had won him the gold medal. Tragically, he lost his right arm, his shooting arm, six months later. But just four years after this he went to the Olympic Games in Melbourne, where he won his second gold medal with his left hand. He had determined not to be limited by his limitations but, instead, to see his possibilities.

Tim Hansel says, "Limitations are not necessarily negative. In fact, I'm beginning to believe that they can give life definition, clarity, and freedom. We are called to freedom of and in limitations—not from. Unrestricted water is swamp; because it lacks restriction, it also lacks depth." [15]

If you want depth—if you want power, real freedom, and clarity— you need to learn to live with your limitations and to embrace them. And if you're going to maximize your life you need to learn to *X out the negatives* and live with the belief that you can do whatever you want in life. As you begin to master this life skill, as well as the two other attitudinal life skills (making things happen and achieving personal significance), you will have the foundation needed to move on to your belief principles.

Action Steps

1. What is the major problem in your life right now? How are you handling it? Write down your feelings, thoughts, and previous actions related to this problem.

2. Choose joy. Write down how you will respond as you embrace the above problem as a friend, rather than treating it as an intruder. Be specific about how you will think, feel, and act. Then practice this process repeatedly until it becomes a habit.

3. Choose an area in which you should believe the best (yourself, life, problems, people). Now, put in place the methods recommended in this chapter to change your attitude. Again, write down specifically how you will think, feel, and act, and practice these until they become an instinctive part of you.

4. Choose a person in your life to whom you can be accountable to practice the above changes for one month. This can be your spouse, friend, or someone else you can trust. Choosing someone who will encourage and yet give you honest feedback is the ideal.

ROOT BELIEFS

Section

2

Have you ever wondered why you do what you do? Why do you lose your temper, eat food you don't want to, spend money on things that aren't satisfying, engage in activities that just waste your time?

I believe we do these things because we have become slaves to the world around us—to our backgrounds, our friends and associates, the media, and other purveyors of the culture's values. The problem is: those values may not be yours. In fact, I would assume most are not.

The only way to change this trend and move toward the maximization of your life and profession is to plant and deepen *belief roots*. And the two major beliefs that you need to frame the direction of your life make up the next two chapters: "Internalize Right Principles" and "March to a Mission."

"Internalize Right Principles" deals with the development of a personal, principle-based value system. Either you must develop your own clearly defined values rooted in right principles, or you will continue to be led by the culture. In this chapter, I explain how to identify and build right values into your life. These right values must form the foundation to your life and empower you to practice what I call "rightness living." The fulfillment and satisfaction you experience as you begin to align your time and resources around your values will be one of the greatest journeys of your life.

"March to a Mission" will further help you frame your life and activities around a deliberate, well-thought-out sense of mission. In this chapter, I offer specific steps for you to follow as you articulate your purpose and mission in life. And I help you work through your beliefs about the major roles you have and specific goals you want to achieve in your life.

These two belief principles will give you the framework, centeredness, confidence, and power to achieve authentic success in your personal and professional life.

Chapter 4

Internalize Right Principles

How to Do the Right Thing

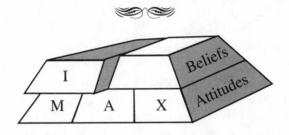

You never know a line is crooked unless you have a straight one to put next to it.

—*Socrates*

Roseanne is one of America's most popular comediennes. Her TV show *Roseanne* has been seen all over the world. Who would have thought, however, that San Diego's Jack Murphy Stadium would be the stage for what could have been *the* most memorable highlight of Roseanne Barr's comedic career? Her irreverent rendition (and accompanying gestures) of the National Anthem at the opening of an early 1990s baseball season will probably be remembered long after all her TV shows are forgotten. For all the feeling we Americans have about freedom of expression, Roseanne's performance evoked the wrath of most Americans.

Why was the response so strong? I believe it was because people finally were saying, "Enough is enough!" While most of us might not be able to articulate the basis for our values, we all have a basic sense of what is right and wrong—and we feel personally affronted when that decency is threatened.

However, when it comes down to daily living—to the choices we make at work and at home, to what we model for our children—it's hard to find the same ethical backbone in society that should be the framework for our collective actions. I believe this lack of a collective ethical backbone is the biggest factor contributing to the breakdown of morals and ethics in our society today.

Why is America discussing values in the nineties? Because we are moving away from the underlying values that molded our nation, and the inevitable result of this trend is clear from history: When there are no values, the society falls apart. *Period.*

One of the surprise best-sellers of the eighties was Alan Bloom's *The Closing of the American Mind.* Bloom's thesis is revealed in the book's subtitle: "How Higher Education Has Failed Democracy and Impoverished the Souls of Today's Students."[1] Bloom makes a strong case that the current decline in education has been caused by a senseless society. He castigates modern education for teaching relativity rather than truth. Educators, he says, no longer distinguish between right and wrong, not only out of fear of lawsuits but also because they themselves can't make the distinction. Bloom contends they see the world through fog-shrouded glasses.

Indeed, we have moved away from values that are rooted in universal principles. We see this in virtually every realm: big Wall Street firms topple regularly. Moguls deal away their lives and their wives. Politicians change their stands on issues with as little thought as it takes them to come to a conviction in the first place. Religious leaders, who we certainly think would embrace and model right values, embarrass us regularly. No area of our culture is free from the imprint of valueless thinking.

Syndicated columnist Cal Thomas wrote the following in a recent book on ethics:

> It was anything but coincidental when just five weeks before the Stock Market crisis the *Wall Street Journal* carried a story in its September 8, 1987 edition with the headline: "Ethics Are Nice, but They Can Be a Handicap, Some Executives Declare."
>
> The story reported on a survey conducted by the research firm McFeely Wackerle Jett. It asked 671 managers their views on the subject of ethics and business. The managers contended that ethics can impede a successful career and that more than half the executives they know would bend the rules to get ahead.
>
> "I know of unethical acts at all levels of management," one fifty-year-old executive quoted in the study said. As for his

rationale for being unethical at times, he said, "I have to do it in order to survive."

For him, survival became the end, not honesty or truth. When such thinking becomes dominant in a culture, that culture is doomed.

The McFeely study also found that older executives generally think they are more principled than their younger counterparts. This is easily understandable given the sociological and moral upheaval younger men and women have gone through during the past twenty-five years.

The study quoted a fifty-nine-year-old vice president at a Midwest company as saying, "Young M.B.A.s and lawyers are taught opportunism, cleverness and cunning. Fairness and equity aren't given equal time or importance."[2]

One of the best pieces of documentation on this decline in the American culture is a study completed in 1991 entitled "The Day America Told the Truth—What People Really Think about Everything That Really Matters." The authors—James Patterson, chairman of the J. Walter Thompson Company, and Peter Kim, the firm's director of research services and customer behavior—document the problems Americans have in ethics in "the most massive in-depth survey of what Americans really believe that has ever been conducted."[3]

The authors noted: "Americans are making up their own rules and laws. . . . We choose which laws of God we believe. There is absolutely no moral consensus in this country, as there was in the fifties and sixties."

Their study indicates that although 90 percent of the respondents said they believed in God, only 20 percent ever talked to a priest, minister, or rabbi about a personal problem. Almost one in three married respondents weren't sure they still loved their spouses; many admitted having affairs; six in ten believed a prenuptial agreement was a good idea. In fact, only one in three listed "love" as the main reason for his or her marriage. Nearly 50 percent of those surveyed said there is no reason ever to get married.

Some 72 percent didn't know their next-door neighbors, and seven in ten said there are no American heroes. A whopping 60 percent said they had been victims of major crimes, and one in seven carried a gun or had a gun or two in his or her car.

Other interesting findings were:

- Thirteen percent of the populace believes in all the biblical Ten Commandments.

- Nine out of ten Americans lie regularly.

- One-fifth of the nation's children had lost their virginity by age thirteen.

- For $10 million, seven percent of the people would kill a stranger.

- A third of all AIDS carriers have not told their spouse or lover about their disease.[4]

Establishing right principles in our hearts and minds so they affect our decision making is the focus of this chapter on the fourth principle from the MAXIMIZERS acrostic—*internalizing right principles.* In this chapter I want to show you how to identify and build *absolute values* into your life and business that will give you stability and strength, and consequently success and significance. To help you identify and build absolute values, I'll give you another acrostic that will help you focus your thinking on the subject of morals and ethics:

V erify your own values.
A rticulate your own ethical grid and philosophy of life.
L earn the proper perspectives on issues.
U npack right values through action.
E valuate your growth.
S hare these truths (your principles) with other people.

Verify Your Own Values

You need to determine just what value is directing your life.

It's important from the outset to distinguish between principles and values. Basically, a value is your perception of where you're going in life. Your values may change, but principles do not. Your principles are the absolute. They are always true in every circumstance. Your values may change as your understanding of absolutes increases.[5]

The point is that everyone is value-driven. A gang member is directed by his or her values. So is a mass murderer, a priest, and a dock worker. The issue is: Are their values based on right, universal principles or not? Universal principles produce the healthy roots of authentic success. False values not based on universal principles ultimately produce failure.

What is it, then, that you value? When I ask this question of people attending my seminars, they usually try to articulate what they think they *should* value. But that's not the question I'm asking! I want you to identify what you value *right now*. What values are reflective of your present lifestyle? Be honest! A rather rigorous evaluation here is critical; otherwise, you'll live in denial by not identifying the real root areas in your life that may need to change.

You are a model for others, whether you like it or not. We say too glibly, "Do as I say, not as I do." But that's lacking in integrity.

Consider what columnist Jack Griffin writes in his piece entitled, "It's OK, Son, Everybody Does It":

> When Johnny was 6 years old, he was with his father when they were caught speeding. His father handed the officer a twenty-dollar bill with his driver's license. "It's OK, son," his father said as they drove off. "Everybody does it."
>
> When he was 8, he was present at a family council presided over by Uncle George, on the surest means to shave points off the income tax return. "It's OK, kid," his uncle said. "Everybody does it."
>
> When he was 12, he broke his glasses on the way to school. His Aunt Francine persuaded the insurance company that they had been stolen and they collected $75. "It's OK, kid," she said. "Everybody does it."
>
> When he was 16, he took his first summer job at the supermarket. His assignment was to put the overripe strawberries in the bottom of the boxes and the good ones on top where they would show. "It's OK, kid," the manager said. "Everybody does it."
>
> When he was 19, he was approached by an upperclassman who offered the test answers for $50. "It's OK, kid," he said. "Everybody does it."
>
> Johnny was caught and sent home in disgrace. "How could you do this to your mother and me?" his father said. "You never learned anything like this at home." His aunt and uncle were also shocked.
>
> If there's one thing the adult world can't stand, it's a kid who cheats.[6]

We can't expect our kids to do what we *tell* them, as if what we're *showing* them means nothing. The great British statesman Winston Churchill said it well:

It's hard to expect an empty bag to stand up straight.

If we don't have ethics or principles to give us substance and weight—if we're empty in the things that matter—we won't be the kind of models we want to be. Change begins with our value systems. And if the values of our society are declining, it's our fault.

Conduct an audit of your values by answering these questions:

1. How do you spend your discretionary time?

2. How do you spend your discretionary money?

3. Who are your heroes?

4. When you're alone, what do you think about most?

Your answers will demonstrate what your values are. Be honest and record what you are and do now, not what you think you ought to be and do. That will come later.

Try this exercise:

Do a one-week, authentic audit of your life. For an entire week, record how you spend your time, how you spend your discretionary money, who you admire the most, and what you dream about. Keep a daily log, and stop several times throughout the day to record your observations.

Then, at the end of the week, go back and determine the things that you actually valued during that week. Next, ask yourself whether these are the values you want. Are you using your time, spending your money, focusing your dreams, and developing your role models the way you want to?

Articulate Your Universal Principles

What is really important to you? Some people believe that the ethical thing to do is always "whatever will get me ahead."

Take time right now to identify the things that are nonnegotiable in your life—principles you will not violate, no matter what. Include principles that affect your work, your personal life, your family, your finances, your spirituality, etc.

What is your personal philosophy or code of ethics? What is your family philosophy? What is your work philosophy?

I suggest you begin your self-examination with the ten MAXIMIZ-ERS principles set forth in this book. The key is to dig your roots down to the bedrock of *truth* and let that source frame your values.

If you do not articulate these philosophies, the culture will continually push you around. You must identify and promote the values you want to characterize yourself, values based on universal principles. Or, you can expect to spend the rest of your life as a slave to other people's values, your own dysfunctions, cultural pressures, or the values your own bad habits produce. The choice is yours.

Learn the Right Perspective on Issues

Merely discovering what motivates your actions is not the end of this exercise. All of us need to continually look for *truth*; we need to make some actual determinations about right and wrong, about the ethical and unethical, about the moral, amoral, and immoral. And there *are* absolutes—universally accepted natural law principles that govern the universe and how people should live.

In *The Power of Ethical Management,* Ken Blanchard and Dr. Norman Vincent Peale simplify this search for truth with three questions to ask yourself at decisive times. I have added a fourth of my own:

1. Is it legal? (Will I be violating either civil law or company policy?)

2. Is it balanced? (Is it fair to all concerned in the short-term as well as the long-term? Does it promote a win-win situation?)

3. How will it make me feel about myself? (Will it make me proud? Would I feel good if my decision were published in the newspaper, or if my family knew about it?)[7]

4. Is it right? (Do I have any concerns inside as I consider my decision in light of what I understand to be right and wrong?)

In recent years, a substantial amount of effort has been aimed at articulating universal values. This effort includes the publication of such works as *Why America Doesn't Work* (Colson and Eckerd), *The Book of Virtues* (Bill Bennett), *Compassionate Capitalism* (Rich DeVos), *Leadership Is an Art* (Max DePree), *The Power of Ethical Management* (Blanchard and Peale), *The Ethical Executive* (Donald Seibert), *Principle Centered Leadership* (Stephen Covey), and *On My Honor* (Randy Pennington and Marc Bockmon). All of these works are very helpful in leading you to specific tools for the development of your principle base.

> **The Greek philosopher Socrates said:**
> **You never know a line is crooked unless you have a straight one next to it.**

I am especially fascinated with the last book, *On My Honor*. The authors elevate the Boy Scout Oath as a model for running a business as well as any enterprise (family, personal life, community). Imagine building your own enterprises around the concept of this oath.[8]

> **On my honor,**
> **I will do my best:**
>
> 1. To do my duty to God and my country, and to obey the Scout Law:
> 2. To help other people at all times;
> 3. To keep myself physically strong, mentally awake, and morally straight.

Another often forgotten source of universal principles are the biblical Ten Commandments. Consider ABC-TV news anchor Ted Koppel's comments to graduating Duke University students in May 1987:

> We have actually convinced ourselves that slogans will save us. "Shoot up if you must, but use a clean needle." "Enjoy sex whenever and with whomever you wish, but wear a condom."
>
> No. The answer is no. Not no because it isn't cool . . . or smart . . . or because you might end up in jail or dying in an AIDS ward—but no . . . because it's wrong. Because we have spent five thousand years as a race of rational human beings trying to drag ourselves out of the primeval slime by searching for truth . . . and moral absolutes.
>
> In the place of Truth we have discovered facts; for moral absolutes we have substituted moral ambiguity. . . . Our society

finds Truth too strong a medicine to digest undiluted. In its purest form Truth is not a polite tap on the shoulder; it is a howling reproach.

What Moses brought down from Mount Sinai were not the Ten Suggestions . . . they are Commandments. Are, not were.

The sheer brilliance of the Ten Commandments is that they codify, in a handful of words, acceptable human behavior. Not just for then . . . or now . . . but for all time. Language evolves. . . power shifts from nation to nation . . . Man erases one frontier after another; and yet we and our behavior . . . and the Commandments which govern that behavior . . . remain the same.

. . . I caution you, as one who performs daily on that flickering altar, to set your sights beyond what you can see. There is true majesty in the concept of an unseen power which can neither be measured nor weighed. There is harmony and inner peace to be found in following a moral compass that points in the same direction, regardless of fashion or trend.[9]

The question arises: How can we establish the truth in our lives? Let me suggest several things you can do:

1. Read Great Books

A movement has been alive for many years now called the Great Books Movement. This movement urges individuals to read classic literature in order to better understand the underlying principles for the guidance of life. These suggested classics range from Shakespeare to Horace Mann to Goethe to the Bible. The movement senses a tremendous break in people's awareness of the roots upon which great civilizations, including the United States, have been built.

Of course there are many current popular books available today as well, including those suggested earlier. Don't neglect the video and audio market, either.[10] Yet be aware of the danger of gaining massive amounts of knowledge and not translating it into practical living, or what I call wisdom.

The whole concept of wisdom is summed up in the metaphor of an artisan. A wise person is an individual who has learned the craftsmanship of *making a life;* he or she has become an artist in living. So, as you read, think and interact with the material. I always read with a pen in my hand. I make notes, debate the author, ask questions, and identify MAXIMIZERS principles that are at issue. Then I file my notes under each MAXIMIZER principle: 1 equals *Make Things*

Happen, 2 equals *Achieve Personal Significance,* etc. This allows me to organize my thoughts and solidify my principle base. When I finish the book, the key concepts, quotations, and insights can be transferred into a simple 3x5 file or onto the computer.

2. Gain Wisdom through Study Groups

Whether you study a book or deal with issues, doing it in a group can be very helpful for your growing process.

One leader told me a story about his study group. This group was reading the classic best-seller *In His Steps* by Charles Sheldon. The book is based on a fictitious group of individuals who ask themselves the following question in their everyday lives, "What would Jesus do?" One of the group members was in a hotel one day, packing his wife's clothes, when he realized he had included in the suitcase a couple of hangers from the hotel. His recent reading planted the question in his mind: "Would Jesus take those hangers?" His conclusion was no.

This man was developing and establishing right principles in his life. And it was a significant lesson for the group. Before you sneer at such a seemingly insignificant issue, remember that our character and our ethical edge are developed on the basis of our small decisions. It's the "little foxes that spoil the vine."

3. Learn from the Lessons of Life

I believe we can gain great wisdom if we simply listen to life around us. Such lessons may come through a friend's comment, a speaker's message, making a mistake and learning from it, or even facing some form of resistance. If we can learn from life by raising the ears of our inner spirit, we can make significant headway in growing and developing. I've learned many of my greatest lessons by simply becoming more aware of the opportunities I have to grow on a daily basis. We all have daily opportunities to grow and to learn the right perspective on issues—if we'll just look for them.

Unpack Right Values through Action

Now you're ready to start putting your values to work. It's one thing to develop an ethical grid of universal principles (truth) but quite another to work it out in your daily life.

Let me offer a strategy for doing this. Separate your life into three major areas: personal, family, and business.

Now, I am going to choose for you a MAXIMIZERS principle that you can put to work in each one of these areas. The principle is: *zero in on caring for people,* which I develop in greater depth in chapter 7. I call this "servant leadership." It is a code that urges you to build up other people in all possible ways.

In the mid-1970s John Greenleaf, former director of management research at AT&T, wrote a landmark book entitled *Servant Leadership.*[11] Servant leadership, as Greenleaf describes it, focuses on your responsibility to build others, rather than on your rights and perks from being in a leadership position. It is the kind of leadership that says, "I'm here to care for people and help them become successful."

To live by this principle, you have to *burn this value of servant leadership into your mind.* You can do this by writing down a popular quotation or statement on servant leadership. I like this one: "A servant leader is one who gets excited about making others more successful than himself."

Put these words on a 3x5 card and keep it before you during the day. Meditate on it four times or so. Think it through; chew on it; eat it up. Focus on that card as soon as you get up in the morning. Take a break at lunch and think about it. Reflect on it before dinner and then later, just before you go to sleep. Program your mind with this thought.

Next, *think about ways you can apply this principle.* Ask yourself questions about how you can be a servant leader in your personal life. With whom do you have regular contact? Perhaps it's a gas station attendant, a waitress, or people you call on the phone. How can you be a source of encouragement to these people?

One day I walked into my favorite diner for early coffee, and the waitress who'd been serving me for months was in a foul mood. Her service was lousy, her attitude grumpy, and her tone of voice mean. Obviously something was bugging her, and I didn't appreciate the fallout. But I had already decided to practice this concept of servant leadership. So, instead of reacting, I left her a one-dollar tip for my forty-cent cup of coffee. She didn't know what to say. And from that day on, her countenance brightened whenever I walked into the diner.

Think through various situations that will come up in your daily activities and plan your servant-leadership attack before they happen. You're bound to meet a grumpy waiter or waitress every now and then. What will you do?

In the arena of your family, your servant leadership may mean taking very deliberate time to be with your children, perhaps developing dates on a regular basis. These need to be planned, thought out, and activated. In the arena of your business, your servant leadership might be seen in the way you develop your employees or those for whom you have responsibility. Here I recommend reading Ken Blanchard's book, *Leadership and the One Minute Manager*,[12] which can help you master the art of situational leadership. This servant-leadership model allows you to meet people's particular needs and at the same time to help them move toward ultimate success.

Finally, *put the practice of servant leadership to work by planning into your weekly schedule the specific activities you have listed for building servant leadership into your personal, family, and business life.* Make these values tangible, specific actions that you can plan into your schedule. For instance, you can actually mark the times you will be in a restaurant where you can apply servant leadership to a server. You can schedule in dates with your children. You can plan specific activities, words to say, memos to send, time to give to caring for those people for whom you have responsibility.

Above all, move from theory to action. Put feet to this concept!

Evaluate Your Growth

To become truly ethically centered, spend time evaluating your efforts on a daily basis. Keep a journal on your growth for one week, taking time at the end of each day to ask the following questions related to your stated values:

- Did I schedule my principles and philosophy into my daily planner?
- Did I keep my schedule as I planned?
- How did I spend my idle time?
- Where did I spend my money?
- What did I daydream or dwell upon?
- Did my values inside match my values outside?

Or, establish a support group whose members will ask you regularly how you're doing. One reason Weight Watchers and Jenny Craig are such effective weight-loss organizations is the accountability that personal trainers or coaches provide. Whether your motivation is humiliation or being verbally rewarded for making positive headway, the impact of accountability and support works.

Share These Truths with Others

There are right ways and wrong ways to share what you're learning. Let's start with the wrong way.

Years ago I went through a personal sales training course. Afterward, I thought I knew everything about how to relate to people in an open forum.

One night I went to a parade, where I saw a young man walking along the street ahead of the parade, passing out materials to people. I couldn't tell quite what he was distributing, but I was struck with how forthrightly he was forcing his materials on them without even talking to them.

Being a newly enlightened salesman myself, I started to take offense with how he was communicating. After all, I'd just been trained that to sell effectively you must actually communicate. You must speak with people and solicit feedback. Therefore, since he was obviously doing it all wrong, I thought, out of the kindness of my heart and the self-righteousness of my convictions, I would share these truths with him.

So I went up to the gentleman, grabbed him by the shoulder, spun him around, looked at him right in the face, and said, "Excuse me, friend. I appreciate the fact that you have something here to communicate with people, but if you really wanted to be effective you'd communicate directly with them. Why don't you speak to people? It's more thoughtful, it's more sensitive, and it's more effective!"

You know what he said? "Uh . . . uh . . . uh." Nothing but gibberish! He couldn't talk! He had lost his tongue.

As I shrunk into the earth, I suddenly saw eternity. There was this long line, and the man I had just accosted was standing in front, while I was standing in the back—singed. That's how I felt!

I had demonstrated incredible audacity in speaking before I had the data, and it came back to bite me. That was an important lesson I learned from life.

Don't be presumptuous, offensive, or pushy. Don't cram truth down people's throats. Be a friend, be a servant, meet others' needs, and watch how they respond.

Now let's look at the right way to communicate what you've learned.

As you know, I believe we ought to be sharing values in our culture. In fact, I believe we ought to be champions of right values and principles. We can do this by being both *formative* and *reformative* in our communications.

Being *formative* means trying to construct truth in people's lives by talking about and modeling right principles.

For example, I have put my ten MAXIMIZERS principles on my business card in an effort to put values at the forefront of people's thinking. It's not uncommon for people to ask me for several cards to give to friends. I put the principles on my cards because I know that absolute principles work, and I want to help people's lives work. In the same way, as you gain wisdom, you need to share it with others in a way that is not offensive, but positive.

The second way you can build these qualities into people's lives is by being *reformative.*

Most of us usually deal with conflict in one of two extreme ways: one extreme is fight, the other flight. Fighting is getting back at people through verbal or sometimes physical assault. Flight is running away from, suppressing, or repressing a problem.

The proper way to deal with a conflict in a relationship or a difficulty is through positive, loving, assertive communication. This way of dealing with conflict or difficulty is neither fight nor flight. Rather, it is working out a situation through direct, loving, sensitive confrontation of your disagreement or problem. Whether you're trying to build a principle into the life of your child, a coworker, or our culture, there is a way to communicate it appropriately.

Let me suggest some steps you can take to communicate appropriately:

First, communicate *personally.* A rampant tendency exists among people today to want to air things publicly. This often occurs because we are insecure about facing people personally. Be brave and be direct in your personal interaction.

Second, communicate *positively*. It doesn't help to say to someone, "Here are twenty-five things you're doing wrong, and I only want to deal with one of them at this point." Instead, say, "There are many things in your life I wish I had in mine, but here's something I believe you may want to work on."

Third, communicate *practically*. There's nothing worse than identifying a generic problem in someone's life and not giving that person specifics. Once after I spoke to a large crowd, a gentleman came up to me and said, "Dr. Jenson, I don't like you." I responded by saying, "I can understand that. You're just one of many. What don't you like about me?" He thought for a long time and said, "It's your personality." I said, "Could you be more specific?" He thought a bit longer and said, "No, it's your whole personality." I said, "Thanks a lot, I feel really affirmed. The only solution for me is suicide."

That kind of generic feedback isn't helpful. It often *is* helpful, however, to point out specifics.

Finally, communicate *patiently*. We often get upset when others push certain buttons in us. I know this is true for me. It has been frustrating for me to see that I've developed a habit pattern of impatience and anger. I've learned to moderate this pattern over time, and I continually work to alleviate it. But I have to work at it all the time because impatience and anger stifle others' spirits. If I didn't continually work on being patient, I would lose credibility and impact. We have to learn to be patient when we communicate.

Whether you communicate with *reformative* or *formative* activity, you must aim to be a champion for values. Be a servant leader. Don't include yourself in the majority who are afraid to talk about truth, either because they haven't come to any conclusions or are afraid of repercussions. Don't leave a legacy of relativity behind you. Leave a legacy of values, of truth, of rightness. It's your choice.

Once you have committed to building bedrock, universal principles into your life and to embedding the roots of these principles into truth, then you are ready to move on to the next belief principle: March to a mission.

Action Steps

Values Clarification Exercise

1. Where do you spend your discretionary time?

2. How do you spend your discretionary money?

3. Who are your heroes?

4. When you're all alone, what do you think about the most?

5. What do the answers to these questions tell you about your values? Are they the same values you thought you lived by?

Principle Development

1. What are the principles with which you want to form the map for your life? Begin to write these down. Place them prominently before you and begin to build them into your life as your code of conduct and organizing principles.

2. List at least one other person who can form a support group to help you flesh out your values and walk your talk.

Chapter 5

March to a Mission

Beyond Success to Significance

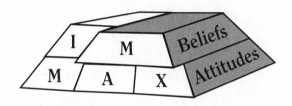

This is the true joy in life. . . . The being thoroughly worn out before you are thrown on the scrap heap. The being a force of nature instead of a feverish, selfish, little clod of ailments.

—*George Bernard Shaw*

We all have rules for our lives. We arrive at some values through thoughtful processes; other values are passed down to us from our parents; still others we develop from we-don't-know-where. Suffice it to say we all live by guideposts—certain principles that form the grid through which we see and do things.

The fifth principle in the MAXIMIZERS model, *march to a mission*, addresses this area of establishing guideposts for our lives. This chapter is about focusing on the present, not avoiding the past or ignoring the future, but rather marshaling your energies toward that part of life over which you have control. This is the opportunity of a lifetime—to change your life by establishing a framework for success. The same opportunity given to Alfred Nobel, which I spoke about in chapter 1, is now yours!

So, what does "march to a mission" mean, exactly? It means living with a sense of destiny, of passion and excitement and meaning. It means knowing that you are living your life in a significant way.

Do You March to a Mission?

I have adapted some questions from Richard Leider's book *The Power of Purpose* to help you examine this area of mission and purpose in your own life.[1] Answer them by circling Yes or No:

1. Do you have a clear picture of where you're going?   Yes   No

2. Have you set targets for your life?   Yes   No

3. Are you satisfied with the targets you've set in your personal life?   Yes   No

4. Do you have a written method to track your progress?   Yes   No

5. Are your values clear and sharp in your mind?   Yes   No

6. Have you written down the values you cherish?   Yes   No

The Power of a Mission

A sense of mission gives *meaning and significance to our lives*. My friend David Rae, past president of Apple Canada, often says that if a man has a "why" for living he can stand any "how." In other words, if someone has a sense of purpose, he can endure all the problems he faces in getting to his goal.

David Rae has conducted research among his peers in the Young Presidents Organization, discovering that most CEOs are less afraid of dying than they are of not making a contribution to their world. Indeed, Harold Kushner says: "I believe that it is not dying that people are afraid of. Something else. Something more unsettling and more tragic than dying frightens us. We're afraid of never having lived. Of coming to the end of our days with the sense that we were never really alive. That we never figured out what life was for."

Sixty students at an American university were asked why they had attempted suicide. Some 85 percent said life seemed meaningless. More importantly, however, 93 percent of these students who suffered from apparent lack of purpose were *socially active*, achieving academically, and on good terms with their families.[2] Yet even in the midst of all of these positive things, their lives lacked meaning.

Viktor Frankl said: "More and more people today have the means to live but no meaning to live for."[3] As you develop mission in life, you develop a *mooring*—something that anchors you and results in stability. This mooring helps you to see things with greater clarity, which in turn results in inner strength.

To help you gain mooring and stability, I suggest you develop a mission statement for your life. A mission statement will serve as a beacon, guiding you for the rest of your life in the right direction. Whatever you do from that point on will be anchored in the principles and values you hold precious. And as you develop your mission statement and begin to live it, you will grow not only in meaning and significance, but also in your sense of mooring and stability.

A sense of mission also helps us to develop *greater motivation.* You see, a mission serves as a *source for starting and sustaining* a project. So often today, people get stuck going around and around in circles, captive to their habits, unable to motivate themselves to make a start.

John Fobre once analyzed what he called "processionary caterpillars." These caterpillars are genetically programmed so that if you stick the nose of one against the tail of another, it will follow the other indefinitely. Fobre did this with a group of caterpillars, putting them all nose to tail so they formed an entire circle. The caterpillars circled around and around for seven days before they finally died from exhaustion and starvation. They just couldn't break out of their cycle of existence.

Mission takes us away from an endless cycle of existence. It creates a motivation for us to move ahead with purpose and direction. It gives us a sense of destiny. It gives us a reason for getting out of bed in the morning. We need to live with the spirit behind the challenging words of George Bernard Shaw: "This is the true joy in life. The being used for a purpose recognized by yourself as a mighty one. The being thoroughly worn out before you are thrown on the scrap heap. The being a force of nature instead of a feverish, selfish, little clod of ailments and grievances complaining that the world will not devote itself to making you happier."[4]

Beyond meaning, mooring, and motivation, a sense of mission also gives us *momentum* or speed. Someone once said, "Focus produces velocity." And having a mission helps you stay focused.

Putting feet to the concept.

A mission also helps produce cognitive dissidence, that is, you set goals that will stretch you beyond what you normally would do. Cognitive dissidence is what Cortez produced in 1519 on the shores of Veracruz, Mexico, where he landed with seven hundred men to take Mexico. As the men stood facing their new land, smoke rose above their heads. Turning around, they saw all eleven ships being burned. Cortez said, "Men, don't panic, don't worry. I set the ships aflame. You see, we only have two options: We take Mexico or we die." That act created cognitive dissidence. Those men decided they'd better achieve their objective, or they were going to be in deep trouble.

Now let's set about producing an actual mission statement. First, we'll take a look at four areas of life that need to be included when we talk about mission: purpose, vision, roles, and goals.

Purpose: Why Do I Exist?

Why do you exist? Why are you here? What is your purpose for living? Develop a two- or three-sentence purpose statement for your life. Your purpose statement can apply to an individual, a family, a business, a community, a nation, or any organization you may be a part of.

Success is the progressive realization and internalization of all that I ought to be and do.

Go to the resource questions at the end of this chapter to help you with this question. Answering it can take from thirty minutes to two hours, depending on the depth in which you want to respond. Perhaps the reiteration of my definition of success will help you to begin the process: Success is the progressive realization and internalization of all that I ought to be and do.

With this concept in mind, try to build your own definition of success. This will help you move toward defining purpose.

Vision: So What That I Exist?

How do you envision the world as being different because you exist? Ask yourself these questions:

1. How do I want myself to be different?

2. How do I want my family to be different?

3. How do I want my business to be different?

4. How do I want my relationships to be different?

5. How do I want my community to be different?

6. How do I want the world to be different?

Many people find these questions easier to answer if they try to look at their lives from the standpoint of old age.

Visualize yourself sitting in a rocker on a beautiful autumn afternoon. You are ninety years old and have lived the most productive and positive life you can imagine. Now, what does your life look like? What is true of your impact on your personal life, marriage, family, business, community, finances, friends, etc.? Write down this *ideal scenario* of your life.

Creating a visual picture will help you in developing a mission statement. Again I have provided resource questions at the end of this chapter to help you with this exciting approach to your future.[5] Remember, this process of vision is more powerful motivationally than your statement of purpose. You must visualize how your life will impact others if you are to be properly motivated for the long run. And this mental future scrapbook will empower you to accomplish your vision.

Roles: Where Do I Accomplish My Mission?

So often we only focus on mission in the area of business. Many of my executive friends grow squeamish about developing the same type of mission-mindedness and actual mission plan for their personal lives.

This resistance leads me into my *attack mode.* I point out how ludicrous it would be to build a business by merely articulating the purpose and vision and then saying, "Okay, troops, go do it." No leader would say that. He or she would move into a very specific strategy in each vital area of concern: production, marketing, finance, administration, sales, etc. Each area would have specific goals along with strategies to accomplish them.

In the same way we all have specific areas in our personal lives that demand attention if we are going to authentically succeed. But we have to identify those areas and develop goals and specific strategies for each one.

Take some time to write down all the various roles you play in your life, especially regarding responsibilities. Just as in your business, you have a role in your family that is specific and vital. Maybe you're the sole provider or sole parent. Maybe you're the encouraging one or the disciplinarian. You have a role as a spiritual leader as well.

I see my roles as revolving around seven Fs:

1. *Faith.* I begin with my role in relationship to God, because I think faith is critical. How do I develop my faith relationship?

2. *Fitness.* How fit am I mentally, emotionally, spiritually, physically, professionally? My overall fitness is important because fitness plays a vital role in every area of my life.

3. *Family.* My family is a top priority. I have roles as both a spouse and a father. But also I'm a child and a brother, and I need to relate to my extended family.

4. *Friendship.* My friendships include intimate relationships, casual relationships, neighborhood relationships, and professional relationships.

5. *Finance.* This area addresses your family or personal budget, taxes, estate, and college-fund planning. It ensures that you keep focused on the short- and long-term financial needs of your family.

6. *Firm* (or career). This category includes all the aspects of your job. You might play many roles as leader, subordinate, peer, teacher, mentor, etc.

7. *Fun.* This includes hobbies and enjoyable activities where you can really relax and renew yourself.

Goals: When and How Do I Accomplish My Mission?

For each role you need to develop specific, logical goals. What, at the end of your life, will you want to have accomplished in that area? What would you like to see in your children at the end of your life? What legacy do you want to leave? Which values, character traits, areas of service, and spiritual lessons do you want to teach your children?

Once you've written down these specific goals, develop further specific, short-range goals that encompass this year. If one of your goals for your children is for them to become authentic lovers of people—to have a heart and a compassion for others—then what one thing can you do this year to help them develop such character?

Now move the goal from this year to this week. How can you build something into your schedule *this week* that will begin to achieve this life goal in your children?

Once you have developed this fourfold process—purpose, vision, roles, and goals—you have the parameters of your mission statement.

Now, combine these elements into a short paragraph and/or phrase that encompasses the essence of each one. This summary, along with the four comprising elements, can be adjusted throughout your life.

The development of your mission statement is critical to everything else in this book. It's imperative that you take the time to thoughtfully consider what I've suggested and to commit those thoughts to paper.

Learning to March to a Mission

Once you articulate your mission, how do you learn to "march" to it? Four basic skills will help you hone your craftsmanship in this area. These skills are: seeing your purpose clearly, wanting it desperately, accomplishing it wholeheartedly, and following it faithfully.

Let's unpack these four skills:

1. See Your Purpose Clearly

You need to know where you're going. You can't win a race unless you know where the finish line is.

If you're going to see your purpose clearly, you need to observe several principles. First, your purpose needs to be very *particular.* You need to particularize or specialize your mission statement through goal development. Write out your goals and make them measurable. Make them specific. Make them achievable. Make them inspiring. Then build your goals into your schedule.

In being proactive and taking control of your life, you need to have a particular sense of purpose. Grab your destiny! When you wake up in the morning, say, "I am here for this reason!" and reiterate your purpose and statement of vision.

Second, you must have a *personal* sense of purpose. Have you ever asked yourself *why* you do what you do?

I am reminded of the man who came home with a roast. His wife asked him why he didn't cut off the end of the roast. He asked, "Why would I?" She thought for a moment and said, "Well, I don't know. But I always have."

He reiterated, "But *why*?" Again she said, "I don't know. I just always have. So did Mother."

He called his wife's mother and asked her why she always cut off the end of the roast. She answered, "I don't know, I just always have. Like Gramma has."

He then called Gramma and asked why she always cut off the end of the roast. She said simply, "My roaster was too small."

We too often live that way, that is, not knowing why we do things the way we do. Why do you spend your money the way you do? Why do you use your free time as you do? What causes you to dress as you do? Often the reason has nothing to do with your mission in life. Instead, we often do things in a certain way because of what our parents or friends or associates expect of us.

A third point is to make your purpose *preeminent.* Your mission needs to be the unifying factor around which you organize the rest of your life—and you've got to be willing to pay the price for it. Martin Luther King Jr. said, "If a man hasn't discovered something he will die for, he isn't fit to live."

2. Want Your Purpose Desperately

This second principle has to do with your constant motivation. How deeply do you desire your mission?

Socrates was walking by the water one day when a young man asked him, "Socrates, may I be your disciple?" Socrates didn't say anything; he merely started to walk into the water. The young man followed, asking again, "Socrates, please let me be your disciple." But Socrates kept his mouth shut and walked farther into the water. The young man still followed, pleading, "Socrates—" At that point Socrates turned around, grabbed the young man by the hair, pushed him under water, and held him there until he knew he could take no more. The man came up gasping for air. Socrates looked at him and said, "Young man, when you desire truth as much as you desire air, then you can be my disciple."

How desperately do you want something? After you have put your vision, purpose, roles, goals, and guiding principles into print, think about them all the time. Read them over and over. Rehearse them in your mind. Pray for their accomplishment. Talk about them. Interact with people concerning your vision. Tell them what you want to do. Let others hold you accountable.

Remember that life is short. So, accomplish what you truly want to accomplish. Develop a deep sense of the preciousness and shortness of your life. And live in light of that!

3. Accomplish Your Purpose Wholeheartedly

Be committed to moving ahead. There's a difference between involvement and commitment, as typified in the story of the pig and the chicken. The two animals were walking along one day when they happened by a church. The sermon title on the sign outside was:

"How can we feed the starving masses of the world?" The chicken turned to the pig and said, "I know. We can feed them ham and eggs." The pig said to the chicken, "For you that's an involvement. For me that's a total *commitment.*" The pig had to lay down his life; the chicken just had to produce a few eggs. And I'm not just talking about involvement when I talk about *your* desires; I'm talking about *commitment.*

W. H. Murray wrote:

> Until one is committed there is hesitancy. The chance to draw back. Always ineffectiveness. . . . The moment one definitely commits oneself then providence moves too. All sorts of things occur to help one that would never otherwise have occurred. A whole stream of events issues from the decision raising in one's favor all manner of unforeseen incidents and meetings and material assistance which no man could have dreamt would have come his way.[6]

I have learned a deep respect for one of Goethe's couplets: "Whatever you can do, or dream you can do, begin it. Boldness has genius, power and magic in it."

You must first commit. If you're going to accomplish your purpose wholeheartedly, enthusiastically, and fully, you've got to commit yourself to act.

4. Follow Your Purpose Faithfully

In short, *don't quit.* Stick with your purpose regardless of whether things are up or down. Booker T. Washington said, "You measure the size of an accomplishment by the obstacles you have to overcome to reach your goals."

A father was discussing with his son why the young man should not quit high school as he was proposing to do. "Son, don't quit," said the father. "Think of all the great leaders of history who never quit. Abe Lincoln didn't quit. Thomas Edison didn't quit. Douglas MacArthur didn't quit. Elmo Mcklinklo."

"Huh?" said the son. "Who's Elmo Mcklinklo, Pop?"

"See, you don't remember him. He quit," said his dad.

How are you doing right now in your application of this principle—*march to a mission?* Once your commitment to marching to a mission is established, you will have solidified your *belief roots.* Then you will be free to begin to follow through with *right commitments.*

Action Steps

Purpose

1. Do you believe you have a destiny?

2. What are your unique gifts, abilities, and skills that indicate this sense of destiny?

3. What sources or activities give you the greatest sense of satisfaction? Can you see how they might fit into your destiny?

4. What is your innermost desire? What makes you happy to think about achieving?

5. Are you working toward the desire you described in the last question?

My purpose in life is to . . . .

Vision

1. What makes you pound the table?

2. What would cause you to weep if you left it undone during your life?

3. How would you see the world differently at the end of your life if you brought your vision to reality? (Include the implications of your life on your profession, your family, and the world in general.)

Roles

1. What do you consider to be the major roles in your life?

2. Look at the following seven areas. Articulate specific activities or interests under each area that you must achieve to fit into the vision of your innermost desire:

Faith
Fitness
Family
Friendships
Finance
Firm (Career)
Fun

Goals

1. For each of the above mentioned roles write at least one thing (and no more than four) that you must now pursue if you want to achieve your goal. For instance, under the area of family, you might write, "I must help my children develop a positive self-concept." Or, "I must teach them basic skills for living."

   Note: In all things, make a positive conscious commitment. Don't equivocate!

2. Work out a weekly schedule of the things you must now do to achieve your innermost desire. Fill in these items one by one on your weekly calendar. This is what you must do to establish your mission. For more tools in this area contact:

Future Achievement International
11828 Rancho Bernardo Road, Suite 12335
San Diego, CA 92128-1999
(619) 487-3177
(619) 487-9212 (fax)
future8@earthlind.net

ROOT COMMITMENTS   Section

3

This final section addresses the basic *root commitments* you must make and fulfill daily if you are to authentically succeed. To the extent that you can embrace and practice these principles, you will maintain a dynamic, maximized life.

These five principles begin with "Integrate All of Life." This "balance principle" shows you how to maintain dynamic equilibrium in all areas of your life, in your family as well as in your work. Moreover, it gives you techniques for balancing your attitudes of structure and spontaneity as well as your goals of results and relationships.

The second commitment principle is to "Zero In on Caring for People." The point of this principle is to learn to *love people and use things,* not vice versa. This relational principle is consistently violated, yet you cannot continue to violate it and expect to authentically succeed. This chapter urges you to develop dynamic relationships using skills that create a unity of spirit in relationship. As you learn to focus on honoring people, you will be given five specific tools with accompanying techniques to build this unity.

If you consistently practice these principles, and the craftsman's skills attached to them, you will authentically succeed in people development and in all relationships.

"Energize Internally" is the third commitment principle. This is your taproot; without it you have no ultimate power. You may make it through life, but you will not authentically succeed. The fact is that without help no one is capable of doing everything I propose in this book. And the help you need is based on building your inner character and cultivating your spirit.

Too often people split the material and spiritual part of their existence. That just doesn't work. You are a whole person—mind, emotion, body, and soul. All of these human components need to fit and work together for your life to work as a whole. This chapter gives you specific craftsman's techniques in building your spirit and deepening your spiritual life. It also explains how to become character-based and not performance-led. This "inside-out" living is meant to change your approach to life and give you inner peace, power, and impact in all areas.

The fourth principle of commitment, "Realign Rigorously," details how to get from point A to point B in the best way possible. Here I explain that life is not a pure path, but a critical one. That is, life is filled with the need for adjustments day in and day out. If you are to authentically succeed at work and at home, you must forever adjust. And this chapter gives you the tools needed to do just that. As you begin to utilize these tools, you'll discover your life to be a tapestry of multicolored experiences and challenges, not constant dead ends and frustrations.

The final principle commitment is "Stay the Course." The tendency we have when learning any new truth is to try it for a while and then quit from discouragement, boredom, frustration, or simple lack of will. In this chapter I provide very specific craftsman's tools that will enable you to stick with it. As you commit yourself to practicing these skills daily, you will find renewed motivation and empowerment to continue. In fact, you'll be so energized with this new way of looking at change and challenges that you'll begin to see significant growth in your personal and professional life. The result will be greater personal completeness and powerful impact.

Chapter 6

Integrate All of Life

How to Have It All

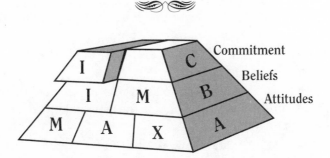

If I had my life to live over again, I would dare to make more mistakes next time. I would relax. I would be sillier. I would take fewer things seriously. . . . I would eat more ice cream and less beans. I would perhaps have more actual troubles but fewer imaginary ones. You see, I'm one of those people who lived seriously and sanely hour after hour, day after day. I've been one of those persons who never went any place without a thermometer, a hot water bottle, a raincoat, and a parachute. If I had to do it over again, I'd travel lighter.[1]
—An eighty-five-year-old woman
from the hill country of Kentucky

Think about the reflection in the words above. Isn't it true of the end of many lives? What would you say if you had to finish this sentence: "If I had my life to live over, I would . . ."? Now is the time to ask that question, so you can begin to live in a deliberately balanced way and erase any "I wish I would have's."

How would you like your life to be played out? What kind of impact would you like to have? What areas are important to you?

How can you integrate all the areas of your life into one great, productive whole?

Harold Kushner wrote: "What is life about? It is not about writing great books, amassing great wealth, achieving great power. It is about loving and being loved. It is about enjoying your food and sitting in the sun rather than rushing through lunch and hurrying back to the office. It is about savoring the beauty of the moments that don't last, the sunsets, the leaves turning color, the rare moments of true communication. It is about savoring them rather than missing out on them because we are so busy and they will not hold still until we get around to them."[2]

What keeps most people from living life to the fullest is usually a preoccupation with one or two aspects of daily life. That's why I want you to look at success in a broad number of areas, not in just one or two. You cannot call yourself successful when your business is growing but your family is failing. Success must be balanced. It must be put in the proper perspective.

In this chapter on integrating all of life (or "having it all"), I will address the subject of balance in three basic areas—your priorities, your attitudes, and your goals. Hopefully, you will begin to see why this MAXIMIZERS principle is so important. Then I'll suggest some practical steps you can take to move toward balance in all three of these areas.

At one time, people who succeeded in all vital areas of their lives were considered mature and well-balanced. These days the rule of thumb is to elevate a successful career (or some other outward goal) above family and personal integrity. Tragically, the idea of balance is reserved for the more public part of our lives: Do I look fit? Do I look successful? Do I look intelligent?

My answer to this attitude is: *nonsense. Nonsense!* There is a principle of life that says, "Only to the extent that we manage our personal lives and our families can we successfully manage in the public arena." To separate the personal and professional is not only dangerous, it's deadly for both individuals and society.

How Did We Get Out of Balance?

Linda and Richard Eyre, in their book *Life Balance*, wrote, "With industrialization came urbanization. People began living closer to each other and comparing themselves in more ways with more people. Mass media and advertising came along to help our wants outpace our needs. Picking out one little thing and trying to know more about it and do better at it than anyone else became the most predictable path to the newly revalued prizes of prominence and prosperity.

"The single-mindedness required was bad for balance. More thought, time, and effort went into work, less into family and personal growth; more importance was placed on structure, less on spontaneity; more attention went to achievements, less to relationships."[3]

The Eyres further point out that we've moved from the industrial age to the information age. Machines are more sophisticated. Access to information and technology has grown dramatically. "Theoretically," they note, "we have more leisure time, more freedom, more wealth and convenience, and therefore more opportunity to broaden ourselves, to take time for all of our priorities, and to balance our lives."

Yet, concurrently, specialization is getting narrower. Competitiveness and materialism combine to require us to be "work oriented, highly structured, and 'in the fast lane' just to keep up!"[4]

All of this creates an incredible tension inside us, and we are driven to move ahead more frenetically in the area of activity. Balance is lost, and we feel out of control.

Results of Imbalance

We see the downside of imbalance in our culture today, ranging from extreme burnout on one end to a lack of passion about life on the other.

As one author has said, *burnout* is when "a job is a job is a job is a job." Christina Maslach, one of the earlier researchers of this problem, says that burnout is "a syndrome of emotional exhaustion, depersonalization, and reduced personal accomplishments that occur among individuals who do people work of some kind."[5]

One of my favorite figures in all of history is King Solomon. He was Israel's leader at a time when that nation was flourishing. He had in his grasp all the power, prosperity, position, prestige, and pleasure anyone could ever want. And yet he got so caught up in those things, his personal life got completely out of whack. Listen to his conclusion on the whole experience:

> So I hated life, because the work that is done under the sun was grievous to me. All of it is meaningless, a chasing after the wind. I hated all the things I had toiled for . . . because I must leave them to the one who comes after me. . . . So my heart began to despair over all my toilsome labor under the sun. For a man may do his work with wisdom, knowledge and skill, and then he must leave all he owns to someone who has not worked for it. This too is meaningless and a great misfortune. What does a man get for all the toil and anxious striving with which he labors under the sun? All his days his work is pain and grief; even at night his mind does not rest. This too is meaningless.[6]

Solomon lived with emotional and mental exhaustion. As Christina Maslach wrote: "Burnout—the word evokes images of a final, flickering flame; of a charred and empty shell; of dying embers and cold, grey ashes . . . once fired up about their involvement with other people—excited, full of energy, dedicated, willing to give tremendously of themselves for others . . . (burnout victims) did give . . . and give and give, until finally there was nothing left to give anymore. The teapot was empty, the battery was drained, the circuit was overloaded—they had burnout."[7]

Are you experiencing burnout? Take the following inventory:

1. More and more, I find that I can hardly wait for quitting time to come so I can leave work.   Yes   No

2. I feel like I'm not doing any good at work these days.   Yes   No

3. I am more irritable than I used to be.   Yes   No

4. I'm thinking more about changing jobs.   Yes   No

5. Lately I've become more cynical and negative.   Yes   No

6. I have more headaches (or backaches, or other physical symptoms) than usual.   Yes   No

7. Often I feel hopeless, like, "Who cares?"   Yes   No

8. I drink more now or take tranquilizers just to cope with everyday stress.   Yes   No

9. My energy level is not what it used to be. I'm tired all the time.   Yes   No[8]

Whether you are experiencing intense burnout or are just showing the early warning signs, my solution will always move you toward greater balance. The way to deal with burnout is to build a healthier, holistic lifestyle.

The opposite extreme of burnout is more typical. That is the individual who exists but is not living. Such a person's life lacks passion. He or she may have thrilling moments from time to time, but life is not savored or enjoyed.

What about you? Is your life in balance or out of balance? Are you maximizing all critical areas of your life, or only one or two? Are you a single-event athlete, or could you compete in the pentathlon of life?

It takes constant work to integrate your life and stay balanced, and if you don't consistently make midcourse corrections, the most pressing urgencies of the day will drive you. Then it becomes impossible to develop in all the areas of your life, and your success and significance become greatly jeopardized.

Following are some techniques to help you in three major areas—priorities, attitudes, and goals.

Balance Priorities: Business and Basic Relationships

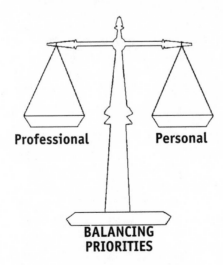

Professional   Personal

BALANCING
PRIORITIES

The most common area discussed in regard to balance is *priorities*. Most of us know it is a difficult chore to balance work with the other areas in our lives. If you're going to balance business and other basic relationships, you need to take some definite steps:

1. Rule Your Impulses

The starting point for balancing your priorities is to take charge of your internal drives. You can rule your impulses only by being disciplined. Consider this penetrating confession of the undisciplined life of the great playwright Oscar Wilde:

> The gods had given me almost everything. But I let myself be lured into long spells of senseless and sensual ease. Tired of being on the heights I deliberately went into the depths in search for new sensations. What the paradox was to me in the sphere of thought, perversity became to me in the sphere of passion. I grew careless of the lives of others. I took pleasure where it pleased me and passed on. I forgot that every action of the common day makes or unmakes character and that therefore what one has done in the secret chamber one has someday to cry aloud from the housetop. I ceased to be lord over myself. I was no longer the captain of my soul and did not know it. I allowed pleasure to dominate me. I ended in horrible disgrace.[9]

This man had a tremendous impact in his field, but because he gave in to inappropriate impulses he ultimately failed in other, more critical areas.

Be cautious of any type of impulse, including drivenness. Be careful not to do your work for the purpose of receiving the approval of others or to fill some unmet need in your life. Work was not given to us to meet all of our needs; it simply can't.

Gordon MacDonald, author, pastor, and speaker, uses these qualifications to identify a driven person:

1. A driven person is most often gratified only by accomplishments.

2. A driven person is preoccupied with the symbols of accomplishment.

3. A driven person is usually caught in the uncontrolled pursuit of expansion.

4. A driven person tends to have a limited regard for integrity.

5. A driven person often possesses limited or undeveloped people skills.

6. A driven person tends to be highly competitive.

7. A driven person often possesses a volcanic force of anger that can erupt any time he senses opposition or disloyalty.

8. A driven person is usually abnormally busy.[10]

Live with a sense of urgency, but don't be driven. Rule your impulses.

2. Reorder Your Priorities

The second skill needed in balancing priorities is to place your priorities in the proper order. Rabbi Harold Kushner reminds us of our need to keep first things first:

> Ask the average person which is more important to him, making money or being devoted to his family, and virtually everyone will answer family without hesitation. But watch how the average person actually lives out his life. See where he really invests his time and energy, and he will give away the fact that he does not really live by what he says he believes. He has let himself be persuaded that if he leaves for work earlier in the morning and comes home more tired at night, he is proving how devoted he is to his family by expending himself to provide them with all the things they have seen advertised.
>
> Ask the average person which means more to her, the approval of strangers or the affection of people closest to her, and she won't be able to understand why you would even ask such a question. Obviously nothing means more to her than her family and her closest friends. Yet how many of us have embarrassed our children or squelched their spontaneity, for fear of what neighbors or strangers might think? How often have we poured out our anger on those closest to us because we had a hard day at work or someone else did something to upset us? And how many of us have let ourselves become irritable with our families because we were dieting to make ourselves look more attractive to people who do not know us well enough to see beyond appearances?[11]

Underlying Kushner's questions is a confusion about priorities. We can vehemently hold to the bottom-line priority, but if we don't live it, we're deceiving ourselves.

The best paradigm for prioritization I have found is in the New Testament, in the words of Jesus of Nazareth. In the episode I'm thinking about, Jesus was being interviewed by a group of religious leaders. They were experts in the Old Testament law, and they spent their time studying and classifying some six hundred laws. These men wanted to trip up Jesus, who had been gaining a following at their expense. So they posed this question to him: "What's the greatest law?" Then they stood ready for a debate.

Jesus answered them simply, "Love the Lord your God with all your heart, mind, soul, and strength, and love your neighbor as yourself."[12] That's it. He said that all we need to do is to love God with all our being, and to love our neighbor as ourselves, and we'll win.

In that simple statement we find the key to the prioritization of all our lives. You can visualize this prioritization in terms of three concentric circles. The outside circle represents others in your life; the middle circle represents yourself; and the center circle represents God, or the spiritual core of your life.

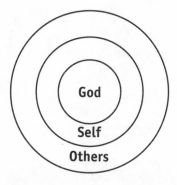

The priorities Jesus set up have been respected throughout history, and they work by taking the focus off ourselves. Whenever we set ourselves up as most important in life, people suffer—spouses, children, clients, neighbors, parents, friends.

> **Love the Lord your God with all your heart, mind, soul, and strength.**

Whatever your perception of God is, He must be in the center of your life to provide you with the healthy balance you need. Don't put yourself in the center; you'll end up frustrated. You're not God. You're not that good. No one is. So put God in the center of your life.

How do we love God? I'll talk about this more later, when I discuss energizing the inner life. But for now let me say that there are two primary ways to love God: First, you must cultivate a relationship with God as you understand him. Second, you must learn to do what God says to do.

You can work on building your personal relationship with God in the same way you build a relationship with anyone: You interact with that person, listening, responding, depending, and communicating. In the same way, you can respond to and obey God as you understand him by finding the principles that God elevates as absolute. Once you identify those principles, live in light of them.

Second, you need to love yourself. "Love your neighbor *as yourself.*" This does not mean selfish, narcissistic love—the kind that focuses only on your own concerns and interests. It means, rather, taking care of yourself. You must develop yourself mentally, emotionally, physically, and spiritually so that you are healthy and can function at an optimal level.

Many people spend so much time caring for others or for their work that they let their own lives atrophy. This leads only to devastation in their impact on others. We must be internally healthy in order to win.

Think about the metaphor of a saw. If you're going to cut down a forest, it's better to periodically stop and sharpen the saw before going back to work. The interruption for saw-sharpening may seem a nuisance. But without it, the saw will grow increasingly dull and will have decreased effectiveness.

Finally, love others. Where do we find others? They are the people around us—at work, at home, in the neighborhood, at the hardware store, on the tennis court, in our churches or synagogues or temples, and on the freeway. Every day and all day long we're to love God, we're to love ourselves, and we're to love others.

How do we learn to balance our love for God, ourselves, and others? We do it by applying the following principles:

1. Realize it's not either/or: you can't either love God or love yourself. You can't either love your family or love other people. You need to love God, yourself, and others all the time.

2. Constantly reflect love for God, self, and others.

3. Realize that balance is not static. It's dynamic.[13]

Think of Balance in Terms of a Marble and a Bowl

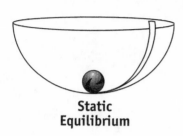

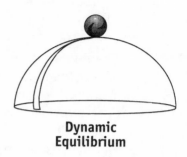

**Static
Equilibrium**

**Dynamic
Equilibrium**

Many people think life should be like a marble sitting at the bottom of a bowl. This is a static equilibrium, with no pressure on the marble. It just sits there comfortably.

The problem is, the bowl is in the wrong position. We need to take that bowl and turn it over so that it sits on its rim. Now, we gently put the marble on the very top of the bowl's upturned bottom so that it's ready to fall in any direction. That is the right view of balance in life!

We constantly have tension. Which bills should I pay this week? Which clients should I woo? Who needs to see me before the weekend? Should we go out to dinner with or without the kids? Which set of in-laws gets to host us at Christmas this year? Should I finish this report or be on time for dinner?

How do you deal with this kind of constant tension? First, you embrace the principle that life is going to be dynamic and not static. If the marble starts rolling down too far in one direction, you need to shift the bowl to get it back to the top.

The best way to stop the marble from rolling off the bowl is to consistently and persistently answer these two questions in the context of your predetermined purpose and priorities:

1. What is the greatest need right now?

2. What have I previously neglected? What have I let go?

If you come home at night and find your children hurting because of some present need, you should zero in on that as a priority. Or, if you go to work and find some difficulty in an administrative area, you may need to get involved and change your appointment schedule. Or maybe you realize you haven't talked to your mother in over a month; you need to shut your door and pick up the phone.

Take a hard look at the major areas of your life—faith, fitness, family, friends, finances, firm (business activities), and fun. And ask yourself, "What is the present need in each? What am I neglecting?" Keep making dynamic, equilibrium-oriented changes, constantly reflecting on your life mission as your anchor. That's called creating balance, or reordering priorities based on values. And balance creates the constantly integrated life.

3. Readjust Your Schedule

The third ingredient to balancing business, family, and other basic relationships is to *let your priorities determine your schedule.* Look at your schedule and keep changing it to reflect your reordered priorities. You can do this early in the morning, late at night, or anytime throughout the day. There are countless new notebooks out there just waiting for you to personalize them with *your* schedule!

Stephen Covey in his book, *First Things First*, provides one of the finest paradigms I've yet seen for proper schedule adjustment. His solution to avoiding the "tyranny of the urgent"[14] is to zero in on scheduling our priorities instead of prioritizing our schedule. This can be done in a very simple and uncumbersome way.

At the beginning of each week, put together a list of activities for the week using your vision, purpose, life roles, and life goals (the areas we addressed in the last chapter). In your average week you have activities to accomplish in all vital areas of your life: business, personal, and family. I suggest you begin with your major life roles, those you articulated in the previous chapter, "Marching to a Mission."

Beginning with these roles, identify activities under each. Then develop specific activities for the week. If your week is like mine, you'll average somewhere between fifteen and twenty-five various activities. These can range from having time alone to think, ponder, and pray, or having a date with one of your children, to multiple activities at your job. Once you've listed all the activities of the week, prioritize them from one to the end-number of activities you've listed. Prioritize them by asking the two questions we mentioned before: What is the greatest need right now? And, what have I neglected previously? These questions will force you to look at the priorities in your life holistically, and not just at those in one or two areas.

Right now Western cultures are experiencing a period of downsizing. Large companies are becoming smaller. And, increasingly, business executives are trying to get more and more out of fewer workers. The net effect is that people are being pressured to put more time into their jobs.

This problem may be intensified in your life if you have workaholic tendencies. "True workaholics are typically driven individuals for whom work is a compulsion or addiction. They can't shift from work for relaxation or recreation without feeling anxiety or guilt, and they often impair their organizations in the short run and long run as well," says Jody Johnson of the Maryland Consultant Group in Timonium, Maryland.[15] Even when pressured by family and friends to take a vacation, a workaholic likely will bring the job along in one form or another—books to read, phone calls to make, plans to complete. In this case, work may become the center of life, a god, because the workaholic's self-concept is inextricably tied to work accomplishment.

If you are an employer, you must address such workaholism and champion the kind of personal and professional balance I am talking about. Without doing this, you will not only be negligent in caring for your people, but you'll actually be doing harm to your company's bottom line.

In an article entitled "That Loyalty Thing," Michael H. and Timothy S. Mescon pointed out that with increasing downsizing and reengineering and "right sizing," there is also a growing concern about the loyalty of employees. Despite Gallup survey findings that 87 percent of eighteen- to twenty-nine-year-olds were challenged by their jobs and had a strong sense of loyalty to their employers,[16] the rules of the game have dramatically changed.

To combat this, there is a growing movement among business leaders to redirect corporate efforts toward building a solid, stable, loyal employment force through personal and family development and support. Here are a few examples of this recent trend:

> **The Leixlip plant in Ireland** is in full production of a wafer-thin Pentium computer chip. The company has succeeded in melding together empowerment and constructive confrontation as well as extensive training through its Intel University. This training focuses on helping people develop professionally and personally and is big on people maximizing their personal and professional lives.[17]

WearGuard Corporation, the nation's largest direct marketer of work clothes and rugged wear, has more than one thousand employees. The vice president for Human Resources and Employee Services says: "We believe we get better work from employees who aren't worried about problems at home." One of the things that distinguishes this company is the "breadth of services, policies and programs" for families. For instance, the company offers a snow-day program for school-age children and a daily on-site day care for more than one hundred children. During school vacations, the company runs on-site programs for older children; during summer vacation, it runs Camp Draugreaw (that's WearGuard spelled backwards). For the health and fitness of its employees, WearGuard offers a state-of-the-art health club and a variety of wellness programs. Chief executive Bruce Humphrey points to "an atmosphere where people are more comfortable," and talks about how these services lead to higher productivity, creativity, a willingness to take risks, and greater loyalty to the company.

Putman Investments offers its two thousand Boston and Quincy, Massachusetts, employees emergency child care at fifteen dollars per family per day, adoption reimbursements, a school vacation program, flex time, job sharing, telecommunicating, resource and referral counseling, discounts at nearby fitness centers, self-production programs, and more. According to Phyllis Swersky, president of Work/Family Directions, a Boston-based consulting firm, "It's only a matter of time until most companies become family-friendly. That's partly because specialists now can measure more precisely the dollar value of the family-friendly programs." Her consulting firm studies demonstrated that, on average, for each dollar spent on such programs, employers realize a six-dollar gain in increased employee output because of additional motivation, employee time saved, employee retention, lower health-care cost, and reduced absenteeism.[18]

The Mescons cite research that identifies six keys to building employee loyalty:

1. Build an educated workforce.

2. Improve the quality of the work environment.

3. Open communications.

4. Make an impact on personal and family life.

5. Be a skill builder.

6. Cultivate teams.[19]

Note that all of these points concern building healthy individuals. And a rapidly increasing number of executives and companies are emphasizing personal and professional balance today because *they understand the power of healthy individuals.* Due to the internal motivation of individuals, company officials have seen greater relational harmony, better quality work, and a decrease in stress-related sickness on the part of their employees. The bottom line: substantial financial increases.

Life is like juggling crystal balls and rubber balls; success depends on knowing which is which.

Roy Roberts, a fifty-five-year-old vice president of General Motors Corporation and general manager of the GMC truck division, states, "Life is like juggling crystal balls and rubber balls, and success depends on knowing which is which. My crystal balls are my religion, my faith, my work in this country. Everything else is a rubber ball. You can let it drop, wait for a week or month, let it bounce. Life is about choices. Life is about balance."[20]

Gary Wilber, a former CEO of Drug Emporium, Inc., a discount drug chain based in Columbus, Ohio, and founded by his father, resigned from his position after being diagnosed with bone cancer. "What I finally realized or was forced to realize was, frankly, that I didn't enjoy what I was doing," Mr. Wilber said. "There are probably a lot of people out there like me who end up doing something, and they get caught up in a career. What happens is, you find yourself twenty years later down the road and something fortunately happens and you say, 'Why?'"[21] He urges graduates to go slowly and bring the various areas of their lives under control and into focus.

Now let me turn to the second major area of balance—balancing *attitudes.*

Balance Attitudes: Structure and Spontaneity

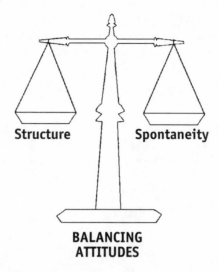

Structure   Spontaneity

**BALANCING
ATTITUDES**

Structure and spontaneity are the tensions that face our attitudes. Many people lead highly structured lives. They live as if successful time management means getting as much done as possible in every minute of their day. Our written goals lock us into a structure that won't let us go. Structure, of course, is important and necessary. But when it becomes the end and not the means, it keeps us from the spontaneity that allows us to buy up the opportunities of life.

Your goal should be to develop some degree of balance between structure and spontaneity. For instance, if you're so busy "getting the job done" that you can't help your child at a point of his or her need, you'll miss not only the need but also the child. Any time the structure of your work (or life) prevents you from spontaneously loving or caring about another person, you're out of balance. People are more important than schedules.

Richard Eyre wrote:

> I took my young son on a hike one rare day. I knew it was important to be together, and he was excited. There was a plateau I figured we would climb to so we would have a level place to camp.
>
> The first part of the hike was great. We talked. We enjoyed being together. But we weren't moving very fast. I started pushing

him to walk faster. I got a little upset at our slow pace. I finally found myself carrying his pack and almost dragging him.

We made it to the plateau just in time to set up camp before dark. My boy fell asleep before I had the campfire going. When the flames grew and hit his face, I saw tear stains.

I realized that there are always two goals. One is to get there. The other is to enjoy the journey. Too much emphasis on one can ruin the other.[22]

Let me offer you some ways to balance your attitudes. I suggest these three specific steps: (1) tighten goals and loosen plans; (2) think process, not just product; and (3) treat interruptions as guests (respond, don't react).

1. Tighten Goals and Loosen Plans

Goals are like beacons in our lives. They show us a direction. I'm a big believer in the retricular activator, that is, the portion of the brain that is able to respond to the power of goals. When you set a specific goal, your mind begins to work toward achieving that goal. One of the great motivating factors in the lives of athletes and other high-performance achievers is that they are able to see very clearly the successful accomplishment of their goal in their mind's eye before they even begin to practice.

One of the ways you can learn to balance structure and spontaneity in your life is by setting specific goals. It may seem incongruous to link structure and spontaneity. But the fact is, you need to tighten your goals to release time for spontaneity. For instance, a simple goal to meet with your executive team weekly is more focused when stated, "I will meet with my exec team every Wednesday at nine o'clock." With that kind of structure in place, you can see where your windows of flexibility lie.

2. Think Process, Not Just Product

A second way of balancing your attitudes is by thinking *process* rather than *product*. I believe success is a journey—a progressive realization and internalization of all I was meant to be and do. That means I'm progressively growing intellectually, and I'm progressively growing in my character and conduct. Indeed, success is tied up in the little moments of the day. It's the little thoughts, the little habits, the little acts that determine our success. Success is not just the end result, but the process of achieving it as well. In fact, the degree of success in the product of our lives is in direct proportion to the degree of success we have in the process.

I first learned the concept of "buying up the opportunities around me" many years ago while doing graduate studies. I used my lengthy commuting time to improve my vocabulary for one of my language classes, all the while trying to reduce the time by driving as fast as I could, leaning on my horn at every irritation. In short, I was studying, moving fast, and approaching my destination as quickly as possible. Yet, it was then that I began to understand, through Ruth's input, that life is not just about *chronos,* the Greek word meaning a linear concept of time; it's also about *kiros,* time in the moment, quality time, moments to be experienced and savored. Life is more about quality than about quantity.

So I conscientiously put aside my behind-the-wheel memory work; I stopped racing and leaning on the horn, being rude and unfriendly to the people around me. Instead, I listened to tapes and began to think and meditate and pray, building my spirit. I was intent on creating within me a balanced persona with the side benefit of being more alert and effective when I took my tests and wrote my papers and listened to lectures. Soon I was kinder, more patient, and more sensitive because I had begun to understand that success meant living in a process and not constantly going for a product.

3. Treat Interruptions as Guests

The final step in balancing your attitudes of structure and spontaneity is learning to treat interruptions as guests. I spoke about this earlier in the chapter "X Out the Negatives," but now I want to readdress it from a different perspective.

One of the major flaws I see in many executives is the inability to handle interruptions. Many react to interruptions. instead of responding to them. Rather than seeing value in an interruption, they instinctively react by running away from it, thinking that it will inhibit them from being successful.

Yet the fact is: those interruptions may be the key to our success—if we learn what we need to from them. "A rabbi once asked a prominent member of his congregation, 'Whenever I see you, you're always in a hurry. Tell me, where are you running all the time?' The man answered, 'I'm running after success, I'm running after fulfillment,

I'm running after the reward for all my hard work.' The rabbi responded, 'That's a good answer if you assume that all those blessings are somewhere ahead of you, trying to elude you and if you run fast enough, you may catch up with them. But isn't it possible that those blessings are behind you, that they're looking for you, and the more you run, the harder you make it for them to find you? Isn't it possible indeed that God has all sorts of wonderful presents for us—good food and beautiful sunsets and flowers budding in the spring and leaves turning in the fall and quiet moments of sharing—but we in our pursuit of happiness are so constantly on the go that He can't find us at home to deliver them?'"[23]

I wrote earlier about the time when my son asked me to play basketball with him and I hesitated. Well, the same opportunity presented itself again, and that time, without hesitation, I dropped what I was doing and moved with him toward the basketball court. You see, the book I was writing—the very book you're reading—could wait for another time. But my son and that opportunity could not. In fact, as I worked aggressively on this chapter, my son's imminent high school graduation kept tapping me on the shoulder. And as important as this book was, the things that really count to me are my relationships with my family and those meaningful people around me. If I lose there and win in other areas of my life, I'll be in real trouble.

One good tool I have found that helps me learn to handle interruptions and opportunities as they come is the *serendipity line*. Serendipity is when you find something of special value while in search of something else. This is a concept that I learned from Linda and Richard Eyre in their helpful book, *Life Balance*. Their serendipity line is a very simple tool. It involves taking your daily planner and drawing a line down your schedule sheet. At the end of the day, you record on the left-hand side all the structured activities, meetings, appointments, to-do's. On the right side of the serendipity line, you write down everything you did that day that reflected an appreciation for the process—how you stopped to smell the roses, how you stopped to listen to an employee or a colleague. Did you stop to meditate or pray because of a need, or because of thanksgiving? At the end of each day, and then at the end of the week, evaluate how much richness was gained in your life because you responded to the serendipitous moments.

To experience this kind of sensitivity to opportunities, try practicing the following:

1. Practice being very aware of your circumstances and the people around you.

2. Listen actively and empathically.

3. Be thankful first when an interruption enters your life.

4. Embrace every experience as a meaningful and ordained opportunity to grow, develop, and become all that you need to become.

As you learn to balance your natural inclination toward either spontaneity or structure, you'll begin to find new liberty and authentic success in your attitudes and life.

This brings us to the last major area of life balance.

Balance Goals: Results and Relationships

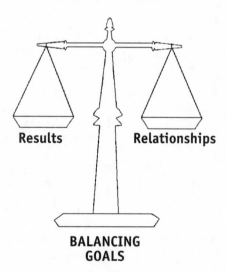

Results   **Relationships**

**BALANCING
GOALS**

It's likely that most people who read this book are heavy on the result/goal side of life. You probably write measurable specific goals when it comes to business results. But I'll bet you never write goals for your relationships. If you do, they are probably vague goals such as, "Don't forget our anniversary this year." But have you written goals for yourself to spend time with your spouse, your children, your parents, your friends?

I urge you to build relationships more aggressively into your frame of reference. People are vital, significant, and worth the time it takes to build right relationships. Research indicates that 85 percent of all employees who are fired are let go because of relational conflict or lack of relational skills, not lack of technical skills. If you're going to be effective in your business—not to mention your personal, family, and social lives—you must learn to be a relational pro. Value people and build relationships into your structure. Yet don't just do this for pragmatic, self-preserving reasons; do it because it's *right*.

1. List Your Goals

Begin by listing your goals, both relational and result-oriented, into your schedule. Most time management is geared toward working on result goals. But let me suggest to you a rather radical paradigm shift: *Now implement your goal-setting strategy with your various relationships.* Here are several examples:

- You see an employee or associate who is having difficulty getting along with other people. Therefore, you set a goal and schedule it, aiming to help this person develop relational skills through your mentoring and help.

- You begin to realize that one of your children is developing emotional distance from you. Therefore, you schedule an appointment to get together with that child and spend concentrated listening and caring time with him or her.

- A good friend has been struggling in a job search. You set a goal and schedule time to call that person and encourage him or her with networking or other help.

- You realize it's been a while since you've taken a deliberate vacation from work (even if only a weekend) or spent concentrated time with certain relatives or friends. So you begin the challenge of scheduling a vacation together with them—and you follow through with it!

My wife, Mary, and I have listed several families with whom we never want to lose touch—friends who would drop everything for us should we need them. (These friendships have proven to be excellent role models for our children.)

Next, we arrange our schedules to spend time with them. Sometimes that means accepting speaking engagements in or near the cities they live in. Sometimes it means vacationing together or spending holidays together.

Who are your friends? Sometimes friendships develop and last with very little attention. But in a mobile society like ours, friendships break up more often than they are supported. If you haven't made your list yet, write out those families you hope to have as friends forever. Then drop them a line or call and tell them so.

2. Listen to Your Intuitive and Logical Areas

A second tool for developing balance in your goals is to listen to both sides of your mind—that is, both the intuitive and the logical.

Though the left brain/right brain theory is still being debated, let's assume that the left brain is logical and likes to accomplish quantitative, measurable goals.

The right brain, on the other hand, is much more intuitive and idea-oriented. It deals with insights and is much more responsive to relational goals.

It takes work to adjust throughout the day, to make sure that you don't just restrict yourself to your results-oriented, goal-centered, accomplishment-focused left brain, but that you also allow yourself to reflect, be more intuitive, and be more relational.

I regularly see this difference between left- and right-brain functioning fleshed out in my marriage. I am much more left-brain-oriented than my wife, Mary. She's the creator, the artist, who likes to create atmosphere. People love coming to our home because they feel comfortable and stimulated here.

One of the upsides to Mary's creative and intuitive capabilities is her assessment of people. I must confess that in my various positions over time, I have often recruited the wrong person for the job. I've made enough mistakes that I have learned to ask my wife's perspective on virtually every person with whom I'm going to work. One reason I hired a president and CEO of my former company was because he not only impressed me with his result capability, but he got a perfect ten from my wife through her relational and intuitive grid!

All of us, regardless of our particular giftedness, need to learn to listen to both sides of our brains.

3. Love People, Use Things

The final tool needed to balance your result goals and relationship goals is to learn to *love people* and *use things.*

Loving things and using people is all too often our modus operandi. Let's face it—loving something inanimate, like a swimming pool, is a lot less work than loving a person. A pool is predictable; it doesn't go anywhere or ask for anything. It doesn't have mood swings or temper tantrums. It doesn't need you to be sensitive.

The people in our lives cause us the most trouble, don't they? If you weren't married, you wouldn't have to share the garage. If you didn't have children, you wouldn't have to deal with adolescent rebellion. If you didn't work with a team, you wouldn't have to share the glory. But good lives, right lives, aren't like that. They're made good by the people in them. Rich living means being deeply involved in others' lives—taking the pain along with the pleasure and experiencing profound sorrow because you've loved so profoundly.

You will only experience rich living as you move your attention away from things as a source of satisfaction and focus it on people. All things come and go. The only "things" that count are people.

When we die, we leave it all behind. And before people die, most of them look back and are always interested in the same things: family, friends, relationships, impact, quality, and character. Those are the real rewards of life, the things that really count.

How much is your life counting?

Action Steps

1. Answer the question I proposed at the beginning of this chapter: If I had my life to live over, what would I do differently?

2. Evaluate your level of accomplishment in the three major areas of balance, on a scale of 1 to 10 (1 being poor, 10 being outstanding):

   Balance Your Priorities (business and basic relationships)

Rule Your Impulses	1 2 3 4 5 6 7 8 9 10
Reorder Your Priorities	1 2 3 4 5 6 7 8 9 10
Readjust Your Time (scheduling)	1 2 3 4 5 6 7 8 9 10

Balance Your Attitudes

Tighten Goals and Loosen Plans	1 2 3 4 5 6 7 8 9 10
Think Process, Not Product	1 2 3 4 5 6 7 8 9 10
Treat Interruptions as Guests	1 2 3 4 5 6 7 8 9 10

Balance Your Goals

List Your Goals into Your Schedule	1 2 3 4 5 6 7 8 9 10
Listen to Your Intuitive and Logical Sides	1 2 3 4 5 6 7 8 9 10
Love People and Use Things	1 2 3 4 5 6 7 8 9 10

3. Now move toward some specific action:

   a. List one relationship at work and one in your personal life that you need to develop.

   b. Write one goal this week for improving each of those relationships, and schedule this goal into your planner.

Chapter 7

Zero In on Caring for People

How to Change People's Lives

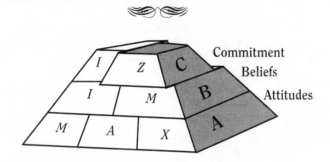

In the right key one can say anything. In the wrong key, nothing; the only delicate part is the establishment of the key.

—George Bernard Shaw

I t's a cold, blustery day. The deep-black clouds blanket and engulf the sky like the deep-brown earth that will soon cover the coffin being lowered the last six feet of its journey. A small crowd of people hangs around for the final moments of this graveside service.

The service is short. But then, so was the life of the deceased. Death came so suddenly.

The date of the funeral: one year from today. The deceased: *you.*

Who will weep at your funeral? Who will care enough about your passing to truly grieve? Whose lives have you touched so deeply that you have left them as your true legacy?

This chapter will address this human-relations principle—*zero in on caring for people.* This principle demands an extended chapter because its scope is so great. Our entire lives are built around people, and there are basic, absolute principles and attendant skills that must be learned if we are to authentically succeed in our relationships.

Deep relationships today are not offered the way they once were. Daniel Yankalovich, in his book *New Rules in American Life*, wrote:

> The hunger for deeper personal relationships shows up in our research findings as a growing conviction that a me-first, satisfy-all-my-desires attitude leads to relationships that are superficial, transitory, and ultimately unsatisfying. Our surveys show that 75 percent of Americans now recognize that while they have many acquaintances they have few close friends, and they experience that as a serious void in their lives. Moreover, two out of five—41 percent—state they have fewer close friends than they had in the recent past.[1]

Why do Americans tend to have difficulty in developing deep relationships? Perhaps it's because we have moved away from acknowledging the importance of deep relationships and have become too involved in extraneous activities that don't encourage them. And in the process we have abandoned the most critical issue of our lives.

When I ask top performers around the world what is most important to them, they don't talk about their work. They speak instead of relationships—of marriage, family, friends, colleagues, partners, and community. And when I ask them how they would live their lives over again if they could, their answers almost always reflect the same concern—for *relationships*. They tell me they've realized people count and that their fundamental mistakes in life have rotated around their mistreatment of family, friends, and colleagues.

You may be like many others in our culture who have lost sight of this fundamental principle of life—the need for caring, building up people, and creating unified teams of productive, affirmed, maximized individuals.

Harold Kushner, the rabbi with such a profound outlook on life, shares a lesson he learned one day at the beach. He was watching two children, a boy and a girl, build an elaborate sandcastle with everything a good castle needs—moats and turrets and passages. Just when it looked as if the castle might be finished, a big wave came unexpectedly and knocked it down. Kushner says he fully expected tears from the children. He was surprised when they laughed, grabbed hands, and moved off to more stable ground to build another castle. Here is the lesson he learned: "All the things in our lives, all the complicated structures we spend so much time and energy creating, are built on sand. Only our relationships to other people endure. Sooner or later, the wave will come along and knock down what we have worked so hard to build up. When that happens, only the person who has some-body's hand to hold will be able to laugh."[2]

More and more, people are looking for deep intimacy in relation-ships, not only to fulfill their own need for good friendships, but also to develop a vehicle for their contribution to society. The ability to develop such personal intimacy—by zeroing in on caring for people—is essential to becoming a maximizer.

Teamwork

The Z in the MAXIMIZER model, "Zero in on Caring for People," is the key to developing intimate relationships and to changing peo-ple's lives. How we change others will be in direct proportion to the level of love we put into our relationship with them.

Unabashed caring is the essence of "teamness," which is funda-mental for powerful families, friendships, communities, and entire cultures. I am delighted to see a growing trend toward teamness in the business realm.

Jon Katzenback and Douglas Smith, in their highly popular and influential book, *The Wisdom of Teams*, document powerfully the benefit and absolute necessity of teamness in the business arena:

> The record of team performance speaks for itself. Teams in-variably contribute significant achievements in business, charity, schools, government, communities, and the military. Motorola, recently acclaimed for surpassing its Japanese competition in pro-ducing the world's lightest, smallest, and highest-quality cellular phones with only a few hundred parts versus more than a thou-sand for the competition, relied heavily on teams to do it. So did Ford, which became America's most profitable car company in 1990 on the strength of its Taurus model. At 3M, teams are critical to meeting the company's well-known goal of producing half of each year's revenues from product innovations created in the prior five years. General Electric has made self-managing worker teams a centerpiece of its new organization approach.

> Nonbusiness team efforts are equally numerous. The Coali-tion's dramatic Desert Storm victory over Iraq in the Gulf War in-volved many teams. A team of active duty officers and reservists, for example, lay at the heart of moving, receiving, and sustaining over 300,000 troops and 100,000 vehicles with more than 7,000,000 tons of equipment, fuel, and supplies between the late 1990 buildup through and beyond the end of hostilities in 1991. At Bronx Educational Services, a team of staff and trustees

shaped the first nationally recognized adult literacy school. A team of citizens in Harlem founded and operated the first Little League there in over forty years.[3]

In this fascinating book, the authors list the qualities of powerful teams. One of those qualities is a "*unique social dimension* that enhances the economic and administrative aspects of work. *Real teams do not develop until the people in them work hard to overcome barriers that stand in the way of collective performance.* By surmounting such obstacles together, people on teams *build trust and confidence in each other's capabilities.* They also reinforce each other's intentions to pursue their team purpose above and beyond individual or functional agendas. Overcoming barriers to performance is how groups become teams. Both the meaning of work and the effort brought to bear upon it deepen, until team performance eventually becomes its own reward."[4]

At their best, these teams are relationally intensive—the members authentically care for one another and build a healthy unity that surpasses normal or even good human relationships.

One of the finest businesses in America is Stew Leonard's supermarket in Norwalk, Connecticut. When asked about the secret to its success, the management said it was people—caring about and serving people. Whether serving ice cream and cake to those in the check-out line so they wouldn't mind waiting or displaying photos of sixty thousand people who have shopped Stew Leonard's on the back wall, the company demonstrates that it cares. Mr. Leonard himself strolls up and down the aisles asking everyone how he could make grocery shopping more pleasant. His enthusiasm for serving others carries over to his employees who also want to be a part of the good they see.

Indeed, there is a move today toward people-intensive operations. Whether it involves serving a customer, coaching the business associates and partners, training a child in the home, or building a personal or professional network of friends and associates, the common link is the vital need to build and sustain relationships.

Megatrends author John Naisbitt, in an insightful chapter entitled "From Hierarchies to Networking," described the powerful motivation behind this business trend. He wrote, "The failure of hierarchies to solve society's problems forced people to talk to one another— and that was the beginning of networks. . . . In a sense, we clustered together among the ruins of the tumbled-down pyramid to discuss what to do. We began talking to each other outside the hierarchical structure, although much of our previous communication had been channeled inside.

"As friends, as individuals, as members of small groups or large organizations, we exchanged resources, contacts, and information with the speed of a telephone call or a jet airplane ride, with the high touch of our own voices set against the din of a world swarming with too much data and too much knowledge."[5]

The beginning of networking highlighted for men and women in the marketplace their need to brush up on relational skills. After all, your networking is a success or failure based on your ability to work with people. And sooner or later your networking associates become your friends.

The Ultimate of Teamness: Unity

Successful networking—that is, really great teamwork—is built upon the principle of unity. The deeper a relationship goes, the greater the unity that will exist in that relationship. It is such unity that creates winning teams in a marriage, a family, a place of worship, a business, or a community.

When I speak of unity, I do not mean *union*. Union takes place when we are joined together organically, as in marriage, a business partnership, or some other organizational match. Certainly you can be in a union but have no unity.

Nor am I referring to *uniformity*. Uniformity occurs when we do things the same way. I believe "group think" can be dangerous at times. If we are too much alike, we stop growing, sharpening, and being sharpened by the people around us. For example, my wife and I have a high level of unity, but we are very different. She likes symphonies and museums. I like pop music and line dancing. Her ideal day is to sit inside on a rainy afternoon and read a good book. My ideal day is lots of sun, a rack of meetings in the morning, a good speaking event, a rigorous two hours of basketball with my son and his buddies, and communicating somewhere around the world with my computer via the Internet.

Finally, I am not speaking of *unanimity*. Unanimity takes place when we totally agree. Certainly we should be agreeable and gracious, but we will not always agree. Forced unanimity can stifle a relationship. Dr. Wayne Dyer says, "In counseling I always think it is important to help anyone to resist automatic conformity to anything, because it detracts seriously from a person's basic human dignity by elevating other authority to a level higher than one's own. This is true for dominated children, wives, husbands, employees or anyone else: If you can't think for yourself, if you are unable to be other than conforming and submissive, then you are always going to be gullible, a slave to whatever any authority figure dictates."[6]

I am speaking of *unity*. Unity begins with giving up your own agenda to develop a better one. It's combining your uniqueness with that of another or others to create something new. It's choosing to be more excited about the success of the team (or the other person) than your own success. It's a spirit of oneness that seeks to build up those around you and to be open and honest in the process. It is rooted in genuine caring (a commitment and action, not merely an emotion).

Such unity is founded on a healthy view of people. To have unity, we must recognize others not as things to be used, but as precious individuals, created for greatness, to be built up and assisted in maximizing their own uniquenesses—all of which allows for healthy, productive institutions in our society.

One Hewlett-Packard research and development manager spoke of a healthy view of people this way:

> Virtually every day, a couple of the engineers in my section get calls from competitors inviting them out to lunch to talk about their futures. A key aspect to my job, obviously, is to keep this group motivated, enthusiastic. . . . The best managers are the ones whose people want to get up in the morning and work for them. The secret is making it clear to your people that you care, that you're really interested in them as individuals. They need to know that you appreciate their efforts and that their accomplishments are recognized.

If you want to both maximize and develop craftsmanship in your life, you must master the roots of right relationships. These roots are many, but they can be categorized with the easy-to-remember acrostic UNITY:

U plift one another
N eed one another
I ntimately relate to one another
T rust one another
Y ield to one another

Uplift One Another

The place to begin developing unity in relationships is to learn to *build up other people.* There are two Greek words, *para* and *kaleo,* from which I draw much of this concept's meaning. *Para* means "alongside," and *kaleo* means "to call." Together these words simply mean, putting your arm around someone, calling him alongside, and encouraging him. It means helping to change another's attitude so he or she is willing to go back into battle. It means encouraging, exhorting, and stimulating a person to positive action.

We can uplift people, build unity, and manifest genuine love by applying four skills:

1. Complimenting

The foundational skill needed to uplift those around you is complimenting. Mark Twain said, "I can live for two months on a good compliment." And Charles Schwab, the great steel executive, noted, "I have never seen a man who could do real work except under the stimulus of encouragement and the approval of the people for whom he is working."

We need to develop a habit of complimenting people around us, not for their looks or their egos or for our own ulterior motives. That is mere flattery. Some sales training programs actually teach it. But *beware!* Flattery is dangerous, manipulative, and wrong because it is not character-based. It is based on external circumstances that are not internally motivated.

Learn to compliment people by praising them for something that illustrates their personal and character growth. True compliments encourage people to progress *in truth.* At the same time, you must consciously determine to express your compliments positively. It's too easy to be critical, sarcastic, or flippant.

The American Institute of Family Relations asked parents how many positive statements and negative statements they make to their children. The results? The average parent makes ten negative statements to every positive one to his or her children. In another setting, elementary teachers were asked how many positive statements it takes to overcome a negative statement to a child. Research found that it takes four positive statements to overcome every negative one.

Ten negatives to one positive. Four positives to overcome one negative.

Think of those ratios. We can't ignore the impact of our words!

You may have grown up in a home where you were put down all your life. As a result, you may have learned the habit of putting down others. It also may be a defense mechanism that you think preserves your self-esteem.

In his book about children and self-esteem, *Hide or Seek*, psychologist Dr. James Dobson provides us a thumbnail sketch of the background of Lee Harvey Oswald. Oswald's assassination of President John F. Kennedy—and subsequently his own murder—were the capstones to a life of rejection.

Oswald's childhood was friendless and loveless, marked primarily by rejection from his mother. Though he had above-average intelligence, he was not successful in any area of his life. He dropped out of high school, left the Marines with a dishonorable discharge, and married a woman from another country who, over time, treated him as abusively as his own mother had. According to Dr. Dobson's account, there appeared to be not one supportive, caring person in Oswald's life. Perhaps to Oswald, the assassination was his final attempt to be noticed.[7]

Lee Harvey Oswald left a legacy of destruction and devastation. What might have happened if just one person in his life had actively cared for him? And what kind of legacy are you leaving through those whom you influence?

Whatever your situation, break the cycle of put-downs and concentrate on uplifting others through compliments. Begin the habit of demonstrating your caring through building up other people. Utilize every tool you can to help others change their lives. Help them believe again in their own abilities and personal assets.

2. Expressing Confidence

A second way you can learn to uplift others is to express confidence in them. How do you respond when people fail you or your organization? Do you give up on them or shame them? Or do you still try to express some degree of confidence?

Harry Hopman built an Australian dynasty in world tennis. Do you know how he did this? He took a slow player and nicknamed him "Rocket." And he took a weak, frail kid and nicknamed him "Muscles." Rod "Rocket" Laver and Ken "Muscles" Rosewall became two of the greatest tennis players of all time. Why? Because someone believed in them.

You can also express confidence in others and articulate appreciation for them through *rewards*. The simple fact is people do what they will be rewarded for. And one area most of us need to reward more often is risk taking. Too often we discourage risk taking and thereby discourage greatness. Great results often have equally great risks attached to their achievement.

Dale Carnegie said it well: "Take a chance! All of life is a chance. The man who goes furthest is generally the one who is willing to do and dare. The 'sure thing' boat never gets far from shore."

A famous story is told of Tom Watson, the founder of IBM. One of Watson's subordinates made a horrendous mistake that cost the company $10 million. When he was called into Watson's office, he told his boss, "I suppose you want my resignation." Watson answered, "Are you kidding? We just spent ten million dollars educating you."[8]

3. Comforting

The third skill that needs to be sharpened as you learn to encourage people is comforting.

As difficult as it may be, there are times in our lives when we simply need to keep our mouths shut and be available to others who are hurting.

Our neighbors of seven years have suffered through multiple problems—job loss, mental distress, an imminent move, and the serious illness of a parent. Suddenly, one night the news came that the man's mother had died. For several reasons he could not attend the funeral (though one of our other neighbors comforted him by providing an airline ticket). He and his tender spouse were experiencing deep grief. So my wife, Mary, urged me to hold a mini-memorial service for this man's mother at the exact time of the funeral. And we in turn persuaded our friend to write a "farewell eulogy" to and for his mother and to fax it to those attending the funeral.

At the time of the funeral, we all sat in our gazebo and remembered "Dottie." We shed tears and offered some words of encouragement. Though we didn't say much, our neighbors were comforted.

Remember, your own tough times can prepare you to empathize with others. So lean into your portfolio of grief. Turn your pain into gain for someone else by simply *being there.*

4. Coaching

The final way to uplift those around you is coaching.

People are encouraged when they see growth in themselves. But growth doesn't just happen. It is ignited and fanned by caring people who help us develop a skill, adjust an attitude, build a mental framework, or gain an insight. These people are coaches. And you are a coach, a mentor, an educator, and a leader. The big question is: How effective are you?

A great leader knows the needs of those around him and seeks to assist them in their development. For instance, a great dad will coach his kids—not just in Little League, but in right values, attitudes, and commitments. A great business leader will coach and mentor his associates and employees in skills and attitudes needed to accomplish their agenda.

How do you coach? First you determine what is needed. Then you help people get there through the appropriate means. John Greenleaf calls this "servant leadership" in his book by the same name.

The apostle Paul said, "Warn those who are idle, encourage the timid, help the weak, be patient with everyone."[9] Use the right method at the right time. If someone is unruly or deliberately out of line, admonish or discipline that person strongly and deliberately. If someone is fainthearted or overwhelmed, then encourage or comfort that person. If someone is weak or given to constant, nagging problems, then come alongside and help him or her.

Author Ken Blanchard recommends a very specific procedure in his book, *Leadership and the One Minute Manager.* He calls this technique "situational leadership."

1. Agree on two to three specific goals to be achieved.

2. Agree on the level of competence and commitment the person has in each goal. She may be committed and not competent or vice versa or any other combination of the two.

3. Apply one of the four methods [of coaching], depending upon the answers to number 2.

The following chart illustrates how this procedure works:

If committed and competent:	delegate (let them go)
If competent but not committed:	support (get roadblocks out of their way
If committed but not competent:	coach (show them how)
If not committed or competent:	direct (tell them and show them how)[10]

If you have an employee, child, or friend who needs help in some area of life, you can use this specific strategy to be of assistance.

For example, my son Matt and I wrote a book entitled *Fathers and Sons*. It is all about how we have grown in our attempt to build the ten MAXIMIZERS principles into our lives. It is intended to help parents and children talk about and take steps to inculcate these principles.

Matt needed certain skills to accomplish his part of the book's writing. He had to be able to organize his thoughts, write, edit, input data into the computer, research, and stay on track. But he had various levels of commitment and competence in each area. If I were to chart his skills at that time, they would look like this:

Research	Committed, somewhat competent
Using the scanner	Committed, not competent
Writing	Committed, competent
Staying on schedule	Slightly committed, competent
Creating the outline	Not committed, not competent

As Matt's father, I needed to adjust my mentoring/coaching appropriately to accomplish three things: (1) to finish the book in a reasonable time frame; (2) to help Matt develop some skills he would use in the future; and (3) to be a man of integrity who cared about my son.

Specifically, here is what I did:

I coached Matt particularly in the area of research. He's a good reader and has the ability to see the big picture, but he didn't know where to find some of the information we needed. So I pointed him to the right books and showed him what to look for.

As to staying on schedule, I knew Matt knew what to do. But as an eighteen-year-old who had just finished high school and was saying good-bye to his friends before moving on to college, his tendency was to stay up late at night and get up late in the morning. This, of course, cramped his scheduling. So, I helped him by charting a deadline and placing it on our office door. This assisted him in setting a daily starting time. I also motivated him with financial rewards for keeping on schedule.

In the area of the outline, I showed Matt the general scope of the project and told him how I wanted us to proceed. Even though I was the architect of the general content, I wanted Matt to contribute his own material.

You encounter people around you every day who are longing to grow. And your job is to serve them by building them up through complimenting, expressing confidence, comforting, and coaching.

Need One Another

The second major principle in the UNITY acrostic is to develop a healthy interdependence through needing one another. There are healthy and unhealthy ways to relate to individuals. Let me point out some of the unhealthy ones.

The diagram on the next page graphically illustrates negative interpersonal connections.[11]

All of the areas outside the center are wrong—over you, in you, for you, off of you, under you, without you, against you, or in spite of you. Rather, you want people to relate to you in a way that is loving and leveling, caring and confronting, living in relationship and in truth. That's a healthy and growing kind of relationship. And that type of relationship builds team unity, whether it's at home, in the office, or in the community.

Other people provide the whetstone to sharpen our skills, character, and convictions. They become sounding boards (and sometimes sandpaper) to smooth off our rough edges.

William Glasser, a major figure in modern psychology, came to a similar conclusion. In his landmark book, *Reality Therapy*, he stated: "We must be involved with other people, one at the very minimum, but hopefully with more than one. At all times in our lives, we must have at least one person who cares for us and whom we care for ourselves. If we do not have this person, we will not be able to fulfill our basic needs. . . . One characteristic is essential in the other person: He must be in touch with reality himself and able to fulfill his own needs within the world."[12]

Needing other people is a two-way reality—*other people need you* and *you need other people.*

1. Others Need You

If you have a position of leadership—whether as a parent, an employer, or a manager—it's not hard to believe that other people need you. You are where the buck stops; your feedback is essential. And you feel needed.

You must fully embrace this reality, privilege, and responsibility if you are going to authentically succeed. Your family needs you. Your friends need you. Your coworkers and associates need you. Your customers need you. Your church or synagogue or temple needs you. Your community needs you. And each of these relationships will suffer if you don't accept your place as both a needed and needy human being.

Consider the man interviewed by Gail Sheehy in her best-seller, *Passages*. This man left his wife and moved in with an eighteen-year-old girl he had just met. "'The difficult thing for me to justify is leaving Nan [his ex-wife] high and dry because she hasn't done anything wrong. She's still in that other world where we were all brought up to live according to plans. . . . What I've learned from the young people I've met out here is that there are no commitments.' In other words, happiness is having no commitments, no one to answer to (which is the literal meaning of the word 'irresponsible'), no one whose needs or problems will ever get in your way or tie you down."[13]

This type of irresponsibility is a major element in the breakdown of the worldwide culture. People are abandoning their responsibilities to others in the home, workplace, and community at large.

Authentic success involves taking responsibility to *care*, knowing that part of your "calling" or "mission" on this earth is to positively touch others and to care for them. This responsibility is not just the job of the social worker, rabbi, pastor, or psychologist. It's *your* job. *You* are the only person in the world who has your contacts and privileged relationships. You alone have this responsibility, this stewardship of caring. Now, the question is: What will you do with your responsibility to care?

2. You Need Others

This is the other side of the same coin.

I am in a public position in which I speak regularly and receive much positive affirmation. I have people say, "Thank you for helping me" in various ways all the time. So I don't have much of a problem believing that others need me.

My problem is the other side of the equation—that is, believing that I need other people. There's a popular psychological test called the Firo B. It shows where you are in this regard on an "inclusion" and "exclusion" scale—in other words, how much you want to *include* versus *exclude* people in your life, and also how much you want them to include or exclude you. On this test you receive two scores, ranging from zero to ten. Zero means you don't want anyone in your life; ten means you want everybody.

The last time I took the test my score was a zero/zero. That means I am an extreme loner. Often this revelation confuses people because I'm friendly and outgoing and have highly developed social skills. But the truth is, I like being by myself.

My struggle is to recognize my need for other people—to keep me in balance, to point out blind spots, to round out my rough edges, and to complement my life.

This tendency to exclusion has led me to develop specific friendships, which come in three different forms: casual, committed, and covenant friendships.

The *casual* group represents your acquaintances and the people you see periodically or relate to at a somewhat superficial level. The *committed* friend is one who cultivates your friendship and is there for you. You have significant things in common and like being together. The *covenant* relationship represents those few people in your life (starting with your spouse) who will always be there. These people love you enough to confront you on your soft spots, but still believe in you. They are fans of yours, a support, an encouragement, and a source of open and honest communication. You can struggle together with them.

How do I cultivate each of these friendships? By practicing the UNITY acrostic. These principles of caring and establishing unity are what make for vital, deep friendships. And the specific step that has helped me most in developing covenant friendships was my formation of the accountability group I mentioned in an earlier chapter. It's easy for me to get off target in the area of needing others, so I have people hold me accountable.

> **"Here are five questions I hope to God no one ever asks me. Whenever you see me, ask me those questions."**

Accountability, as I referenced in another chapter, is when you turn to someone and say, "Help me here." It is when you turn to someone and say: "Here are five questions I hope to God no one ever asks me. Whenever you see me, ask me those questions."

When I meet with my group of men every week, we ask one another hard questions—potentially embarrassing questions—such as:

- Did you consistently give your employer an honest day's work?
- Did you do anything this week that could hurt your reputation?
- Were you in any compromising situation with someone of the opposite sex?
- Did you take quality time to build up your children?
- Was your integrity impeccable?

If you're serious about developing positive qualities in your life, you will need to say to a few others, "I want you to hold me accountable. You have access to my life, and if you ever see anything in me that needs to change, tell me. You're my friend, and I know you want the best for me."

All of this builds the right foundation for the next three UNITY subprinciples.

Intimately Relate to Others

There is an increasing fear of intimacy in today's culture. Psychologist Herbert Hendin points to an "involvement trap" that causes people to reject the caring that would make them vulnerable to rejection and disappointment. Hendin states, "Twenty years ago, detachment and inability to feel pleasure were considered signs of schizophrenia. Today, people believe that emotional involvement invites disaster, and detachment offers the best means of survival. In our work, in our play, even in our sexual lives, we want to be like machines (we speak of being 'turned on'), performing but not caring too deeply."[14]

Intimacy is the center letter—"un**i**ty"—and central principle in my concept of people-building. Intimacy is central because, without it, there can be no real unity. Remember, unity is oneness—and oneness requires a deep, abiding intimacy. It is about being one with someone else—being open, honest, and unashamed in the presence of another. Wouldn't you like that? A key to true intimacy is *communication.*

Do you know what the word *intercourse* means? Of course, it probably brings to mind sexual union. But the word actually means much more. It is an old English term for "discussion," "interaction," "communication." That's what social intercourse is.

When we communicate, we ought to aim for the same openness and honesty, the same mental and emotional connectedness, that we find in a thrilling and meaningful sexual experience. Considering this, do you think differently now about communications?

Under this critical principle, I am going to address two aspects of communications—*connecting* (first understanding and then being understood) and *clarifying* (learning how to resolve conflicts).

1. Connecting

Effective communication takes place when the picture in my mind becomes the same as the picture in yours. This is easy to say but not so easy to do.

Think about the past week. Did you experience a miscommunication? Perhaps you directed one thing, but your employee did something else. Or, perhaps you said something that offended someone unintentionally. Or, maybe you were hurt by someone's comment.

The fact is, we misconnect often—perhaps even most of the time. Someone said:

Norm Wright, in his fine book *Communication: Key to Your Marriage,* defines communication as "a process (verbal and nonverbal) of sharing information with another person in

> "I know you believe you understand what you think I said, but I am not sure that you realize that what you heard is not what I meant."

such a way that the other person understands what you are saying."[15] In other words, you must *connect* if you are to communicate. Communication is not just talking . . . not just listening . . . not just repeating back what another person says. It's not just understanding words spoken to you. Communication is *connecting*. It is seeing and feeling things the way your partner does. It is getting into his or her shoes and catching that person's perspective.

Let me give you a personal example. My wife Mary and I went out for a quiet dinner some time ago. She had just returned from a conference that made her think about her future and about the different life roles she had at the time. She came home confused and discouraged about her direction and needed to talk.

As she poured out her heart, I, of course, formulated a nice plan of action for her to take. I knew it would solve her unease and give her direction.

Yet, as I expressed my thoughts, Mary politely told me she didn't want to hear my plan. She didn't want me to fix her problem; she just wanted me to listen. Just talking about it—putting it all into words in the presence of someone who cared—was all she needed to do.

Most women are like Mary. And for a marriage to be most fulfilling, both partners need to check their perspective. Women are generally more intuitive and sensitive and often more effective communicators than are men. A woman will often seek to communicate at a deeper level than a man does.

When Mary and I talk about goals and dreams, mine are usually measurable and specific, while hers are more general and life-encompassing. When we talk about our children, for example, I address the bottom line concerning grades or behavior. But Mary wants me to know how our kids feel about themselves and for me to think about what I can do to boost their self-esteem. When we talk about friends, I like either the husband or the wife based on whether he or she is a good tennis player. Mary looks for soul mates in friends, whether male or female.

Checking your perspective in your marriage communication can make all the difference in the world. So, you ask, how do I connect? First, work hard to understand the other person's perspective. This does not mean you'll always agree with that perspective, but you must try to understand it.

Most people spend too much time trying to get their own view across and not nearly enough trying to understand the other's view. And by doing so they are saying to that person, "You're not very important . . . your views are stupid . . . you're not worth listening to."

How does it make you feel when someone doesn't listen to you or try to understand your perspective? Simply put, it hurts.

You can learn to sharpen your understanding skills by first learning to listen. Don't just work on parroting back the words you hear. Rather, listen for what the other person is trying to say and try to understand how he or she feels. Ask probing questions.[16]

Beware of improper listening. This kind of listening fakes interest. It selectively tunes in only to points of interest and self-protectively doesn't hear any threatening messages.

Healthy listening is based on making the other person and his or her views a priority. And it seeks clarification by asking questions such as, "Are you telling me that . . . ?" or "What did you mean when you said . . . ?"

Here are some keys to healthy listening:

Focus on:	Rather than:
what is being said	the way it is being said
the meaning	the words
clarification of valid points	defense of incorrect accusations
questions	indictments
understanding	judgment

Remember that the goal of your listening is to see from the other's perspective—to empathize and to feel with that person. *Sympathy* is when someone hits his thumb with a hammer and you say, "Oh, I'm so sorry." *Empathy* is when someone hits his thumb with a hammer and you say, "Ouch!" You feel with the other person. If you can accomplish that kind of empathy, you'll be well on the road to connecting.

The second aspect of connecting is your ability to communicate in such a way that people understand *what you mean.*

Your meaning is communicated not just through your words, but also through your tone and body language. In fact, the weight we give to each of these factors is as follows:

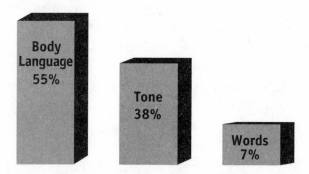

Obviously, one of the skills you need to cultivate is that of understanding and effectively utilizing your nonverbal skills.

I'll never forget the day in my college speech class when my professor pointed out my posture as a perfect example of the body language of a bored student. To all appearances, I fit the bill. I was slouched in my seat with my neck resting on the back of the chair and my legs stretched out in front of me. I'm sure I looked as if a nap were forthcoming.

Yet I learned two distinct and indeed opposite lessons that day. First, my professor was wrong. I was sitting that way to ease the strain on my lower back, which I had broken playing high school football. Second, body language does send a message—and unless you're given the opportunity to correct the message it sends, it will stand as it appears.

You probably can see in your mind's eye postures and body languages that communicate various attitudes—the shy person with her arms crossed over her chest, who won't meet your eye or initiate a conversation; the friend who stares into space in the midst of your conversation or who watches everyone else in the restaurant except you; the person who looks at you, listens carefully, and responds thoughtfully; the guy who grimaces at "red flag" words; the woman who strokes her boyfriend's arm as she talks.

Years ago I worked on a business team with a man I deeply respected. But every time we were in a meeting, he got angry at someone and exploded. His outbursts of anger disturbed me deeply, and

I became quite offended by his behavior. Finally, I decided to clarify the situation with him.

After one of our more contentious meetings, during which he performed true to style, I took him out for a meal. I began our conversation by asking: "Mark, are you aware that you often express extreme anger in our meetings?"

"Anger?" he retorted. "Not me. I never get angry. I don't know what you're talking about." He truly meant what he said.

I responded, "What would you call it when someone raises his voice to a near shout, the veins bulge in his neck, his face turns beet red, and he points his finger two inches from the face of the person he is addressing?"

"I do that?" Mark asked.

"Bingo," I said.

That simple conversation began a new sense of self-awareness for my friend and colleague. We even devised a sign for me to show him when he was starting to blow (I put my finger against the side of my nose). You see, he had a blind spot, and he was not communicating what he wanted to. He was, in fact, alienating the people around him instead—of moving them toward his perspective.

Self-awareness is a very significant factor in connection. It's part of the work you must do to ensure effective communication. In fact, it really is the only thing you *can* do that ensures it. By knowing your own bents and predilections, you can free yourself up to consider the others' perspectives.

Indeed, communication is a complex activity that involves your whole person. So, work hard to align your verbal and nonverbal communications. Otherwise, you may find that your actions are sabotaging your intent!

Connecting is further confused by the five levels of communication that take place:

1. *Cliché.* That's when we say things out of habit. "Hi, how are you?" you say to a friend, who answers, "Fine."

2. *Telling facts*—about others. There's a negative word for this—*gossip*. When we talk about someone in this way, it feels as if we're not revealing much about ourselves. But in reality, gossip reveals quite a bit about our character or lack of it.

3. *Opinions.* At this level we share how we view things. It's a little riskier because if an opinion is rejected, it feels like a fundamental part of the opinion-sharer is rejected too.

4. *Feelings.* This is when we start to share what's going on inside of us, when we begin to become transparent.

5. *Genuine transparency and honesty in communication.* This level (and in many cases the fourth one) is a level of communication you will not have with a large number of people.

COMMUNICATION LEVELS:	MEANING	DEGREE OF TRANSPARENCY:	NUMBER OF PEOPLE
1. Cliché	Non-sharing		
2. Fact	Sharing what you know		
3. Opinion	Sharing what you think		Degree of:
4. Emotion	Sharing what you feel		• Trust • Commitment • Friendship
5. Transparency	Sharing who you are		

From *Why Am I Afraid to Tell You Who I Am,* John Powell. Chart used by permission from Family Life

Our natural tendency toward self-preservation can scare us into staying at the cliché and gossip levels in far too many relationships. And, as William James said, "It is only by risking our persons from one hour to the next that we live at all." Sharing opinions and feelings is vital to building oneness and unity in relationships, even casual ones. And close relationships are vital to a good life.

"Some people are like medieval castles," says Judson Swihart. "Their high walls keep them safe from being hurt. They protect themselves emotionally by permitting no exchange of feelings with others. No one can enter. They are secure from attack. However, inspection of the occupant finds him or her lonely, rattling around the castle alone. The castle dweller is a self-made prisoner. He or she needs to feel loved by someone, but the walls are so high that it is difficult to reach out or for anyone else to reach in."[17]

The way we open up and experience ongoing communications is through connecting. But, the way we keep it ongoing and dynamic is through clarifying issues on a day by day basis.

2. Clarifying

Clarifying is the art of focusing on issues so that conflicting perspectives are resolved in the most positive way possible. Inevitably, there are times when you hit an impasse. You can't make someone else respond. All you can do is communicate and clarify in the right way; you cannot be responsible for the results. You are responsible only for getting the point across.

© Steve Bjorkman. Used by permission.

In my "How to Change People" seminar, I spend a great deal of time focusing on interpersonal skills, training people in how to communicate intimately, and teaching them how to resolve conflict. Most people have never learned how to build intimate relationships. Yet intimacy is a prerequisite for thriving families, friendships, businesses, and communities. And clarification, or conflict resolution, is critical to establishing intimacy.

The fundamental balance in clarification is to speak the truth in love.

Speak the truth:	Speak in love:
confront	care
level	learn

Can you see the balance in this chart? You must be honest, but in your honesty you must not seek to harm. You must deal with the issue and not wallow in self-pity.

Unfortunately, much of the "assertiveness training" that has been popular in recent years has become a license to practice what I call "offensiveness training." It is based on an honest desire to help people speak up and speak out. But now the pendulum has swung to encourage people to become fighters, demeaning the people around them and having negative long-lasting results.

If you are going to create unity and oneness and effectively clarify issues, you must learn and hone the skills of appropriate, balanced assertiveness.

What is your perspective on clarifying issues or conflict resolution?

Conflict Resolution: What Is Your Opinion?

- It is okay to modify the truth to avoid unpleasantness.

  Agree or Disagree

- An argument is a destructive force. Agree or Disagree

- The wisest course to take when having an argument is to remain silent or leave the room. Agree or Disagree

- In the communication process, it is best to discuss certain matters and not others. Agree or Disagree

- It is a sign of emotional immaturity for a person to be angry with another individual. Agree or Disagree[18]

> **As iron sharpens iron, so one man sharpens another.**

Now let me give you some guidance. First, conflict is inevitable. It will happen. It is natural. And it isn't necessarily bad. In fact, conflict is often the key to building relationships. Conflict sharpens us. As the proverb says: As iron sharpens iron, so one man sharpens another.[19]

Just as iron striking iron causes sparks in the process of honing and sharpening a tool, so the sparks created in our disagreements may be the manifestation of the sharpening of our character, sensitivity, commitment, integrity, and authentic love. So expect conflict. Don't run from it or deny it. Learn to embrace it and learn from it.

Second, strong emotion is not a bad thing. In fact, strong emotions have launched some of the greatest actions and movements of all time. A hatred of poverty and a deep love for both God and humankind spurred Mother Teresa to do her incredible work in Calcutta. Deep hatred of inequality and injustice motivated Martin Luther King Jr. to spearhead the civil rights movement.

Anger or frustration also can motivate you to find solutions in the clarification process. But keep in mind that deep emotions can also be destructive and debilitating.

If you can activate the following principles consistently and persistently, you'll be well on your way to mastering clarification.

Trust One Another

The hinges on the door to intimate, unified relationships are greased by the level of trust you have in and with those around you. This fourth principle is simply "believing the best" about people. It doesn't demand that you abandon your discernment of inappropriate behavior. In fact, as mentioned in the previous principle, you must consistently clarify and address conflicts and problems.

Trust underscores the need not to develop harmful imaginations about others—misreading nonverbal communication, misjudging motives, or making false accusations. Forming preliminary assumptions is a sure way of closing another's spirit—not only stopping present communication but hardening the arteries of its future flow.

I remember showing up at a friend's house some years ago. I was supposed to bring some chairs. When I rang the doorbell, my friend opened it and said, "Hi, Ron. Where are the chairs?"

"Oh, I forgot," I responded. My friend glared at me and barked, "That figures!"

I thought, *"That figures?" He thinks I'm no good. He thinks I can't follow through. He thinks I'm useless.* Then I thought, *Who does he think he is? The creep. I bet he's got a problem or twelve!*

Then I realized I had one of two options. I could believe the best about what he was saying—although that was pretty tough—and just forget it. Or, I had to ask him what he meant—and it was obvious to me what he meant, which seemed even tougher to swallow.

Finally, a couple of weeks later, I saw my friend again and questioned him on the incident. "You know the other day when I was at your house and forgot to bring the chairs? And you said, 'That figures'?"

He interrupted me. "I shouldn't have said that," he said.

"That's what I thought," I responded. "But in any case you said it. And I was wondering what you meant."

"Well," he began, "all that day, in every meeting, someone had forgotten something. It just figured."

He wasn't telling me, "Jenson, you're a jerk." He was saying, "My day's been terrible."

The next time you find yourself wondering what someone means when he says or does something questionable, why not go up to that person and ask him what he meant? You'll be amazed at how often you misread a situation.

Just that one little question, "What is his/her motive?" can make us stop, think, and give the benefit of the doubt to someone we truly love and don't want to hurt.

Yield to One Another

Now, this last letter in the UNITY acrostic may not sound too appealing to you. But if you really want to change people's lives, you learn to yield to them.

You may say, "That is stupid!" It's not stupid. Continual fighting produces only bruises, breaks, and resistant people. But when you learn to yield appropriately, at the right time, you'll take all the hot air out of an argument and allow others to respond positively.

Real commitment is seen in our willingness to yield to others. This spirit is evidence of a selfless, caring love for others. Without it, you communicate merely a self-centered, ego-driven, superficial relationship, which is based on outward conditions and performance, not real commitment.

And how do you yield to others? You submit yourself to those absolute principles that govern your thoughts, emotions, and behavior. C. S. Lewis spoke eloquently on this issue:

> It would be quite wrong to think that the way to become [loving] is to sit trying to manufacture affectionate feelings. Some people are cold by temperament. . . . The rule for us all is perfectly simple. Do not waste time bothering whether you "love

your neighbor"; act as if you did. . . . When you are behaving as if you loved someone, you will presently come to love them.

> If you injure someone you dislike, you will find yourself disliking him more. If you do him a good turn, you will find yourself disliking him less. . . . But whenever we do good to another self, just because it is a self, made (like us) by God, and desiring its own happiness as we desire ours, we shall have learned to love it a little more or, at least, to dislike it less.[20]

Malcolm Muggeridge wrote reflectively about the Calcutta he saw in the company of Mother Teresa: "The biggest disease today is not leprosy or tuberculosis, but rather the feeling of being unwanted, uncared for, and deserted by everybody. The greatest evil is the lack of love and charity, the terrible indifference towards one's neighbor who lives at the roadside assaulted by exploitation, corruption, poverty, and disease."[21]

How do you put this concept of yielding to work in your life? Simple: You do it every day—at work, at home, in social settings, even on the road.

Imagine this scenario at home: You're late—again—and during dinner your wife says, "When are you going to get your priorities straight and give some attention to me and your children?"

How would you feel? Angry, embarrassed, bitter. And what would you normally do? Yell back? "Look! I'm the one who keeps food on the table." Or, "Why don't you get a job so I don't have to work extra hours?" Or, perhaps more likely, "Shut up!"

Let me suggest a radical strategy. *Yield.* That's right—yield. I don't mean to imply that your wife is totally right and that you are totally at fault. But think of the message you convey to your wife and children if you yield:

What You Say	What the Family Actually Hears
"Honey, I apologize. You're right."	humility and openness to talk
"I'll try to be home at six, four work days a week."	flexibility, caring for your children and spouse
"What would you like me to do?"	honoring family by seeking advice

What will you lose by yielding? Absolutely nothing. Your authority is increased because your humility enhances your credibility. Your family's respect for you is elevated because your open spirit and healthy yielding reflect a deeply-held value of the people around you. Putting others first is a sign of character, not compromise.

Years ago I was driving home from a conference with an employer. We were good friends, I thought. But out of the blue he said to me, "Ron, I have a big problem with you. In fact, I have many." He then enumerated all sorts of problems he saw in me.

I was outraged and shocked. After all, this guy was loaded with problems himself! I honestly felt he was jealous of my success. It was no secret that the people in our organization gravitated toward me much more than toward him. Yet I had tried to be loyal and supportive of him.

This was the straw that broke the camel's back. I kept silent during his dump on me. Then I went home and started writing down all of *his* problems. I filled out the front and back of three 3x5 cards. And I wrote in teeny, tiny letters.

I was ready to confront this offensive individual, but I sought the advice of a graduate professor of mine. After laying out the problem, I asked him how I should confront my associate. His response was specific and concise: don't!

"Don't?" I exploded. "This guy deserves it! Besides, he needs to know his own problems. It's the least I could do."

My wise mentor responded that the associate might need some clarification. But for now, he needed my loyalty and humility. He pointed out the universal principle that in yielding to others we grow in our character and humility—and others are opened up to learn what they need to learn as well.

Ruth said the following to me one day in the midst of a heated argument over how to handle a bitter detractor. "Ron, if your enemy is needy, meet that need. That will take all of the wind out of his sail. But if you fight him, he will fight back and his spirit will close. And you never want someone's spirit to close if you can help it."

Dying to yourself ensures growth in others. This is true of great mothers, effective executives, winning professionals, and successful employees. As we grow in humility, those around us open up to change. And we grow as well.

In the end, I determined to follow my prof's advice. I went back to my employer and asked specific questions about how I could grow. I looked for specific opportunities to make him successful, and I supported him publicly and in private.

Ten months later he called me into his office. He said, "Ron, do you remember a while back when I lambasted you? Well, I want you to know I was wrong in the way I did it and in most of what I said. Frankly, I think I was jealous. And your behavior has shamed me into realizing this. I'm sorry! Will you forgive me? And tell me—what can I change in me?"

Of course I forgave him. In fact, I had tossed out the 3x5 cards months earlier. His flaws had diminished in my mind as I had focused on helping him to succeed.

But does yielding always produce such fruit? Certainly not. Yet it is the only way of *potentially* producing that kind of fruit and authentically succeeding at creating *unity*.

Do you want to make a difference in people's lives? Are you willing to set aside your own agenda and to encourage the success of others? Do you want to zero in on caring for people?

You know what you have to do. You have to die—to your own will, your own way, and your own wisdom at times. You've got to let others live by your dying. If you allow yourself to go under the heat of an obnoxious person who asks for a lot and gives very little—if you can learn to handle that heat and at the same time yield in your responses in a loving but a positive way—you'll find that people will be willing to change. You can make that kind of difference in their lives.

Action Steps

Uplift One Another

1. Identify the two most critical people in your life—one from your personal life and another from the professional side. Recalling the four subprinciples of Uplifting One Another (complimenting, expressing confidence, comforting, and coaching), what specific step can you take this week to begin to create the "right key"?

2. Determine where you can practice each of the four subprinciples this week.

Principle	Action Step
Complimenting	e.g., take Bill out to lunch and tell him how much I appreciate his positive attitude at work.
Expressing Confidence	e.g., remind Mary how vital her role is to me and the children. Create a computer banner expressing this to hang on the garage.
Comforting	e.g., take your newly divorced associate out for lunch and *listen*.
Coaching	e.g., teach my son how to change a tire.

Need One Another

1. Who are the six most critical people who need you at home and at work?

2. Who are your committed friends?

3. Who are your covenant friends?

Intimately Relate to One Another

1. In which specific relationships do you need to become more vulnerable to enjoy closer friendships?

2. How can you display this openness?

3. Identify one major conflict that needs clarification.

Trust One Another

Identify one area where you have violated this principle. What will you do to resolve it?

Yield to One Another

Where do you need to put this principle to work? With a boss, a friend, a coworker, a spouse, a child? Identify your strategy (time, place, conversation, etc.). Do at least one thing this week to demonstrate yielding.

Chapter 8

Energize Internally

How to Experience Ultimate Personal Power

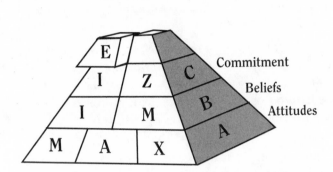

... in the midst of economic plenty we starve spiritually.
—Norman Vincent Peale

Facing an early death from brain cancer, "bad boy" Lee Atwater, President Bush's 1988 campaign manager, found his perspective changed:

> The '80s were about acquiring—acquiring wealth, power, prestige. I know. I acquired more wealth, power, and prestige than most. But you can acquire all you want and still feel empty. What power wouldn't I trade for a little more time with my family? What price wouldn't I pay for an evening with friends? It took a deadly illness to put me eye to eye with that truth, but it is a truth that the country, caught up in its ruthless ambitions and moral decay, can learn on my dime. I don't know who will lead us through the '90s, but they must be made to speak to this spiritual vacuum at the heart of American society, this tumor of the soul.[1]

Listen also to Jeff, a single, twenty-six-year-old advertising executive, who feels the spiritual vacuum even while enjoying the best of times:

> My life has been terrific the last few years—lots of money, women, friends, all sorts of activities and travel. My job is good and I am good at it. There is even a good future—I will probably be promoted this year and make lots more money and have freedom to do what I want. But it all seems to lack any significance for me. Where is my life leading, why am I doing what I'm doing? I have the feeling that I am being carried along without ever making any real decisions or knowing what my goals are. It's sort of like getting on a road and driving along fine, but not knowing why you chose that particular road or where it is leading.[2]

Lee Atwater and Jeff graphically illustrate what I believe to be the greatest need of the hour in America and many other parts of the world—a return to spiritual roots and character-centeredness. These are the true bases for ultimate personal power. It's who you are at your core—your inner person, your depth of faith, your spiritual virility—that's the real source of ultimate power.

In your concentration on the roots of your life, energizing your inner life is the taproot. A taproot is the "main root of a plant, usually stouter than the lateral roots and growing straight downward from the stem."[3] Without it, the rest of the plant will quickly rot and die.

All the principles within the MAXIMIZERS model have significant stand-alone capability. But this principle of energizing the inner life and its accompanying implications are absolutely necessary to accomplishing the overall goals we've established. You must have an irrepressible, inner strength that flows from your character and an ever-deepening spirituality. Your character is the root of that strength—and your spirituality is that which brings life to the root. So, if you can focus only on one principle, this is it!

I want to talk again about the Jewish king Solomon. Nearly three thousand years ago, he reigned as Israel's wisest and most magnificent king. According to the Bible, God appeared to Solomon early in his career and asked him to name anything he wanted God to give him. Solomon requested only a discerning heart, that he might rule the nation with justice.

People from around the world came to consult this great king. He had it all! Consider this list:

- He was a builder of magnificent cities and structures (the temple and Solomon's palace).

- He was a man of unparalleled wealth in his time (1400 chariots, 12,000 horsemen).

- He was author of 3,000 proverbs, 1,005 songs (Proverbs, Song of Solomon, Ecclesiastes).

- He was an expert in botany and zoology.

- He had 700 wives and 300 concubines.[4]

But, even though Solomon had it all, he departed from his spiritual roots—and the net result was increased flaws in the fabric of his character. The ultimate result was a divided kingdom, a lost empire, family destruction, and personal depression, shame, and grief.

Summing up his life and all that it gave him, Solomon said, "Meaningless! Meaningless! . . . Everything is meaningless . . . a chasing after the wind."[5] At the end of the Book of Ecclesiastes, which describes the ups and downs of Solomon's life, he shares his final words of wisdom.

> Now all has been heard;
>   here is the conclusion of the matter:
> *Fear God* and *keep his commandments,*
>   for this is the whole duty of man.
> For God will bring every deed into judgment,
>   including every hidden thing,
>   whether it is good or evil.[6]

Solomon implied that only two worthy pursuits exist: "Fear God" (cultivate your spirituality) and "keep his commandments" (obey truth from the heart; cultivate character).

I urge you to follow these two pursuits. For just as this once-great king left his spiritual roots and paid the consequences, so have many in our culture today done the same. Earlier in this book I recorded the famous words of French statesman Alexis de Tocqueville, who said America's greatness flowed from the goodness of her people. He also said, directly preceding this quotation, "Not until I went into the churches of America, and heard her pulpits aflame with righteousness did I understand the secrets of her genius and power."[7] He saw a "rightness" flowing out of a deep spirituality.

In this chapter I will answer three questions: Why is this principle so critical? What do "character-centeredness" and "spirituality" mean? And how do you cultivate them?

Why Is This Principle So Critical?

1. It's the Source of Our Strength

The title of this chapter gives away the answer: Your life is energized by your character. Your power and ultimate success will flow out of your character—that is, who you are on the inside—which is profoundly influenced by your spiritual depth and maturity.

The case for this source of energy for life has been powerfully made in such recent works as *The Culture of Disbelief* by Stephen Carter[8] and *The Book of Virtues* by Bill Bennett.[9] Both of these books have been outstanding sellers; the latter was number one on the New York Times Bestsellers List for more than twenty weeks. Why? Because people are looking for deeper and more profound answers to the growing problems of our day. We have abandoned our concentration on the inner person—our character and spirit—to go after the fruit of this life. But the reason we enjoy so much abundance today is because of *the application of this principle in earlier generations.* In essence, we are leeching off the lives of our ancestors and leaving our culture in ruin.

C. S. Lewis said it well:

> We remove the organ and demand the function.
> We make men without chests and expect of them virtue and enterprise.
> We laugh at honor and are shocked to find traitors in our midst.
> We castrate and bid the geldings be fruitful.[10]

We want the fruit but are unwilling to concentrate on the roots. Or, as John Updike writes, "The fact that . . . we still live well cannot ease the pain of feeling that we no longer live nobly."[11]

Bill Bennett illustrates this problem. "I recently had a conversation with a D.C. cabdriver who is doing graduate work at American University. He told me that once he receives his master's degree he is going back to Africa. His reason? His children. He doesn't think they are safe in Washington. He told me that he didn't want them to grow up in a country where young men will paw his daughter and expect her to be an 'easy target,' and where his son might be a different kind of target—the target of violence from the hands of other young males. 'It is more civilized where I come from,' said this man from Africa."[12]

Bennett concludes, "I submit to you that the real crisis of our time is spiritual." Note his analysis:

> Specifically, our problem is what the ancients called *acedia* [which] is an aversion to and a negation of spiritual things. Acedia reveals itself as an undue concern for external affairs and worldly things. Acedia is . . . an absence of zeal for divine things. And it brings with it, according to the ancients, "a sadness, a sorrow of the world." It eventually leads to a hatred of the good altogether. And with hatred comes more rejection, more ill-temper, sadness, and sorrow.[13]

Interestingly enough, Bennett's research centered on the writings of two literary giants with completely different backgrounds, whose views on the rise of acedia were amazingly coincidental. He writes that the late novelist Walker Percy, when asked what concerned him most about the future of America, answered, "Probably the fear of seeing America, with all its great strength and beauty and freedom . . . gradually subside into decay through default and be defeated, not by the Communist movement . . . but from within by weariness, boredom, cynicism, greed and in the end helplessness before its great problems."[14]

Alexander Solzhenitsyn, Bennett's other profound influence, spoke in his 1978 Harvard commencement address of the West's "spiritual exhaustion." The great Russian writer said, "In the United States the difficulties are not a Minotaur or a dragon—not imprisonment, hard labor, death, government harassment and censorship—but cupidity, boredom, sloppiness, indifference. Not the acts of a mighty, all-pervading, repressive government but the failure of a listless public to make use of the freedom that is its birthright."[15]

"What afflicts us," said Scottish author John Buchan, writing a half-century ago, "is a corruption of the heart, a turning away in the soul. Our aspirations, our affections, and our desires are turned toward the wrong things. And only when we turn them toward the right things—toward enduring, noble, spiritual things—will things get better." Buchan foresaw the:

> . . . coming of a too garish age, when life would be lived in the glare of neon lamps and the spirit would have no solitude. . . . In such a [nightmare] world everyone would have leisure. But

everyone would be restless, for there would be no spiritual discipline in life. . . . It would be a feverish, bustling world, self-satisfied and yet malcontent, and under the mask of a riotous life there would be death at the heart. In the perpetual hurry of life there would be no chance of quiet for the soul.[16]

Bennett concurs:

There is a disturbing reluctance in our time to talk seriously about matters spiritual and religious. Why? Perhaps it has to do with the modern sensibility's profound discomfort with the language and the commandments of God. . . . Whatever your faith—or even if you have none at all—it is a fact that when millions of people stop believing in God, or when their belief is so attenuated as to be belief in name only, enormous public consequences follow. And when this is accompanied by an aversion to spiritual language by the political and intellectual class, the public consequences are even greater.[17]

As Dostoyevsky wrote in *The Brothers Karamazov*, "If God does not exist, everything is permissible." I believe we are now seeing "everything."

2. It Is the Basis for Enduring Societies

Consider America's spiritual roots. Our significant decline as a country can be directly attributed to our increasing abandonment of our spiritual roots. A helpful starting point is to remember where we have come from.

Have you ever wondered why in the 1770s America's population of just three million produced such brilliant leaders as Thomas Jefferson, Benjamin Franklin, George Washington, John Adams, James Monroe, James Madison, and a host of others? Can you think of any names today, in our population of 250 million, that can match those in the list above?

In answering this question, Zig Ziglar, the popular sales trainer, posed the question: "Could it be that what those early Americans were taught had a direct bearing on their performance and accomplishments? For example, according to the Thomas Jefferson Research Institute, in the 1770s over 90 percent of our educational thrust was aimed at teaching moral values. At that time most of the education was handled in the home, church, or in church-supported schools. By 1926 the percentage of moral training had been reduced to 6 percent, and by 1951 the percentage was so low you could not even measure it."[18]

Consider the words of George Washington in his first inaugural address. He pledged "that the foundations of our national policy will be laid in the pure and immutable principles of private morality. . . He further proclaimed, "There is no truth more thoroughly established than that there exists in the economy and course of nature an indissoluble union between virtue and happiness."

Or reflect on the sentiments of the great Abraham Lincoln: "The only assurance of our nation's safety is to lay our foundation in morality and religion."

The point is obvious: Character-centeredness flowing from spiritual roots is the ultimate source of our power individually, institutionally, and societally. Therefore, I contend that you must weave this principle into the fiber of your life. Your spiritual roots will empower the growth of your character through the establishment of moral bearings, daily internal reformation, heightened perspective, and the control of your basic impulses. *They will root you!* And unless you accept this premise, you will overlook the very taproot of your life and never experience ultimate power. Listen to the words of William Faulkner in his 1950 Nobel Prize acceptance speech: "I decline to accept the end of man." Humankind will not merely endure but will prevail because, as Faulkner said, we alone among creatures "[have] a soul, a spirit capable of compassion and sacrifice and endurance."

3. It's the Secret to Our Satisfaction

Character-centeredness is not only the source of real strength but also the key to a life of satisfaction. In his outstanding book *The Pursuit of Happiness*, David Myers addresses what makes people happy. This becomes clear in the subtitle of his book, "Discovering the pathway to fulfillment, well-being and enduring personal joy."[19]

Dr. Myers takes a scientific-research approach to measuring happiness, and his discoveries align very closely with my research on authentic success. He concludes that happiness and fulfillment are by-products of certain attitudes and perspectives, and not significantly affected by externals. Dr. Myers then elaborates extensively on how and where these traits are developed. He begins with a discussion on the welcome decline in materialist values, citing Ronald Inglehart's worldwide studies of shifting values:

> "We see this most clearly in the demise of secular Marxism in Eastern Europe. But in the West, too, a new generation is maturing with decreasing concern for economic growth and social order . . . and with increasing concern for political freedom, personal relationships, and the integrity of nature. This emerging 'post materialism' provides fertile soil for a new consciousness that questions prosperity without purpose, money without meaning. After two decades of rising concern for 'becoming well-off financially,' the percentage of American collegians rating this a very important life goal finally began to taper off during 1989 and 1990." Concludes Inglehart, "A renewed concern for spiritual values" is beginning.[20]

Such hunger can be seen in multiple arenas today, ranging from the growth of Islam worldwide, to the resurgence of the church in America and many Eastern European countries, to the explosive growth of the Eastern, mystic religions.

Perhaps you're a person who has retreated from religion or spirituality of any kind in part because of the extremes you see. Be careful not to throw out the baby with the bathwater. Instead, open your spirit for maximum growth. As Dr. Myers verifies, "Survey after survey across North America and Europe reveal that religious people more often than nonreligious people report feeling happy and satisfied with life."[21]

What Does Faith Offer?

Why do researchers find such positive links among faith, mental health, and happiness? Because faith and spirituality provide a place to belong (community), a sense of purpose (commitment), and a perspective on life (contentment). Let me discuss each of these briefly:

1. A Place to Belong, or Sense of Community

University of Pennsylvania researcher Martin Seligman attributes today's widespread depression to "rampant individualism . . . without commitment to the common good." Our expectations have soared, yet:

"Life is inevitably full of personal failures. Our stocks go down, people we love reject us, we write bad papers, we don't get the job we want, we give bad lectures. When larger, benevolent institutions (God, nation, family) are available, they help us cope with personal loss and give us a framework for hope. Without faith in these institutions, we interpret personal failures as catastrophic.[22]

"Part of what's missing," says California sociologist Robert Bellah, "is a sense of connectedness, belonging, mutuality, being part of a people."

All of us, at one time or another, have experienced a sense of community—whether at camp, on a long bus ride, in a fraternity or sorority house, on a football team, or at a high school reunion. But somehow, as we get older and society celebrates more and more the individual rather than the group, and more of us work out of our homes, and our houses don't have porches, and our streets don't have sidewalks, and our computers do our communicating; we slowly lose our connectedness.

Interestingly, Myers observes that all around the world today, "the most common communal setting for finding such social identity and support is the local religious community." In America, a local religious community—be it a church, synagogue, or mosque of some kind—is within walking distance of almost everybody. And it is within these groups of people that one can find the supportive social ties that provide a stability to life. Yet, amazingly, as a culture we are only growing more disconnected.

One of the more phenomenal movements of today is a group called PromiseKeepers. This is a multidenominational, multicultural network of men that began gathering in 1991. The group grew from 1,200 to 21,000 in 1992, to 55,000 in 1993, to more than 400,000 in 1994. The purpose of the movement is to encourage men to "make and keep their promises."

Can you imagine hundreds of thousands of men coming together for an intensive weekend simply because they want to make and keep their promises? They want to be men of integrity. They want to be spiritual and moral servant-leaders in their homes, businesses, communities, and all other spheres of influence.

One of the major results of these meetings has been the establishment of support and accountability groups for men who share the seven common commitments of PromiseKeepers—honoring God;

pursuing vital relationships with a few other men; practicing spiritual, moral, ethical, and sexual purity; building strong marriages and families; supporting the church; building unity by reaching beyond racial and denominational barriers; and positively influencing the world.[23]

2. A Sense of Purpose, or a Commitment Worth Dying For

It is the sense of mission I addressed in chapter 5 that is embraced more fully and deeply by those of an abiding faith. The nineteenth-century Polish poet Cyprian Norwid wrote, "To be what is called happy, one should have (1) something to live on, (2) something to live for, (3) something to die for. The lack of one of these results in drama. The lack of two results in tragedy."[24] The search for meaning motivates all of us at one time or another. Indeed, it's unsettling to live as an adult for very long without making a few forays into the "meaning of life" questions.

Clinical researcher Seligman states that finding meaning demands "an attachment to something larger than the lonely self. To the extent that young people now find it hard to take seriously their relationship with God, to care about their relationship with the country or to be part of a large and abiding family, they will find it very difficult to find meaning in life. To put it another way, the self is a very poor site for finding meaning."[25]

Psychiatrist Viktor Frankl came to a similar conclusion after he observed lower apathy and death rates among fellow concentration-camp inmates who retained a sense of meaning—a purpose for which to live, or even to die. Many of these were devout Jews whose faith provided a deeply internalized purpose that gave them a reason for living and for resisting their oppressors.[26]

Note the findings of a recent national Gallup survey, analyzed by Princeton University sociologist Robert Wuthnow. He found "that spirituality begins to move people toward being compassionate only when a threshold of involvement in some kind of collective religious activity has been reached."[27]

3. Perspective on Life, or Contentment

Faith in the future produces a healthy view of self, life, and eternal issues in the here-and-now—that is, a healthy sense of contentment.

For instance, as people of faith grow in their spiritual depth, their sense of awe of God gives them a healthy perspective of themselves.

They have a greater capability of identifying their soft spots (*sins* in their terminology) and dealing with them (through forgiveness).

David Myers tells a moving story of the power of faith being demonstrated in works of incredible selflessness:

> With Nazi submarines sinking ships faster than the Allied forces could replace them, the troop ship *SS Dorchester* steamed out of New York harbor with 904 men headed for Greenland. Among those leaving anxious families behind were four chaplains, Methodist preacher George Fox, Rabbi Alexander Goode, Catholic priest John Washington, and Reformed Church minister Clark Poling. Some 150 miles from their destination, *U-456* caught the *Dorchester* in its crosshairs. Within moments of a torpedo's impact . . . stunned men were pouring out from their bunks as the ship began listing. . . . On board, chaos reigned as panicky men came up from the hold without life jackets and leaped into overcrowded lifeboats.
>
> The four chaplains . . . distributed life jackets, and coaxed the men over the side. . . . The chaplains handed out the last life jacket, and then, with ultimate selflessness, gave away their own. As [one of the crewmen] slipped into the waters he saw the chaplains standing—their arms linked—praying in Latin, Hebrew, and English. Other men, now serene, joined them in a huddle as the *Dorchester* slid beneath the sea.[28]

Spiritual depth does make a difference. It motivates one to a higher cause in this life and thereby stimulates and feeds the roots of authentic success.

By this point, you can see the benefit and necessity of cultivating the spiritual and character base in your life. Let me take a few moments now to provide specific suggestions to develop your inner life of spirituality and character development.

Energizing your inner life involves at least two specific needs: your need to *concentrate on being,* and your need to *cultivate spirituality.* Let me elaborate on each of these.

Concentrate on Being

We are a nation of people consumed by "having." We not only want to have material things, but knowledge and information as well. We even want to have the intangibles of love, inspiration, and happiness. Ownership seems to be the king of virtues, no matter what the commodity, and yet we are a society of notoriously unhappy people—lonely, anxious, depressed, and dependent. In fact, we are learning that the more we have, the less satisfied we are.

If we're going to concentrate on "being," we need to begin with the internals—character. Instead, we have become so preoccupied today with how we appear in public, we tend to focus on our outward performance not our inner character. This often results in pretending to be someone we aren't. We project one life and live another. This results in a lack of internal motivation and power to live and behave the way we ought. It also results in manipulation of others.

That's why we need to get back to character. We must live from the inside out. And there are numerous character qualities that we ought to be developing.

Taking clues from the great philosophers, religious statesmen, and successful leaders, we can boil these desirable character qualities down to a focus on the concept of authenticity. Authenticity is at the heart of this book. To be authentically successful, you must be the same on the inside as you are on the outside. This means being a person of integrity. You must align your inner, private life and outer, public life with the same principles. It is from here that real energy flows. Some of the most ludicrous logic on this matter in recent days has come from Washington, D.C. In defense of their incongruous lifestyles, many of the nation's leaders have tried to convince us that their private lives are unimportant and shouldn't have any bearing on their performance at work.

Don't ever buy that philosophy in any way, shape, or form! These individuals are role models for your kids and my kids. We should all be *very* concerned about their personal lives. Our public servants have been given a responsibility in their leadership positions to model a certain lifestyle. To separate the two sides of life is what Socrates called "dualism." It is unhealthy. Life needs to be integrated.

We must be people of integrity. And that's why, of all the character qualities, I choose to focus on this one. So—how are *you* doing at being the same in public as in private?

A recent study of CEOs from Fortune 500 companies indicates that the most critical factor to consider in hiring or promoting top managers and in gauging the potential for ultimate success is *integrity*. Ironically, traits that were ranked as least important were appearance, likability, and conformity.[29] (I find it interesting that the characteristics many adolescents, the general public, and the mass media find most attractive are the least likely to lead to genuine, enduring success.)

A story is told of a young nurse who was completing her first day of responsibility in the operating room of a large, well-known hospital. "You've only removed eleven sponges, doctor," she told the surgeon. "We used twelve."

"I removed them all," the doctor declared. "We'll close the incision now."

"No," the nurse objected. "We used twelve sponges."

"I'll take the responsibility," the surgeon said grimly. "Suture!"

"You can't do that!" blazed the nurse. "Think of the patient."

The surgeon smiled, lifted his foot, and showed the nurse the twelfth sponge. "You'll do," he said.[30]

Make a commitment to be consistent—inside and outside. The focus of this consistency must be based on your own value system. Everyone has a value system, whether it is determined thoughtfully or thoughtlessly. And we live out our value system either intently with determination, or haphazardly with no attention at all.

Now, take the values statements you developed under the principle of *internalizing right principles* (chap. 4). Ask yourself whether those values are just statements on paper or practices you are consistently building into your life.

The first area you must concentrate on is *being*—who you are, your character. Next, I want to explore the area of spirituality, because the flame of character needs the fuel of spirituality.

Cultivate Spirituality

You may be a person who has never been religiously oriented. But what I am talking about here is *spirituality*. Let me show you the distinction.

When I think of spirituality, I think of our internal lives, internal issues. When I think of religiosity, I think of externals.

When I think of spirituality, I think of relationships—our personal and private relationship with God and our relationships with others in light of that. When I think of religiosity, I think of rules—external obedience to rules.

When I think of spirituality, I think of progressing, growing, and developing in that personal relationship with God. When I think of religiosity, I think of people trying to be perfect and never making it.

When I think of spirituality, I think of transparency, openness, and honesty. When I think of religiosity, I think of a facade—people trying to hide things because of their weaknesses. When I think of spirituality, I think of being winsome, attractive, and compelling. When I think of religiosity, I think of pushy people insisting that I follow their rules.

Cultivating spirituality is building a significant and meaningful relationship with a personal God.

Spirituality	Religiosity
Internal character	External Performance
Relationship with God and others	Rules
Progressive and growing	Pretense to perfection and fixed
Openness and transparency	Pretentious and closed
Attractive and compelling	Pushy and offensive

The *American Heritage Dictionary* defines spirit as "vital principle or animating force with living beings."[31]

Best-selling author Sam Keen has another definition of spirituality: "In every cycle of breath, between the emptying and the inflowing, there is a moment of absolute calm, an instant when history comes to an end. Then, the yearning begins, the divine discontent, the lungs praying to be filled, the body longing to be animated by spirit."[32]

For the sake of simplicity, when I refer to the spirit, I mean the spiritual side of the inner man. Many thinkers say that there are three parts to human beings: body, soul, and spirit. The body (outer man) handles the physical aspects of life; the soul deals more with the mental, emotional, and volitional aspects of life; but the spirit deals with that intangible relationship we are seeking with the supernatural. All three parts of human beings need to be cultivated and integrated for life to be healthy and authentically successful. Without the full development of all three, we function like a two-legged footstool.

The soul is that area where character is developed. But the spirit feeds the soul. It gives perspective and power. As you feed and grow your spiritual life, you gain the perspective needed to initiate and nourish the other roots (principles). Remember Solomon's wisdom at the end of his life: "Fear [or revere] God and keep his commandments." He had a clear-cut order: first, you revere God. That gives you the perspective and urgency to keep the Commandments or apply universal principles in your life. Socrates, arguably one of the finest moral educators in history, demonstrated the hollowness of character without spirit when he said, "All the wisdom of this world is but a tiny craft upon which we must set sail when we leave the earth. If only there was a firmer foundation upon which to sail, *perhaps a divine word*" (italics mine).

Cultivating your spiritual life also helps you gain the power needed to live out these principles. Prayer, faith, hope, and belief in a transcendent source have always been mainstays in helping people achieve the greater—and often the more mundane—experiences in life.

On his deathbed, Napoleon reflected on the ultimate power of the sword and compared it to the ultimate power of spirit when he said, "I die before my time and my body shall be given back to the earth and devoured by worms. What an abysmal gulf between my deep miseries and the eternal kingdom of Christ. I marvel that whereas the ambitious dreams of myself and of Alexander and of Caesar should have banished into thin air, a Judean peasant, Jesus, should be able to stretch his hands across the centuries, and control the destinies of men and nations."

Siddhartha Gautama, whom we know as Buddha, left behind the life of a king in search of this spiritual power and illumination. Understanding the inevitability of aging and death, he sought a way to transcend this human reality. The Jewish leader Moses and the Christian apostle Paul sought this power in their respective deserts. Today men and women of all backgrounds continue to seek power and perspective in the spiritual realm.

In his fascinating book, *Hymns to an Unknown God,* Sam Keen attempts to answer the following penetrating questions:

> What does the concept of spirit mean to us today? Do most of us even have a sense of it anymore? And of those of us who still believe in a place for the spirit, a place called soul, a god, how many have a daily experience of it? Is it possible in this chaotic

day and age to have a sense of the sacred in everyday life, or do we have to check our spirits and our god at the workplace door?

We yearn for something that will give a sense of meaning and purpose to our daily lives, something more engaging than paying lip service to the idea of God or attending worship on the weekend.[33]

A week seldom passes without some friend or stranger speaking to me about the kind of yearning Keen addresses.

An Australian businessman came to visit me several weeks ago to "simply introduce himself." Yet, after a few moments of polite discussion, he began to share his struggles: "I have had everything money could buy," he asserted, "but I became engrossed in my work, emotionally deserting my children and my wife and finding my satisfaction in alcohol." He went on to say that through the help of a friend and involvement in Alcoholics Anonymous he was beginning to put his life back together. But, as he went on, "I know there is more. It must have to do with prayer and spiritual growth."

An artist in his early sixties confided the following to Sam Keen:

After weathering several mid-life crises, I am finally comfortable with myself, have a good marriage, and have gotten my children launched and out of the nest. In the last years I have become moderately famous and financially successful beyond my wildest expectations. I have bought everything I ever wanted—an elegant house, a fine car, adventurous vacations in exotic parts of the world. I have given to the charities of my choice and been generous to my family and friends. As far as I can tell, I don't have any unmet needs or unfulfilled desires. But I yearn for some kind of fulfillment I can't even imagine or name, except to call it spiritual.

Keen responded:

Perhaps your success or failure in love or work has left you with an urgent need to find some greater meaning and purpose in your life. Perhaps a near encounter with disease or death has eaten away at your old certainties and filled you with doubts. Perhaps your despair at the madness of modernity has created a hunger for hope, a need for a new vision of the sacred.[34]

In fact, this hunger for the "sacred" is a dramatically growing trend internationally and within the United States. The November 28, 1994, cover of *Newsweek* expressed it well: "The Search for the SACRED . . . America's Quest for Spiritual Meaning."

The article states that "it's suddenly OK, even chic, to use the S words—soul, sacred, spiritual, sin." In its own poll, *Newsweek* states that 58 percent of Americans say they feel the need to experience spiritual growth and that a third of all adults report having had a mystical or religious experience.[35]

One of the most fascinating discoveries during my years of research and interviews is the vital nature of spirituality in the lives of high achievers as well as the culture at large. For whatever reason, the role of spirituality is often overlooked and not mentioned. Perhaps people think that it is private and personal and therefore not appropriate to be discussed in public. But this lack of attention tends to cause an unhealthy separation of the spiritual and the secular—one that was never meant to be, and one that stifles ultimate authentic success.

In an attempt to let you in on some of my research, I have collated just a sampling of the comments on spirituality that I have gained through my studies and interviews.

- "I caution you . . . to set your sights beyond what you can see. There is true majesty in the concept of an unseen power which can neither be measured nor weighed."—Ted Koppel, ABC News

- "Any journalist worth his or her salt knows the real story today is to define what it means to be spiritual. This is the biggest story . . . of the century."—Bill Moyers

- "I know that God is everywhere and in all things. There is nowhere that God is not, even in me."—Robert Fulghum, best-selling author and speaker

- "I believe each person is made in the image of God. For those of us who have received the gift of leadership from the people we lead, this belief has enormous implications."—Max DePree, Chairman of Herman Miller

- "We are not human beings having a spiritual experience. We are spiritual beings having a human experience." Wayne Dyer, best-selling author

- "You can't out give God. His resources are fully reliable, abundant, and freely offered on your behalf."—Mary Kay Ash, former business executive

- "What keeps our faith cheerful is everywhere in daily life, a sign that faith rules through ordinary things: through cooking and small talk, through storytelling, making love, fishing, tending animals and sweet corn and flowers, through sports, music, and books, raising kids—all the places where the gravy soaks and grace shines through."—Garrison Keillor, A Prairie Home Companion

- "I started praying, asking God to give me compassion, understanding, and a spirit of helpfulness. Even as I prayed, my heart was touched, and I experienced a newfound peace."—Zig Ziglar, best-selling author and sales trainer

- "The capacity to become enthused is a spiritual quality generated from within; it doesn't need pep talks or perks . . . I am valuable because God created me with inner value and worth."—Denis Waitley, author and speaker

- "There is no greater area for putting your faith on the line than in running a business, regardless of the size. We recognize that God is really the owner of all we have."—Carl Lindner III, partner in American Financial Corporation

- "My religious faith . . . satisfies . . . the most fundamental human need of all. That is the need to know . . . that our lives . . . count as something more than just a momentary blip in the universe."—Harold Kushner, best-selling author

- "My job is to do right. The rest is in God's hands."—Martin Luther King Jr., civil rights activist

- "Our first objective (to honor God in all we do) is not simply an expression of some religious or denomination's belief—be it Jewish, Protestant, or Catholic. . . . Rather, it is an affirmation statement that the source of our way of doing business begins with God. We reject the notion that . . . man's reason is the final authority."—C. William Pollard, CEO/Chairman, Service Master, Inc.

These leaders do not all express their spirituality in the same way and do not all have the same faith. But they do have faith, and they seek to cultivate it and integrate it into their personal and professional lives.

For you to authentically succeed you, too, must cultivate this area of your life.

1. Pray

How can you cultivate spirituality? Let me suggest three simple steps. The first one is to learn to experience God—to pray.

I have already mentioned that years ago, when I lived in Philadelphia, a doughnut shop was close to my home. Whenever I got within a mile of the Donuttery, I got a vision of a hot cinnamon roll with butter cascading down the sides. I could smell it, I could see it, I could taste it—and I would salivate just like Pavlov's dog thinking about that cinnamon roll.

In a very real sense, that same response ought to be true of your relationship with God. You ought to be able to virtually touch Him and sense Him and feel Him and taste Him. You ought to experience that God is a caring, compassionate, personal God and to acknowledge His presence in the universe as you go through the day.

How do you do that?

You talk to Him through *prayer.* I don't mean formal, organized prayers necessarily. I mean simply open, honest conversation—telling Him your needs, desires, wants, joys, sorrows, frustrations, and expectations.

"I seek to enter the morning slowly," says best-selling author and speaker Ken Blanchard. My friend Ken, like many others I have interviewed and researched over time, spends from fifteen minutes to two hours for daily solitude, reflection, and prayer.

As one leader said, "I have so much to do that I must spend one hour in meditation and prayer if I am going to get it all done." His point is clear. This time of prayer and reflection gives him the perspective, power, and peace to not only do things right but to do the right things.

One head of a three-billion-dollar corporation told me that he goes through his DayTimer daily, reflecting on the previous day's schedule to determine whether he had perhaps been offensive, inappropriate, rude, or unloving to someone in the course of the day. If he had, he would seek forgiveness from God and, if necessary, from the other person. He said he believed such times gave him real clarity to function effectively at home and at work.

Others communicate their habit of prayer throughout the day—simply offering up words of thankfulness, concerns, struggles, and joys. Their consistent assessment is that these times of active dependence on a supernatural source are the KEYS for overall effectiveness in their lives and in the lives of any who incorporate prayer into the warp and woof of living.

So, become a person of prayer. Begin with some daily time of solitude. Then simply talk to God throughout the day, just as you would to a friend.

2. Meditate on Great Principles

The second thing we can learn to do is to *meditate.*

There is a lot of discussion today about meditation. Most of that discussion surrounds an Eastern religious form of meditation called Transcendental Meditation (TM). TM is based on the assumptions that God is all around us; man is basically good; God is within man; and if we empty our minds, the God within us will bring us to full fruition.

I subscribe to a different type of meditation. The type of meditation that is most helpful to me comes from Hebraic thought. Ancient Jewish writers speak about meditating on the Law, or principles, day and night. The assumption is that emptying our minds, if that is ever truly possible, leaves us with nothing save our own limited resources. What a person needs to do instead is to fill his or her mind with right thoughts that will positively influence his or her lifestyle. For me, the key to growth in the area of spirituality is to meditate on great thoughts and truths that help me grow, develop, and build character into my life.

Learn to meditate. Make it a habit day and night. Allow yourself time in the morning to focus on planning, and perhaps some time to mull over a few of the deeper truths that have enriched humankind. You may also want to stop in the middle of the day to "smell the roses," acknowledging the wonder of the world around you. Finally, before you go to bed, reflect on the day, focus on the kinds of thoughts that make life meaningful to you, and watch what happens as you're changed from the inside out.

3. Express Your Faith

You also can cultivate spirituality by *expressing faith.* Briefly explained, faith is believing that positive things can come out of wherever you are in life. However, faith is only as good as the object in which it is placed. I urge you to think long and hard about the source of your faith. Ask such questions as:

1. Is this faith historically credible?
2. Do I see evidence of changed lives because of this faith?
3. Does this faith adequately address the core issues in my life—meaning, forgiveness, power, direction, values, etc.?

The effectiveness of your faith is in direct proportion to your sense of the reality of a living God. Faith is like a muscle: The more you use it, the bigger and stronger it grows.

Some years ago a friend of mine was absolutely overcome by worry. She worried about everything, and if she didn't have anything to worry about, she would get worried that she didn't have anything to worry about. Then someone helped her to understand some principles about dealing with worry, built on these five phrases: Number one, *fret not*—or don't worry. Number two, *trust* in the Lord. Number three, *commit your way* to the Lord. Number four, *rest* in the Lord. And number five, *wait* on the Lord.

As she reflected on her application of faith she said, "I started to put my faith to work on each of these principles. And after a period of concentrating on these simple principles, I learned I could express my faith when it came to resolving any kind of conflict—whether physical, mental, emotional, spiritual, or financial. My faith grew like a well-toned muscle, until soon I believed for very significant things in my life. Now expressing faith has become a very necessary way of life for me."

Professionals in many fields acknowledge the need for spiritual growth in human beings. What I want you to see is that you can build a relationship with God the way you build a relationship with any close personal friend. It can be meaningful. It can be significant. It can be deepening. And it can be yours. You can talk about it if you want to, or you don't have to talk about it if you don't want to. Just enjoy it and let your spirituality grow and be cultivated.

If you can develop a relationship with God and base your life on character—that is, on "being"—then you're going to be energized internally. And you'll be known more and more as a person of success and significance.

Action Steps

1. How do you differ in your character (the real you) and your personality (your external projection) in the following areas?

Area	Character (inner self)	Personality (outward self)
Personal life	(ex.) I feel hollow and rudderless	I project that I have it "together"
Family life		
Business life		
Social life		

2. How can you create alignment in one of these areas this week? Develop and implement an action plan. For example, take your hollowness and try to fill it by building your roots into truth (read a great book, reflect on the majesty of creation, make a list of everything for which you are thankful and meditate on it several times each day, etc.).

3. Which of the three spiritual development skills do you need to focus on at this time? What fifteen-minute-a-day practice can you implement to begin a twenty-one-day experiment of making a habit of this skill?

Chapter 9

Realign Rigorously

Getting from Point A to Point B the Right Way

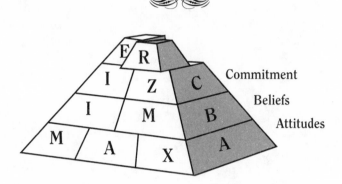

. . . for a conscious being, to exist is to change, to change is to mature, to mature is to go on creating oneself endlessly.

—*Henri Bergson*

You've probably seen the speedway game that kids play in video arcades. Maybe you've tried it. You press the button, and suddenly the images on the screen start moving toward you. You steer your video car around obstacles, you speed up, you slow down, you adjust to quick changes, and sometimes you crash. (I do that a lot.) You watch out for the fire engines. You veer left around the wrecks ahead. Too far—you're off the road! Now back on, step on it, make up lost time.

You can make it to the end, but not without a few crashes. And in the next round you raise your skill level: The car goes faster on the track, more obstacles close in, and you handle more changes per unit of time.

What does it take to stay on the track in this game? A lot of attention and constant midcourse corrections. And so it should be in your work and personal life. That's the principle I am going to discuss in this chapter—how to revise your actions rigorously, or, *how to get from point A to point B the right way.*

Many of us think the old, straight-line approach to getting anywhere is the only right way. But life isn't like that. Life is messy. So midcourse corrections are necessary to a successful, maximized life. We've got to learn how to respond to the needs around us and revise our actions rigorously and consistently.

If you're going to become a pro in making midcourse corrections, then you need to learn to become a craftsman in the following three strategies: framing, focusing, and flexing. These strategies provide the essential building blocks and skills needed to effectively develop the important root of midcourse corrections.

Framing

Framing is developing your overall perspective and sense of parameters about any issue in life. Whenever you face a decision, you need to begin by forming your framework. What's your frame? What are your guides? What will give stability to any decision you make? It entails four major aspects, which become clearer if you can picture the four sides of a picture frame: your overarching *purpose* in this situation and in your life, your *priorities* in this situation and in your life, your *principles* or guidelines in this situation and in your life, and finally, your *peculiarities* (the differences and distinctions that make up you, your strengths and weaknesses).

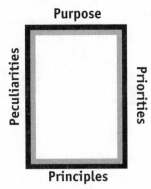

1. Purpose

The first thing you must do to frame your situation is to understand your *purpose.* You must understand your purpose in making this decision as it relates to your overarching sense of purpose and mission in life. If you go back to principle number five in this book, "March to a Mission," you'll have the framework upon which you can make a major decision. Then look at the purpose you need to address with the issue at hand. Ask how it relates to your overall mission.

The most effective leaders have always been people who see the outcome way ahead of time. That's why I'm referring you back to setting down your mission statements in the form of specific goals. Where do you want to go? What do you see as the ultimate outcome of your entire life, that is, your personal life, your marriage, your business, your spiritual life? Develop your sense of vision or faith so you know exactly where you are going.

Thomas Watson, founder of IBM, was asked once when it became clear to him that IBM would become an enormous success. He answered, "Right from the beginning." That kind of response is typical of great leaders. They get a vision of what they want to accomplish, and faith in that vision spurs them on.

Let's imagine that a decision you have to make involves correcting somebody in your workforce. You're trying to decide how to do this. One of the starting points is to ask: What is my purpose here? What am I trying to do? Asking questions like these—and making yourself answer them—requires you to be thoughtful and keeps you from merely reacting to your situation. If your overarching purpose is to help individuals grow because of your commitment to zero in and care for people, your approach to the present situation will be dramatically affected by this perspective.

This concept of *purpose* allows you to see the whole forest while you're dealing with one of the trees. If your perspective isn't big enough, you could miss a great opportunity and make a decision that could have devastating consequences down the road.

2. Priorities

The second major area of framing is the skill of *prioritization.* We've already talked about developing priorities in life under the principle of "integrating all of life." And that's a good beginning place in this area of decision making. If you've clearly developed your prioritization built on the paradigm I have recommended—loving God, self, and then others—you will have a healthy foundation as you move forward to make your decision.

You also need to understand your priorities *in the given situation.* For instance, if in correcting someone, you elevate the circumstances higher than your regard for the individual, you run the risk of making a major dent in your relationship and possibly creating devastating consequences. Remember: If you're here to love God, love yourself, and love others—to truly care, help, build, develop, and maximize people—then that conviction needs to be built into your priority decision. And you need to make your decision and accomplish the actions in accordance with that set of priorities.

3. Principles

The third area of framing is to lean into your *principles.*

I see principles as being similar to train tracks. A train cannot easily move without tracks. Yet sometimes, like a train without tracks, we try to move ahead without the foundation of underlying principles to guide us. Though you might think tracks restrict the freedom of a train, they actually give it freedom to move ahead all the more rapidly. In the same way, your principles rooted in absolutes will guide you in getting any job done more effectively. And you'll be surprised at how freely and creatively your mental agility comes into play in your situation.

If you haven't developed your own philosophy of life (that is, organizing and guiding principles) I suggest you begin with the ten principles in this book, the MAXIMIZERS principles. In any given situation, you can use these as a grid. Simply ask in your situation how the principle of "Making Things Happen" applies. Perhaps you'll conclude that you need to take the initiative to resolve the problem. After all, you are responsible; so be proactive!

Then look at the principle of "Achieving Personal Significance." Perhaps you're holding back from making a certain decision because you lack confidence in yourself. This principle will help you adjust appropriately.

You can follow the same process with all ten of the MAXIMIZERS principles. In fact, let's take the scenario we set up earlier (correcting or disciplining someone at work) and look at how some of those principles could be applied.

Make Things Happen	"I need to take responsibility for this situation and not 'backburner it' out of a sense of feeling like a victim."
X Out the Negatives	"I must be specific in the issue that needs to be addressed, but I must do it in a way that gives this person hope and elevates his attitude positively, rather than creating despair and discouragement. Moreover, I must maintain a positive attitude even though this problem irritates me significantly. I must attack the problem, not the person."
Internalize Right Principles	"I need to be sure I'm following the policies and ethical standards of dealing with this issue in this particular situation. I especially need to show this individual how specific principles and values of the company were violated."
March to a Mission	"I need to remember that I've been called to help people grow. That's part of my mission in life. I need to communicate with clarity that this is exactly what I'm doing, and I need to do it with a good spirit. I also need to show how this individual can make corrections in his life in the days to come based on a more finely tuned and articulated sense of personal mission that aligns itself with the corporate mission of the company."
Energize Internally	"I need a supernatural resource to give me wisdom, sensitivity, and a graciousness as I deal with this individual, because I really don't feel like any of those qualities are in me right now. I need to have the integrity to be open and forthright as well as caring in this situation."
Stay the Course	"I need to show this person that I'm committed to him and that I'm sticking with him—that I'm his fan and his friend and that I want him to win. I'm not going to let one problem derail this relationship."

Do you have a better sense now of how you can take principles and build them into your life as you try to frame your situation?

4. Peculiarities

Finally, you frame by understanding your own *peculiarities*. We talked about this somewhat under principle two, "Achieving Personal Significance," when you looked closely at your personal strengths and weaknesses. In this situation, you'll want to know what your weak tendencies might be in a particular circumstance. For instance, in confronting someone, you may have a basic weakness in speaking the truth because of an underlying desire to be liked. Actually, at the root this is an integrity problem. Therefore you might find yourself grappling with inner conflict and never truly addressing the problem.

If this is the case, be careful. You may need to have someone else with you at first when you're dealing with confrontation problems. Or, you may need to write down your words ahead of time so that you can, with integrity, be truthful as well as compassionate. Then, you may need a friend or associate to hold your feet to the fire to ask you specifically what you said. You can do all of this to protect yourself and others from your weakness.

In the area of framing, it is helpful to have a team of people—or at least one other friend—who can give you an honest perspective. In fact, I recommend developing different types of counselors or mentors in your life.

First, you should have a personal mentor or counselor. This is a friend who knows you well and cares enough for you that he or she can speak the truth to you about your strengths and weaknesses, your consistencies and inconsistencies.

Second is a spiritual counselor. This is a person of wisdom, someone you believe understands truth and will serve as a coach or counselor for you. This is a principled person who has integrity and who will help you grapple with the issues.

The third type of consultant or counselor is a specialist in the area of your concern. For instance, if you're focusing on a family problem, you may want to locate a family counselor or specialist. If you're dealing with an area of management and strategic planning, you may want a strategic planning specialist. Look for a pro in whatever field you want to address.

The fourth and final type of consultant you want is a practical counselor. This is someone who is a nuts-and-bolts, practical person—an individual who'll say either, "It will work," or "It won't work," or "This doesn't make sense," or "Great idea, but it's just armchair philosophy."

Identify the people in your life whom you think are the very best in these four areas. It may be that the personal, spiritual, and practical counselors are the same in virtually every major decision in your life. Probably only the specialist will change, depending upon the need of the moment.

Another way to get the same kind of corporate wisdom is through developing a team of friends with whom you meet on a regular basis. I've mentioned that I have a group of executives with whom I meet about every two or three weeks. We often spend our time reviewing these principles and working on their application in our personal as well as public lives.

If you haven't formed a group that can provide resourcing for you, I urge you to do it. It can be a group of just one other person or two with whom you meet on a weekly basis. Take the initiative to begin something like this so that over time you can become a pro at framing your life and the major issues you face daily.

Focus

The second principle I want to address is the principle of *focus*. Focus is the ability to keep your eye on your goal and the task at hand, while at the same time being mentally agile in dealing with the various contingencies that come into play. This is the skill that allows you to remain directed and not be interrupted by the multiple messages or alternative opportunities that avail themselves to you. In other words, you must learn to focus while being aware of your environment. And that is a real art.

"Laserlike focus is perhaps the most common trademark of the supersuccessful," writes Robert Ringer in his fine work, *Million Dollar Habits.* He adds that "the more certain you are about your purpose in life, the more focused you'll be on living in the present and the more enthusiastic you'll be in your day-to-day work; the more you display enthusism in your daily work, the more likely you will attract the attention of positive, enthusiastic people; the more positive, enthusiastic people you attract, the more successful you'll be; and the more successful you are, the more present-living oriented and enthusiastic you'll be. Thus you set in motion a self-perpetuating cycle of enthusiasm and success."[1]

This concept of focus encompasses two major skills—concentration and constant learning.

1. Concentration

William James stated, "That which holds our attention determines our action." Attentiveness is a skill that allows you to accomplish your desired outcomes in your personal life, family, business, and in the community.

Karl Vesper of the University of Washington illustrates the importance of attention in making key business innovations. He writes in his book, *New Venture Strategies*:

- Leo Gerstenzang thought of Q-Tips when he saw his wife trying to cleanse their baby's ear with toothpicks and cotton.

- Ole Evinrude got angry when the ice cream in his rowboat melted before he got to his island picnic spot, so he invented the outboard motor.[2]

I once heard a story about concentration that grabbed my attention. It was about a chemist who wanted to teach his students the power of observation and focus. He said, "Do exactly as I do," to his group of ten observing students. He took a specimen bottle filled with (you guessed it) specimen. Then he stuck his forefinger in the bottle, took it out, and stuck his middle finger in his mouth. He told his students to do exactly as he had done.

The students freaked out! They thought he had stuck his forefinger in the specimen bottle and then put the same finger in his mouth. So, one by one they all went around and did just that. How disgusting!

The professor watched them. Then, after explaining their mistake, he said, "Ladies and gentlemen, you've got to focus."

Learn to concentrate.

2. Constant Learning

We read a great deal today about the "constantly learning company." This is a modern movement that flows from the "quality management emphasis" popularized by Dr. W. Edwards Deming in his historic work in Japan. One of his emphases is on constant, continual improvement that's rooted in inquisitiveness and progressive learning. In his hallmark work, *The Fifth Discipline*, MIT management guru Peter Senge addresses "the art and practice of the learning organization."[3] "Learning companies" are organizations skilled at creating, acquiring, transferring knowledge, and modifying behavior to reflect new knowledge and insights.[4]

Why this new emphasis on learning? The fact is, our compiled knowledge doubles every year. An advanced degree in any discipline will hold its value for only about six to eight years. In higher technology, knowledge is replaced every two to three years.

In fact, today we even have developed "knowledge workers"— people who are involved in collecting, analyzing, organizing, storing, retrieving, or communicating information. Benjamin Disraeli once said, "The most successful person is usually the one with the best information." Consider:

- The last thirty years have produced more information than the previous 5,000 years.

- Nearly 50,000 books and 10,000 magazines are published in America every year.

- Every single day, researchers and scientists produce 7,000 new scientific papers!

- The average American is confronted with about 140 advertising messages a day, or about 50,000 a year.

- A typical issue of the *Los Angeles Times* contains more information than a typical person in the sixteenth century would encounter in a lifetime!. . . The amount of information available to you now doubles every five years. . . . The average desk in the average office in America has thirty-six hours' worth of work stacked on it—and much of it is reading![5]

Given these rapid refresh rates, knowing *how* to learn is a key to the future.

Learning companies measure learning using the half-life curve, or the time it takes to achieve a 50 percent improvement in a specified performance measure such as defects, on-time production, and time-to-market. That is, bottom-line events are tied to the learning curve.

The critical difference in learning companies is that the *spirit* of learning is encouraged. Each learning step is reinforced with multiple methods at every level and systems are vested to support the changes. (Here's a cautionary note: If the basic beliefs and values of the corporation do not undergird learning, the learning becomes yet another buzzword term and will quickly go the way of other quick fixes.)[6]

According to Roger Martin, the key to the [change] process is *self-examination.* Even highly educated professionals prevent change by engaging in organizational defensive routines to preserve status and security. In searching for problem sources, managers look outside themselves and often outside the company, blaming the customer, the vagueness of goals, or the unpredictability of the environment (one recent study found that 95 percent of failing companies blamed poor economic conditions and only 13 percent said poor management had anything to do with present problems). Organizations defend against change because they are made up of individuals who are working at what "always has worked." Companies, like individuals, think that to change means *they have been wrong all these years.* Not so.[7]

In the same way that companies must constantly be learning, so must you. If you are going to succeed authentically, you must be ever-growing in your knowledge and insight of truth and how to apply it to everyday life at the office, in the home, during your social interactions, and even when alone.

I am constantly inundated with new and interesting information. It comes through the FAX, the mail, magazines, the Internet. Ruth and I regularly discuss my need to pay attention to what is relevant to my life. My time with her helps me to focus on what is important. She once told me, "Beware! As Ecclesiastes reads, 'Be warned: there is no end of opinions ready to be expressed. Studying them can go on forever, and become very exhausting!'[8] And, 'To increase knowledge only increases distress.'"[9] I think she's right.

Therefore, let me suggest a grid for you to use in your own continual learning and handling of the data overload:

1. Know What Is Important to Know. Discipline your reading and mental focus toward only those things that will help you accomplish your overarching mission in life. Certainly, you are free to be entertained mentally; relaxation and refreshment are part of any growth. But if you can keep your mission ever before you, it will help filter what goes into your mind in the first place.

Also, keep observing what enters your mind through the principle grid I have set forth in this book. For instance, constantly ask:

- What principle does this support or violate?

- Is this a universal principle (an absolute) that is always true in every circumstance?

- Under what subcategory does this information fit? (For example, under "Achieving Personal Significance," does it fit under your specialness or your soft spots?)

2. Understand What Is Meant by the Information. Read, watch, listen critically. Try using a pen or marker when you read to highlight points (I almost always do). Then interact mentally with what you read. I often debate the author of a book and write down my points of contention in the margin. It further helps me to ask questions such as:

- What is the real issue here?

- What does she mean by this?

- How does this relate to his earlier comment?

- What is wrong with this idea?

3. Decide What to Do with This Data. There is nothing as pathetic to me as someone who is filled with knowledge and either does not know how to apply it or just won't.

Imagine you are trying to authentically learn how to empathize with someone. You have never developed that skill, so you attend a stimulating and provocative lecture on the subject. And you go home with the desire to put this newfound knowledge to work. But your schedule becomes filled up and nothing ever comes of it.

Months later you read a book on the subject. This time, instead of being motivated, you tell yourself, "I know all about how to do this. I've attended a seminar." You have become both unteachable and proud of the knowledge you do have. Yet you still don't know how to empathize. You only know how to repeat what someone has said about it.

The bottom line: You have gone backward through knowledge, (into hardening and arrogance) rather than forward (authentically empathizing) because you have not cultivated and followed a strategy to develop the truth into a habit and lifestyle.

Some further questions will help here:

- How do I practice this truth?
- Where do I need to change?
- What one skill could I practice today?
- How can I forge this truth into a habit by practicing the "make it happen" principle?

Now you have two options. You can either make midcourse corrections and revise your actions rigorously, which is the easy way, or you can do it, the hard, rigid way. Take it from me—it's better the easy way.

Flexing

Finally, I want to address the principle of *flexing*. You must master the ability in any decision-making situation to constantly adapt to change and to adjust to mistakes in an appropriate way.

Flexibility, or mental agility, is what Charles Garfield defines in his highly popular book, *Peak Performers*, as "the [ability] to change perspective and do the creative thinking necessary to deal with challenges."[10] Earlier I talked about routinely asking the questions: "What have I neglected in the past?" and "What are the present needs?" This takes mental agility. I'm not suggesting you dodge thoughts or feelings or positions, but rather that you allow yourself to see things in perspective. Try to describe things as accurately as you can to yourself and to others so that you can get the best possible perspective on them.

We desperately need to learn the skill of flexibility today because of the unprecedented level of change in our culture. Heraclitus said, "There is nothing permanent except change."

Karl W. Deutsch, professor of International Peace at Harvard, suggests, "The single greatest power in the world today is the power to change. . . . The most recklessly irresponsible thing we could do in the future would be to go on exactly as we have in the past ten or twenty years."

The new data we're receiving must be accompanied by a great ability to make rapid, midcourse corrections and daily adjustments, small or large, in light of these new facts. Such dramatic change can either frighten you or flame you into cultivating the skills and technologies you need to respond to the various options available to you today. "To live is to change," noted John Henry Newman, the English cardinal and writer, "and to be perfect is to have changed often."

The skills needed to become a craftsman at flexibility are three-fold: creativity, adaptability, and learning from mistakes.

1. Creativity

Creativity is not always found in an environment of tranquility and ease. In fact, a creative environment is often a quite chaotic and messy one. Remember: To get the paste out of the tube, you have to squeeze a little.

At the turn of the twentieth century, Charles H. Duell, head of the U.S. Patent Office, recommended to President McKinley that the office be closed down because "everything that can be invented has already been invented." This makes me wonder how he got the job in the first place.

Creativity is the ability to see things in a new way. It is taking a fresh look at the familiar. Public relations executive John Budd wrote: "Creativity is the result of intense focus on a particular problem. It's a logical thought process that maneuvers towards a solution. It occurs not because a person is trying to be original but because a person is attempting something difficult. A truly creative person excludes conventional solutions and searches beyond them."[11]

It amazes me how just a handful of innovative people have kept the rest of the world busy doing things with the ideas they started. I think of Steve Jobs of Apple Computer fame. He started a revolution in the personal computer industry. Two marks of such a creative mind are: (1) an ability to look at facts tangentially (around their edges, not just directly), and (2) an open lack of fear at being dead wrong occasionally.[12]

Everyone has potential for creativity. It is possible for everyone to enhance it, nurture it, and let it flourish, or to block and suppress it. If you are conscious of these conditions, you will either fear or facilitate its emergence.[13]

How creative are you? Here are eight specific steps toward developing this area of craftsmanship in your life:

1. To define a problem or a process, create a metaphor or simile.

2. Learn to challenge the status quo.

3. Get as much information as you can.

4. Learn what works well in one area or discipline and look for principles that will carry over to your field.

5. Work hard.

6. Combine things that already work.

7. Be willing to risk failure.

8. Leave room for the impossible.[14]

2. Adaptability

Another aspect of flexibility is *adaptability*. Adaptability is the ability to handle ambiguity. It means meeting changes with appropriate behavior, imagination, and confidence, even though nothing seems clear. Years ago I read an article in the *Harvard Business Review* that listed qualities of outstanding CEOs. One of the major strengths of these executives was the ability to live with ambiguity for an extended period of time while focusing on the ideal. Isn't that something? We want life to be neat; we want to travel in a straight line. But that's not how it works. Life brings many sorts of ambiguity, even when you have a direct path to follow. And that direct path isn't as straight as it should be. It's comprised of a lot of bouncing back and forth, like a ball in a pinball machine.

When I talk about flexibility, I don't mean just dealing with changing circumstances in the work environment, but also dealing with people. How do you respond to people with different personalities, different backgrounds? You need a great deal of flexibility to handle people and make the kind of midcourse corrections that are necessary.

People aren't alike. We're all different, and we all tend to push buttons in each other. Consequently, certain situations and people drive us crazy. Therefore, identifying problem situations and finding a creative way around them will give you a flexibility that's necessary for midcourse corrections. This applies not just to your work situation, but to your home and your personal life as well.

3. Learning from Mistakes

Not only do you need to apply creativity and adaptability, but you also need to learn from mistakes. This is probably the most fundamental of the principles. I've spoken about mistakes and problems in other parts of this book, but I want to underscore it here: *Mistakes are not only inevitable; they can be extremely valuable.*

Buckminster Fuller is best known for inventing the geodesic dome, the honeycomb sphere that encases many radar stations. He's also known for targeting his ingenuity to almost every practical aspect of living. His inventions were less important to him than his lifelong refinement of the insights that made them a reality.

Fuller spent the last fifty years of his life delivering one critical message: "Humans have learned only through mistakes." That's quite a statement, as is this: "The billions of humans in history have had to make quadrillions of mistakes to have arrived at the state where we now have 150,000 common words to identify the many unique and only metaphysically comprehensible nuances of experience. . . . The courage to adhere to the truth, as we learn it, involves then the courage to face ourselves with the clear admission of all the mistakes we have made. Mistakes are sins only when not admitted."[15]

Harvey Mackay runs one of America's most successful envelope manufacturing companies. I asked this mega-marketer how he handles mistakes. "If you want to double your success ratio, double your failure rate," he says. "Mistakes happen all the time. Every time you make a mistake and learn from it, you build strength and character."

The problem again isn't with making mistakes; it's with not learning from them. The first principle we've got to learn is to *embrace problems, not react to them.* This goes back to the principle of not asking *why* but asking *what.* What can I learn? How can I grow? How can I develop?

Learning from mistakes also means you need to be *teachable.* Whether or not you are teachable is a matter of spirit. The best way I know to be teachable is to ask people around you to help you. If you want to grow personally, find a mentor who's growing and developing and ask that person what he or she does. Learn from that person, practice what that person tells you, and grow in the process. Be teachable.

Invite your friends and your colleagues to point out anything in your life that needs to change. Let them invade your life and show you when there's some mistake you might be practicing. Do it with your spouse. Do it with your children. They won't reject you. On the contrary, they will be encouraged by your example of openness. And since your perspective now is that you're progressing and not pretending to be perfect, this process will allow you to become the kind of special, successful, significant person you want to be.

We're always going to make mistakes. We'll always run into things that don't work. The name of the game is to adjust. Adjust to your own weaknesses and foibles and failures, get your mind back into focus, heighten your flexibility, intensify your concentration, move back to the basics as you seek to frame your situation, be conscious of your weaknesses, and play to your strengths.

If you can learn to apply these principles in your life, you'll be the kind of person who is truly moving toward authentic success. And you'll be set up to follow the final principle of this book—to *stick with it and stay the course.*

Action Steps

1. List any challenge or obstacle you are facing toward the achievement of a particular goal:

Goal	Challenge
i.e., resolving a conflict at work	I am afraid of the intimidating parties involved.

2. How can you frame this situation? Which of your life principles, purposes, priorities, and peculiarities do you need to take into account as you work toward this goal?

principles	I must work toward unity on the team (nonnegotiable).
purpose	I must manifest the integrity of rightness living and doing the hard thing here.
priorities	I must resolve conflicts to get the job done. It's the right thing.
peculiarities	I am not good at this, so I will practice it until I have it down.

3. How can you focus on this issue? What do you need to do to concentrate and continually learn here?

4. How can you be more flexible? Brainstorm several possible ways to solve your problem. Try to be option-oriented; even allow for crazy ideas. Don't edit any until you review the list a second time. If solving this challenge involves responding to people differently, jot down some alternative strategies for making midcourse corrections here as well.

Solution Brainstorm	People Strategies
a.	a.
b.	b.
c.	c.
d.	d.
e.	e.

Now go back and circle the best course of actions—and go to work!

What did you learn from the last major mistake you made?

Chapter 10

Stay the Course

The Most Consistent Leadership Principle in the World

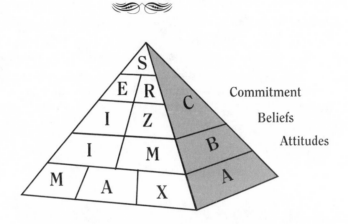

When nothing seems to help, I go and look at a stone-cutter, hammering away at his rock, perhaps a hundred times without as much as a crack showing in it. Yet at the hundred and first blow it will split in two, and I know it was not that blow that did it—but all that had gone before.

—Jacob Riis

Have you ever had a bad day?

"Bad day," you snort. "What about a bad week, bad month, bad year?"

We all have had bad days. And it's when those days come that we get discouraged, overwhelmed, frustrated, and want to give up. "Rainy days and Mondays always get me down." So crooned the Carpenters in 1971, capturing a sentiment that hasn't changed for centuries. Why has Monday gotten such a bad rap? Research shows that dropping dead from a heart attack is more common on Monday mornings than on any other day of the week.

Hopefully your Mondays aren't quite that dramatic. But regardless of how you face your Mondays, a final principle will give you what it takes to win. I call it *staying the course*. Simply put, this means sticking with it.

I have subtitled this principle "the most consistent leadership trait in the world" because the American Management Association (AMA) deems it so. In their research among leaders in various fields, the AMA has found that the one consistent characteristic of outstanding leaders is persistence. Indeed, great leaders often are *ordinary leaders who just wouldn't quit.* They stayed the course.

There are four basic life-craftsmanship skills involved in perseverance: fighting the good fight (life is difficult but worth the work), being faithful (keep focusing on roots, not fruit), finishing the course (you are in a race that demands you finish well), and keep focusing on the future (your impact or legacy will continue beyond your life).

Fight the Good Fight

One of the greatest tragedies of our day in materially wealthy countries is that an insidious apathy and comfort has settled in. Many people have forgotten the reality of life. Life is not meant to be a playground where personal ease and satisfaction are the goals and expected results. It is a precious resource to be invested for the good of others.

Life is a battlefield! You are at war—and you need to act like it!

I remember an animated discussion I had one evening with Ruth. I was frustrated about the apathy all around me and sought her advice. "Ruth," I demanded, "Why don't people care?" She looked at me with a thoughtful stare that seemed to see right through me and said, "They're already defeated."

"Defeated? What do you mean?"

"They are losing the battle day in and day out and are becoming perilously close to losing the entire war."

"Do you mean the day-to-day competition war in the business world?"

"Certainly competition is a reality of business," she answered. "You must compete. But your real competitor is you.

"You see, the real war is for people's hearts and minds. For as our minds go, so go our emotions and will. And there are forces around us daily that constantly push us away from what you call 'rightness living' and woo us toward narcissistic self-destruction.

"There is a bent we all tend to have toward self-preoccupation and raw selfishness. Whether you're trying to gain control of a bad habit or simply seek to satisfy your own desires, you know the battle you face. It's often fun to feed those desires, but if they take charge, you lose the battle. Then all of a sudden you're held captive to your own passions.

"Also, there is the battle we face against higher forces. Now, I don't believe in conspiracy theories. But I do believe there are cultural forces around us that stimulate our negative tendencies.

"Call these forces what you will. But I believe there is a battle going on. At least, I certainly hope there is. Because if all of the horror in Bosnia, Rwanda, the Middle East, Ireland, the inner cities of America, and scores of other places around the world is only to be blamed on man's evilness alone, I pity this world. No, I think there is more at work than just man's inhumanity to man."

"If we are losing the war," I pressed, "then how do we begin to retake the lost ground and get back on the offensive?"

From my subsequent lengthy discussions with Ruth, I came to the following conclusions:

1. Practice Defensive Warfare

One of the first objectives of war is to survive in order to win. Therefore, we must use good defense tactics. We're not fighting an army with moral conventions and with respect for the enemy. We're in the midst of guerrilla warfare. Listen to how an expert in the field describes such warfare:

> Basically, it is an ideological appeal, carefully tuned to justice, honor, pride, and emotion. Its final goal is the capture of the human mind so that the people will participate in a violent struggle. Guerrilla leaders know well that human beings are slaves to their minds. Consequently, once the cause has its grip on the people's mind, they cannot but comply.[1]

So . . . *get angry!* That's right, get angry. You should be incensed with the mental manipulation that surrounds you. Don't let it suck you in. Become angry at it, and let that anger motivate you to change and respond aggressively.

Aristotle said it well, "The man who is angry at the right things and with the right people, and, further, as he ought, when he ought, and as long as he ought, is praised. . . . For the good-tempered man tends to be unperturbed and not to be led by passion, but to be angry in the manner, at the things, and for the length of time, that the rule dictates."[2]

Study Your Enemy. The experts in guerilla warfare I mentioned, further state:

> The guerrillas, who cannot fight except on their own terms, must know enough about their enemy's plans and movements to avoid being trapped into battles which they cannot win; they must have sufficient knowledge of the enemy's weaknesses to make their own strikes as safe and effective as possible.[3]

Begin your fight by writing down the forces you face in the various areas of your life:

- What cultural factors are attacking your "rightness living"? Remember, these are attitudes and thoughts that seep into your frame of reference. Do you really want them there? It's your choice. Do a reality check. Make a list.

- What about your own negative tendencies? Are you being held captive to your own passions? Articulate them and begin applying the principles in this book to take charge again.

- Where do you stand in the area of warfare? Could other forces be moving you in the wrong direction? What might those forces be, and how can you stand against them?

NOTICE: I did not include your spouse, kids, associates, employees, employers, or even your competitors as your enemy. They are *not* the enemy—your battle is with yourself. Be the best *you*—focus on the roots. Don't put the blame on others.

Wear Appropriate Armor. The second way to fight defensively is to wear appropriate armor. Let me suggest that you put on the "armor" of the ten MAXIMIZERS principles. Here is how it can work to protect you:

Category	Principles	Protects
Attitudes	Make Things Happen Achieve Personal Significance X Out the Negatives	Emotions
Beliefs	Internalize Right Principles March to a Mission	Mind
Commitments	Integrate All of Life Zero In on Caring for People Energize the Inner Life Realign Rigorously Stay the Course	Will

These principles all focus on helping to protect your mind, will, and emotions through proper input. As you stimulate the roots of your life (these principles), you will guard against the inappropriate access of the enemy to your mind. And as you begin to reclaim the arena of your beliefs, attitudes, and commitments, you will find renewed safety, energy, wisdom, and power to move into offensive warfare.

2. Practice Offensive Warfare

How will you know you have succeeded in the offensive warfare of life? What will spell victory to you?

We have come full circle in this book. I began by addressing the broad area of success—what it is and what it isn't. And I have driven home throughout that authentic success is the *progressive realization and internalization of all that you were meant to be and do.*

This is victory—to daily, consistently, and persistently build these principles into your life. Your focus on the roots of righteous living will result in the fruit of maximum satisfaction and significance. If you keep your eye on the ball of doing right, you will achieve victory in your battle of life.

Therefore, get active . . . get aggressive . . . get energized . . . and get going! Deliberately get into the war!

Strategy. To win this offensive thrust, you need to develop a very *specific strategy.* It will not just happen. You must plan it.

So, what is your strategy to take the offensive? With what principles will you begin? How will you schedule the inculcation of these principles into your day-to-day activities? And how will you reinforce these principles in your life?[4]

Begin with the *belief* principles. Go back to your value system and articulate the nonnegotiable values in your life based on the chapter "Internalize Right Principles." Then go to the "March to a Mission" chapter and carefully write out and develop your overall mission. This mission includes your purpose, vision, roles, and lifelong goals.

Next, check your *attitude* principles. Are you merely reacting in life or are you initiating according to the "Make Things Happen" principle? Are you "Achieving Personal Significance" by owning up to your soft spots and "X-ing Out the Negatives"?

Finally, make appropriate *commitments.* Maintain balance by "Integrating All of Your Life." Relate to the people around you by "Zeroing in on Caring for Them" as your modus operandi. Constantly "Energize Your Inner Life" as you build a character base and cultivate your spirit. And keep making midcourse corrections as you "Realign Your Life Rigorously." Finally, build the life craftsmanship skills of "Staying the Course" and not quitting.

Do you get the point? You are to take the offensive by *deepening your roots.* As you build these principles into habit, you will take charge of your life and begin to enjoy the fruit of authentic success.[5]

Resources. Once you have determined your strategy, you must identify your *resources.* And since the battle is for your mind, your resources must be of a kind that will help you build the MAXIMIZERS principles into your being.

I suggest you begin by developing an Action Plan (Success) around which you organize these resources. This organization will allow you to filter out irrelevant data, motivate you to look for specific, useful information, and help you build a life message that will give you the capability to help others based on your own life changes and growth.

Your resource organizer should be broken down by principle, with tabs for each one. Each tab should have space for articles, insights, quotations, exercises, and any other craftsmanship tools that will help you hone your understanding and application of these principles. I use this type of resource organizer to keep my eye on the roots in my life. And it can make a dramatic difference in your life if you put it to work. I have made such manuals available to those who desire to go further with the principles of authentic success.[6]

With your organizer in hand, you're ready to begin looking for information that will hone your skills and add to your wisdom. You can find this information in discussions with friends and associates, magazines, books, lectures, moments of reflection, and multiple other areas.

Make the search for wisdom and resources part and parcel of your daily life. I have taken the ten MAXIMIZERS principles and developed a code to help me do this. Principle 1, for example (Make Things Happen), is coded as "M-1." Principle 2 (Achieve Personal Significance) is coded as "M-2," and so on. Whenever I read a book or article or have an insight, I mark it "M-1" or "M-2," and so on through "M-10." Today, if you were to look through the thousands of books in my personal library, the tens of thousands of articles in my filing cabinets, or the hundreds of thousands of Ks in my computer, you would see "M-1," "M-2," etc. as a consistent organizing principle.

Begin to apply this organizing approach to virtually every conversation, reading time, and moment of reflection. Stop daily for some reflective time and write down your insights in your manual. And watch the internal power and fulfillment explode as you activate this process.

One of my best friends once visited our home with his family. We had three rich days together, sharing, playing, and interacting. I watched this friend rise every day, go for a run, and then spend forty-five to sixty minutes reading, reflecting, praying, and recording his insights in a journal. When I asked him how often he did this, he said, "Daily." In fact, this practice was a core value for him to keep growing personally. It was a resourcing tool that had become indispensable.

You may say, "But I don't have time to do that!" Well, he certainly doesn't, either. After all, he is the president and CEO of a major international corporation. He has responsibility for more than seven thousand employees, and the corporation nets more than $3 billion a year. Moreover, his industry is one of the toughest in the world today. Yet this man realizes he can't afford not to take time to keep resourcing.

Keep growing. Read books, look for articles, study people, search for insights, reflect, pray, listen to tapes, watch videos, attend seminars, and find a mentor in authentic-life success. Over time I have collected and organized the best resources for each of these principles and have formed a curriculum that my associates and I communicate via seminars, conferences, audio/video tapes, and printed materials. If you would like information on these, refer to the endnotes for this chapter.[7]

Team Unity. One final principle of offensive warfare is to *cooperate as a unit.* You must work together not only to cover each other's backs, but also to cohesively pursue and defeat the opposing forces in your lives.

Whoever is part of your unit—whether family, friends, or business associates—it is critical that you work together with them. Whatever your battle, you can't do it alone. You are too vulnerable.

Be Faithful to the Principles

Faithfulness is one of the least revered and most needed qualities in our culture today. To be faithful is to "adhere strictly to the person, cause, or idea to which one is bound; be dutiful and loyal."[8] Synonyms of this word include *loyal, true, constant, steadfast, staunch, resolute,* and *trustworthy.*

The concept of faithfulness is as old as culture itself. The following oath was taken by the young men of ancient Athens when they reached the age of seventeen:

> We will never bring disgrace on this our City by an act of dishonesty or cowardice.
>
> We will fight for the ideals and Sacred Things of the City both alone and with many.
>
> We will revere and obey the City's laws, and will do our best to incite a like reverence and respect in those above us who are prone to annul them or set them at naught.
>
> We will strive increasingly to quicken the public's sense of civic duty.
>
> Thus in all these ways we will transmit this City, not only not less, but greater and more beautiful than it was transmitted to us.[9]

If you are to craft the MAXIMIZERS principles into your life, then you must dutifully and faithfully work them into your character by practicing them in both the big moments and the small. After all, one of the greatest traits of an artisan is his or her attention to detail.

So, regardless of whether you are alone or tired or bored, apply these principles. Don't wait for a big event or a big moment; by then it will be too late. Instead, start now to put these principles into practice dutifully and moment by moment. By so doing you will build them into your life as *habits*.

Finish the Course

How many times have you begun a task only to become distracted, discouraged, bored, or frustrated to the point that you didn't finish it? I must admit I have a penchant toward distraction. Because of my high creative bent and my seemingly insatiable hunger for learning, I become absolutely absorbed in information and data collection.

Therefore, I have to work hard at finishing whatever I'm involved in, whether it is a project or my entire life. And so must you!

The primary skill to develop here is *perseverance*. To persevere is to "persist in or remain constant to a purpose, idea, or task in the face of obstacles or discouragement."[10]

Consider these findings from the National Sales Executives Association concerning sales persistence.

- Eighty percent of all new sales are made after the fifth call to the same prospect.

- Forty-eight percent of all sales persons make one call, then cross off the prospect.

- Twenty-five percent of all sales persons quit after the second call.

- Twelve percent of all sales representatives call three times, then quit.

- Ten percent keep calling until they succeed.[11]

Perhaps discouragement stops you. Discouragement simply means to lose your courage. And, once you've convinced yourself you cannot succeed, you train yourself to become hopeless. In an article in *SELF* magazine, William Sloane Coffin Jr. gave this admonishment:

> Our greatest moral problem today is cowardice. It's cowardice that prevents us from coming up with new thoughts. It's cowardice that won't let us open our hearts to each other in more honest relationships. Americans have been taken over by an insurance mentality. We want life to be reliable, predictable, safe. No one wants to take any risks.
>
> The root of this cowardice is fear—fear of an uncertain future. But there's also a kind of internal terror. Common integrity now passes for courage. Rarely do you find a businessman or woman speaking out at any level. We're so anxious to climb higher, we keep our mouths shut.[12]

Ty Cobb and Hank Aaron are not remembered as baseball failures. Yet, Cobb was thrown out of games for stealing bases more times than anyone in baseball history, and Aaron, who broke Babe Ruth's record, struck out more times than 99 percent of major league players. Opera singer Enrico Caruso's voice teacher told him to quit singing and Thomas Edison's teacher called him a dunce. (It took Edison fourteen thousand failures to perfect the light bulb.) Physicist Albert Einstein and rocket engineer Werner von Braun both flunked math.

Do you know how Colonel Sanders built the Kentucky Fried Chicken empire that made him a millionaire and changed the way millions eat? "When he started, he was merely a retiree with a fried chicken recipe. That's all. No organization, no nothin'. He had owned a little restaurant that was going broke because the main highway nearby had been routed elsewhere. So, when he received his first Social Security check, he decided to see if he could make some money by selling his chicken recipe. His first idea was to sell the recipe to restaurant owners and have them give him a percentage of the proceeds.

"Now, that isn't the most realistic idea for beginning a business. And as things turned out, it didn't exactly rocket him to stardom. So he drove around the country, sleeping in his car, trying to find someone who would back him. He kept changing his idea, and he kept knocking on doors. He was rejected 1,009 times—and then something miraculous happened. Someone said yes (to his request for backing). The colonel was in business."[13]

Do you have a "recipe"? Do you have the physical power and charisma of a chunky old man in a white suit? Colonel Sanders made a fortune simply because he had the ability to stick with it. He was able to hear the word "no" a thousand times and yet still knock on the next door, confident it could be the one through which someone would say "yes" to his request for backing.

So, regardless of the circumstances, never, ever give up!

Focus on the Future

Remember the questions I posed to you early in this book: How will you be remembered when you die? What will people be saying at your funeral? I asked these questions because I wanted to shock you into reframing your perspective.

As I have pointed out throughout this book, life is about concentrating on the roots and letting the fruit come as a result. Yet, as you concentrate on building these root principles into your life, you must forever keep in mind the future implications of each decision you make.

If you apply the wisdom inherent in these principles and become a *life craftsman,* you will authentically succeed. You will have fruitfulness in all arenas of your life, and you will have fulfilled your destiny. The legacy you leave will touch the lives of your family, friends, neighbors, associates, and thousands (and perhaps millions) more.

If you choose to practice rightness living and align your life with truth, you will leave a vivid, positive, and powerful legacy. But if you do not choose to embrace these principles, you will leave another kind of legacy—perhaps one of dishonor and disgrace; or, at worst, insignificance; or, at best, mediocrity.

It's your choice. What do you want to make of your life?

There is a type of "moth with no mouth," a species of caterpillar that lays its eggs and then changes into a moth that has no digestive system and thus no way of eating. So it starves to death in a matter of hours. This moth has been designed to reproduce, lay eggs, pass on the life of its species, and die.[14]

Is your life like this? Do you live just to produce children and perpetuate the human race? Or do you have a greater purpose? Does your life really count? Can you truly leave a vital, significant legacy as you maximize your days on this earth? I believe you can and you *must*.

Conclusion

The principles I have shared with you are not just haphazard principles. They are intended to serve as a map—a model, a way of looking at life. And I guarantee you that if you can build these principles into the fabric of your being and let them be the roots for your understanding of life, you'll have the kind of perspective that will make you a success in every sense of the word. And you'll be the kind of significant individual you truly want to be.

Just remember . . . don't quit!

Remember the words of Winston Churchill, who in the dark days of 1941 gave this speech at Harrow School:

> For everyone, surely, what we have gone through in this period . . . this is the lesson: Never give in, never give in, never, never, never, never—nothing great or small, large or petty—never give in except to convictions of honor and good sense. Never yield to force; never yield to the apparently overwhelming might of the enemy.[15]

Action Steps

1. Memorize the MAXIMIZERS acrostic and repeat it four times a day for the next thirty days.

2. Identify which of the four major areas of "Staying the Course" you struggle with most. Identify one specific step you can put feet to this week.

Notes

Introduction

1. Jon Johnston, *Will Evangelicalism Survive Its Own Popularity?* (Grand Rapids, MI: Zondervan, 1980), 49.
2. Harold Kushner, *When Everything You've Ever Wanted Isn't Enough* (New York, NY: Simon and Schuster, 1986).
3. Glenn Bland, *Success* (Wheaton, IL: Tyndale, 1972), 54–55.
4. Kushner, *When Everything You've Ever Wanted Isn't Enough*, 15.
5. Ibid., 15.
6. Ruth is simply a literary technique I am using to personify wisdom. She is rooted in natural law—universal, absolute truths that can be discovered in the realm of creation, the classics, Greek philosophy, spiritual wisdom throughout the ages, and many general religious and philosophical writings, including the Old and New Testaments of the Bible. Whenever I use this technique to paraphrase a specific quotation, I will document it. Otherwise, I will communicate my synthesis of multiple wisdom sources.
7. Interview with Ruth (Prov. 8:4–9).
8. My personal interview experience began in 1973 when another couple, my wife, and I spent seven months touring the United States in a twenty-foot motor home. We covered twenty thousand miles in thirty-eight states and interviewed 350 top professional leaders and executives. This work was foundational to my doctoral work. Since that time I have sought out high achievers who succeed authentically as I define it in this book. I have personally interviewed leaders on five continents and in dozens of countries. They have helped give great clarity to and illustrations for the ten MAXIMIZERS principles.

Chapter 1

1. Irwin Shaw, "The Eighty-Yard Run," a short story.
2. Charles J. Sykes, *The Nation of Victims: The Decay of the American Character* (New York, NY: St. Martins, 1992).
3. Ibid., 1.
4. Ibid., 7.
5. Mike Royko, "A Discrimination Charge Hits Bottom," *Chicago Tribune*, 22 May 1991, (Editorial Section), in Sykes, *The Nation of Victims*, 7.
6. Sykes, *The Nation of Victims*, 9.
7. Adaptation of the parable of the talents in Matthew 25:14–30.
8. Douglas LaBier, *Modern Madness* (Redding, MA: Addison-Wesley, 1986) in Doug Sherman and William Hendricks, *Your Work Matters to God* (Colorado Springs, CO: NavPress, 1988), 27–28.
9. Ibid., 28.
10. Art Williams, *All You Can Do Is All You Can Do* (Nashville: Thomas Nelson, 1988), 61.

11.   Robert J. Ringer, *Million Dollar Habits* (New York: Ballantine, 1990). In this book Ringer develops ten major habits ranging from the practice of reality to simplicity to morality to human relations. It's one of the finest books on habits written, and I strongly encourage a careful reading and study of this book.

12.   G. W. Target, "The Windows," *The Window and Other Essays* (Mountain View, CA: Pacific Press, 1973) in Tim Hansel, *You Gotta Keep Dancin'* (Elgin, IL: David C. Cook, 1985), 57–59.

Chapter 2

1.   James Moore, *Self-Image* (Colorado Springs, CO: NavPress, 1992), 26–27.

2.   Peter Drucker, "Tomorrow's Manager," *Success*, October 1993, 80.

3.   Ibid.

4.   Ibid.

5.   John Powell, *Why Am I Afraid to Tell You Who I Am?* (Chicago, IL: Argus Communications), 1969.

Chapter 3

1.   Martin Seligman, *Learned Optimism* (New York, NY: Random House, 1991). Much of this section summarizes some of Seligman's insights. For further clarification, read this book and other works by him.

2.   Ibid.

3.   Richard Leider, *The Power of Purpose* (New York, NY: Fawcett Gold Medal, 1985), 29. This is one of the best books I have read on handling difficulties, written by a man who has faced serious setbacks in his own life.

4.   Scott Peck, *The Road Less Traveled* (New York, NY: Simon & Schuster, 1978), 15.

5.   Clyde Reid, *Celebrating the Temporary* (San Francisco, CA: Harper, 1974) in Hansel, *You Gotta Keep Dancin'*, 44–45.

6.   Lois A. Cheney, "Feeling Blue" in Hansel, *You Gotta Keep Dancin'*, 107.

7.   Lewis Smede in Hansel, *You Gotta Keep Dancin'*, 53.

8.   Frederick Buechner in Hansel, *You Gotta Keep Dancin'*, 74.

9.   Norman Cousins, *Anatomy of an Illness* (New York, NY: Fawcett Columbia, 1986) in Anthony Robbins, *Unlimited Power* (New York, NY: Fawcett Columbia, 1987), 157.

10.   Hansel, *You Gotta Keep Dancin'*, 83–85.

11.   Karen Abbott, Scripps Howard News Service, *San Diego Union-Tribune*, 13 July 1992.

12.   Ibid.

13.   C. W. Metcalf, *Lighten Up: Survival Skills for People under Pressure* (Redding, MA: Addison-Wesley, 1993).

14.   David D. Burns, *Feeling Good* (New York, NY: Signet Books, 1980). This is an outstanding book about cognitive psychology which postulates that all moods are determined by our cognitions or thoughts. In short, control the thoughts—particularly the negative distortions—and you will control your moods.

15.   Hansel, *You Gotta Keep Dancin'*, 94.

Chapter 4

1. Alan Bloom, *The Closing of the American Mind* (New York, NY: Simon & Schuster, 1987).
2. Cal Thomas, *The Death of Ethics in America* (Waco, TX.: Word, 1988), 50–51.
3. "Poll bares 'The Truth,' if you can believe it," Cox News Service, *San Diego Union,* 29 April 1991, 1, A-Y.
4. Ibid.
5. Covey, *Seven Habits of Highly Effective People.*
6. Jack Griffin, "It's OK, Son, Everybody Does It" in Ken Blanchard and Norman Peale, *The Power of Ethical Management* (New York, NY: William Morrow and Company, 1988), 30–31.
7. Blanchard and Peale, 27.
8. "Boy Scouts of America Oath" in Randy Pennington and Marc Bockmon, *On My Honor, I Will* (New York, NY: Warner Books, 1992), 4.
9. Ted Koppel's 1987 address to graduating students at Duke University in Thomas, *The Death of Ethics in America,* 133.
10. For an annotated bibliography of tools for development in this area, see FAI information at end of Notes.
11. John Greenleaf, *Servant Leadership* (New York, NY: Paulist Press, 1977).
12. Ken Blanchard, Patricia Zigarmi and Drea Zigarmi, *Leadership and the One Minute Manager* (New York, NY: William Morrow, 1985).

Chapter 5

1. Leider, *The Power of Purpose,* 77–78.
2. Ibid., 9.
3. Viktor Frankl in Leider, *The Power of Purpose,* 9.
4. George Bernard Shaw in Leider, *The Power of Purpose,* 3.
5. For more resource tools in these areas of purpose and vision-statement development, see FAI information at end of Notes.
6. W. H. Murray in Charles Garfield, *Peak Performers* (New York, NY: Avon Books, 1986), 123.

Chapter 6

1. Kushner, *When All You've Ever Wanted Isn't Enough,* 145.
2. Ibid., 142.
3. Richard and Linda Eyre, *Life Balance* (New York, NY: Ballantine Books, 1987), 38. This book not only addresses the balance in the three areas I have mentioned (priorities, attitudes, and goals), but also is filled with practical tools on how to develop that balance in your life. It is a tremendous supplement to this chapter and this concept.
4. Ibid., 38–39.
5. Christina Maslach, *Burnout—The Cost of Caring* in Frank Minirth, et al., *How to Beat Burnout* (Chicago, IL: Moody Press, 1986), 14.
6. Ecclesiastes 2:17–18, 20–23.
7. Maslach in Minirth, et al., *How to Beat Burnout,* 147.
8. Ibid.

9. Oscar Wilde in Gordon MacDonald, *Ordering Your Private World* (Nashville, TN: Thomas Nelson, 1984), 15.
10. MacDonald, *Ordering Your Private World,* 31–37.
11. Kushner, *When All You've Ever Wanted Isn't Enough,* 15–16.
12. Matthew 22:34–40.
13. I'm indebted to J. Grant Howard for his work in *Balancing Life's Demands.* The book is geared toward developing a philosophical basis for building life's priorities around this threefold grid.
14. Stephen Covey, *First Things First* (New York, NY: Simon & Schuster, 1994), 88.
15. Jody Johnson in Ellen James Martin, *Kitchener-Waterloo Record,* 28 January 1991, D-2.
16. Michael H. and Timothy S. Mescon, "That Loyalty Thing," *Sky* Magazine, June 1994, 30.
17. Ibid., 32.
18. Lynn Gaines, "Like Family, Not Company," *Boston Globe,* 17 March 1994, 41–42.
19. Mescon, "That Loyalty Thing," 34.
20. Roy Roberts in Matt Murray, "Scratch That Itch and More Graduation Advice from the Top," *Wall Street Journal,* 26 May 1994, B-2.
21. Gary Wilber in Murray, "Scratch That Itch . . . ," B-2.
22. Eyre, *Life Balance,* 101.
23. Kushner, *When All You Ever Wanted Isn't Enough,* 146.

Chapter 7

1. Daniel Yankalovich, *New Rules in American Life.*
2. Kushner, *When All You Ever Wanted Isn't Enough,* 165.
3. Jon R. Katzenback and Douglas K. Smith, *The Wisdom of Teams* (New York, NY: HarperCollins, 1994), 15–16.
4. Ibid., 18 (italics mine).
5. John Naisbitt, *Megatrends* (New York, NY: Warner Books, 1982), 191, 198–99.
6. Wayne Dyer, *The Sky's the Limit* (New York, NY: Pocket Books, 1980), 52.
7. James Dobson, *Hide or Seek* (Old Tappan, NJ: Fleming H. Revell, 1974), 9–10.
8. Robbins, *Unlimited Power,* 312.
9. 1 Thessalonians 5:14.
10. Blanchard, Zigarmi, and Zigarmi, *Leadership and the One Minute Manager* (New York, NY: William Morrow and Company, 1985). My friend Ken Blanchard and his team have developed this concept well and provide very specific training on how to coach others.
11. David Augsburger, *Caring Enough to Not Forgive . . . Caring Enough to Forgive* (Ventura, CA: Regal Books, 1981), 19.
12. William Glasser, *Reality Therapy* (New York, NY: Harper & Row, 1965), 7.
13. Gail Sheehy, *Passages* (New York, NY: Bantam, 1974) in Kushner, *When All You Ever Wanted Isn't Enough,* 62.
14. Kushner, *When All You Ever Wanted Isn't Enough,* 94.
15. Norman Wright, *Communication: Key to Your Marriage* (CA: Gospel Light Publications, 1974), 52.
16. Marriage Conference Manual (Little Rock, AR.: FamilyLife, 1993), 78.
17. Judson Swihart, *How Do You Say "I Love You"?* (Downers Grove, IL: InterVarsity, 1977), 46–47.

18. Adapted from H. Norman Wright, *Communication: Key to Your Marriage* Leader's Manual (CA: Gospel Light Publisher, 1974).
19. Proverbs 27:17.
20. C. S. Lewis, *Mere Christianity* (London, England: Fontana, 1952), 113–14.
21. Malcolm Muggeridge, *Something Beautiful for God* (New York, NY: Ballantine, 1971), 58.

Chapter 8

1. Lee Atwater with Todd Brewster, "Lee Atwater's Last Campaign," *Life*, February 1991, 67.
2. David G. Myers, *The Pursuit of Happiness* (New York, NY: Avon Books, 1992), 178–79.
3. William Morris, ed., *The American Heritage Dictionary* (Boston: Houghton Mifflin Company, 1970), 1316.
4. Carl DeVries, *Zondervan Pictorial Bible Dictionary* (Grand Rapids, MI: Zondervan), 802–804.
5. Ecclesiastes 1: 2, 14.
6. Ecclesiastes 12:13–14 (italics mine). I strongly urge you to study this work in addition to the wisdom that flows from one of Solomon's other works, the Book of Proverbs.
7. Alexis de Tocqueville in Gerald Kennedy, *A Reader's Notebook* (New York, NY: 1953), 224.
8. Stephen Carter, *The Culture of Disbelief* (New York, NY: Basis Books/Harper and Row, 1993).
9. William J. Bennett, *The Book of Virtues* (New York, NY: Simon & Schuster, 1993).
10. C. S. Lewis, "Men without Chests," *The Abolition of Man* (New York, NY: MacMillan, 1978) in Bennett, *The Book of Virtues*, 264–265.
11. John Updike in William J. Bennett, "Getting Used to Decadence: The Spirit of Democracy in Modern America," *The Heritage Lectures* 477 (Washington, D.C.: The Heritage Foundation, 1993), 2.
12. Bennett, "Getting Used to Decadence," 3.
13. Ibid., 5.
14. Walker Percy in Bennett, "Getting Used to Decadence," 5.
15. Alexander Solzhenitsyn in Bennett, "Getting Used to Decadence," 6.
16. John Buchan in Bennett, "Getting Used to Decandence," 5–6.
17. Bennett, "Getting Used to Decadence," 7.
18. Zig Ziglar in Pennington and Bockmon, *On My Honor, I Will*, xvi.
19. Myers, *The Pursuit of Happiness*. This text analyzes the traits that lead to happiness and fulfillment by making extensive, objective use of scientific studies conducted worldwide.
20. Inglehart in Myers, *The Pursuit of Happiness*, 179.
21. Myers, *The Pursuit of Happiness*, 183.
22. Martin E. P. Seligman, "Boomer Blues," *Psychology Today*, October 1988, 50–55, in Myers, *The Pursuit of Happiness*, 189.
23. Randy Phillips, *Seven Promises of a PromiseKeeper* (Colorado Springs, CO: Focus on the Family Publishing, 1993), 1–10.
24. Cyprian Norwid, 1850, Waladylaw Tatarkiewixz, *Analysis of Happiness* (The Hague: Martinue Nijhoff, 1976), 176, in Myers, *The Pursuit of Happiness*, 188.

25. Seligman in Myers, *The Pursuit of Happiness.*
26. Harold Kushner, "You've Got to Believe in Something," *Redbook,* December 1987, 92–94.
27. Viktor Frankl, *Man's Search for Meaning: An Introduction to Logotherapy* (Boston, MA: Beacon Press, 1962).
28. Robert Wuthnow, "Evangelicals, Liberals, and the Perils of Individualism," *Perspectives* in Myers, *The Pursuit of Happiness,* 190.
29. Myers, *The Pursuit of Happiness,* 196.
30. Covey, *Seven Habits of Highly Effective People,* 31–45.
31. Denis Waitley, *Being the Best* (Nashville, TN: Thomas Nelson Publishers, 1987), 54–55.
32. Jeffrey P. Davidson, "Integrity: The Vanishing Virtue," *PMA Adviser,* V, 9:1.
33. *The American Heritage Dictionary,* 1245.
34. Sam Keen, *Hymns to an Unknown God* (New York, NY: Bantam Books, 1994), xv.
35. Ibid., xvi.
36. Ibid., xvii–ix.
37. *Newsweek* in Keen, *Hymns to an Unknown God,* xxi.

Chapter 9

1. Ringer, *Million Dollar Habits,* 100, 107–8.
2. Scott DeGarmo, "Entrepreneurial Types," *Success,* September 1989, 2.
3. Peter M. Senge, *The Fifth Discipline* (New York, NY: Doubleday Currency, 1990). The discussion is adapted from his fine work in this area.
4. Jeff Comer, "The Hearing Organization," *Change* (San Diego, CA: Center for Leadership Development, Fall 1993), 3.
5. Rick Warren, *The Fax of Life,* 29 September 1993.
6. Ibid.
7. Ibid., 5.
8. Ecclesiastes 12:12 TLB.
9. Ecclesiastes 1:18 TLB.
10. Charles Garfield, *Peak Performers* (New York, NY: Avon Books, 1986), 46.
11. O. A. Battista, *Quotations* (New York, NY: G. R. Putnam and Son, 1977), 74.
12. Ibid., 74–75.
13. Erwin DiCyan, Ph.D., *Creativity: Road to Self-Discovery* (New York, NY: Jove Publications, 1978), 15.
14. Adapted from a 1989 Campus Crusade study guide.
15. Buckminster Fuller, "Mistake Mystique," *East/West* (April 1977), 26–28 in Garfield, *Peak Performers,* 215.

Chapter 10

1. Banjit Singh and Do-Wang Mei, *Theory & Practice of Modern Guerrilla Warfare* (New York, NY: Asia, 1971), 28.
2. Aristotle, *Nicomachean Ethics* (384–322 B.C.).
3. Singh and Mei, *Theory & Practice of Modern Guerrilla Warfare,* 44–45.
4. For scheduling and implementation tools, see FAI information at end of Notes.

5. For audio and video tapes as well as printed tools to build these principles on, see FAI information at end of Notes.

6. For more information on the manual and/or file systems tools, see FAI information at end of Notes.

7. For more information on these materials, seminars, and "best of the best" list, see FAI information at end of Notes.

8. *The American Heritage Dictionary,* 471.

9. Bennett, *The Book of Virtues,* 217.

10. *The American Heritage Dictionary,* 978.

11. Waitley, *Being the Best,* 163.

12. William Sloane Coffin Jr. in *SELF.*

13. Robbins, *Ultimate Power,* 13.

14. Kushner, *You've Got to Believe in Something,* 19.

15. *Winston S. Churchill: His Complete Speeches, 1897–1963* (London: Chelson House, 1974), 6499.

About Future Achievement International

Make a Life, Not Just a Living was not just a book project. Rather, it is the centerpiece of the vision of Dr. Ron Jenson to encourage people and equip them with life skills for authentic success. It is a vision built around the notion that we must first embrace a healthier, more complete definition of success—then provide the training and life-skill tools to move one person at a time toward this model of success. Thus, the vision is about a process. FAI was established to facilitate this process by developing a personal leadership/coaching system.

FAI can provide you with a full suite of products and services, including:

- live keynote presentations

- live on-site or remote training programs for business, education, and civic groups

- satellite-based multisite remote learning programs

- video- and audio-based educational packages for individual or group self-study

- MaxTools: a series of learning aids designed to sustain the learning process

For more information, write or call:

Future Achievement International
11828 Rancho Bernardo Road
Suite 12335
San Diego, CA 92128-1999

(619) 487-3177
(619) 487-9212 (fax)
future8@earthlink.net

Index